A Diamond in the Desert

Also by Jo Tatchell

Nabeel's Song: A Family Story of Survival in Iraq

Jo Tatchell

A Diamond
in the Desert

*Behind the Scenes
in Abu Dhabi,
the World's Richest City*

BLACK CAT
New York
a paperback original imprint of Grove/Atlantic, Inc.

First published in Great Britain in 2009 by Septre
an imprint of Hodder & Stoughton
a Hachette UK Company

Printed in the United States of America

ISBN-13: 978-0-8021-7079-8

Black Cat
a paperback original imprint of Grove/Atlantic, Inc.
841 Broadway
New York, NY 10003

Distributed by Publishers Group West

www.groveatlantic.com

10 11 12 13 14   10 9 8 7 6 5 4 3 2 1

For W and L
And for Kate

'Once the realisation is accepted that even between the closest people infinite distances exist, a marvellous living side-by-side can grow up for them, if they succeed in loving the expanse between them, which gives them the possibility of always seeing each other as a whole and before an immense sky.'

Letters to a Young Poet by Rainer Maria Rilke

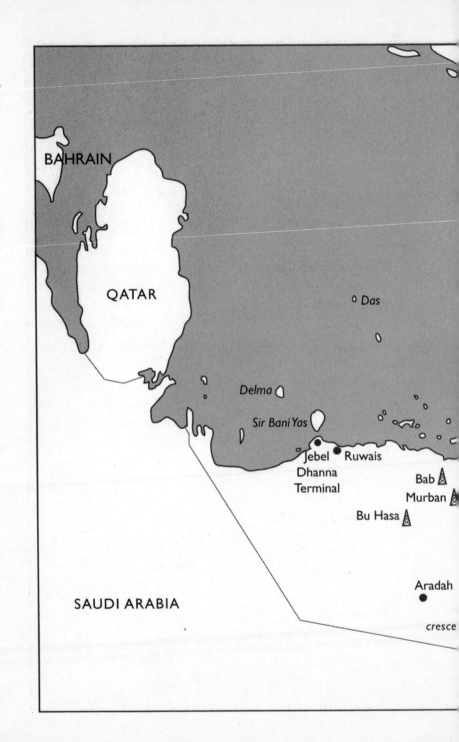

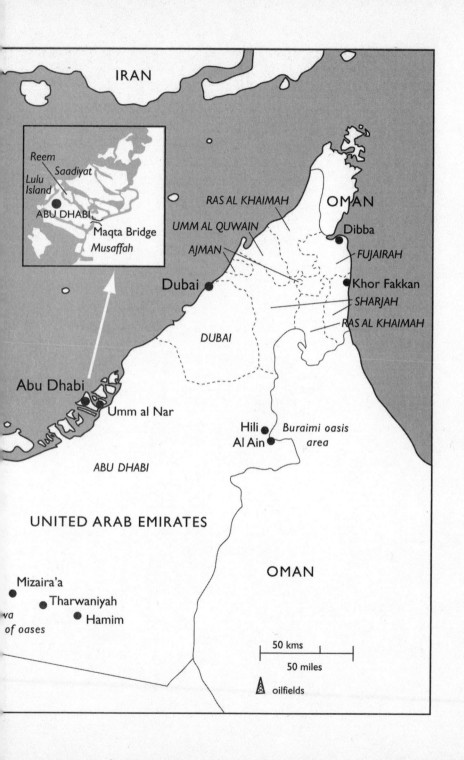

Prologue
1965

A plume of golden dust bloomed high into the desert air behind the Chevrolet pick-up. Edward Henderson was working his way inland from the flat, coastal sands of Abu Dhabi Island towards the red dunes around the Buraimi oasis. The air in the cabin was suffocating, but although it was hard to breathe, the windows and vents had to be kept tightly shut all the way. Even the tiniest crack would allow fine, glassy desert dust to fill the car, dirtying clothes and clogging every crease of his face and lips.

On the seat next to him was a tin of Macintosh toffees and a large metal security trunk, stacked to the brim with neatly tied bundles of money. The pick-up skimmed the slopes, bouncing and jolting along the tracks – it was not for nothing that it was called the Boneshaker. There was no respite: under the harsh sun the journey continued, relentlessly, for hours.

Edward was on his way to see Zayed, the brother of Abu Dhabi's ruler, Sheikh Shakhbut, and representative, or *wali*, of Abu Dhabi's fertile Eastern Region. Zayed was not easily found. He and his entourage circled Abu Dhabi's territory, meeting tribesmen and hunting, rarely settling for more than a few days in any one place. It had become Edward's custom to stop at the home of Zayed's wife, the sheikha: she always knew exactly where, in the dunes around Al Ain, he could be found.

Edward tramped beneath the palm groves towards the mud house, the tin of toffees in his hands. A barefoot servant emerged to greet him, beckoning him into the dim light of the sheikha's quarters.

When she appeared, wrapped in an *abaya*, the thick black robe women routinely wore, and a stiff, inky *burka* that covered all of her face but the eyes, she settled herself on a rug behind a gently clicking screen of beads. '*Salaam alaikum*, bin Hender. Come. Sit.' As they shared news of family and developments in Abu Dhabi, the sheikha intermittently extended a hand with fruit or dates through the beads. Edward took what he was offered, and, after a while, placed the tin of toffees on the floor between them. Her hand reached for the tin and pulled it towards her.

The sheikha deserved whatever he gave her, for she was not only generous, but helpful. However whimsical her instructions might seem, Edward knew he would come upon the tents and flags on the horizon just where she had said they would be.

◆ ◆ ◆

Zayed's retainers watched the pick-up approach and gathered, waving him in from the dunes, their robes billowing in the wind. To Edward, it always felt as though they had been expecting him. And perhaps they had. Life here was lived in perpetual readiness for the arrival of guests. The Bedu code of hospitality was sacred.

There was much commotion over his arrival. The men lined up to embrace him, then took him to the large rug spread in front of the pitched tent where Zayed sat. The two men embraced and rubbed noses. They had met more than ten years earlier when Edward had been with Petroleum Development Trucial Coast Ltd, the joint venture between major international oil companies operating in the Trucial States – the seven tribal sheikhdoms, Abu Dhabi, Dubai, Sharjah, Ajman, Umm al Quwain, Ras al Khaimah and Fujairah, spread along the south-eastern Arabian peninsula. As the consortium had begun to plug the desert emptiness with rigs and derricks, Edward had fostered diplomacy in an effort to bring stability to a region whose leaders had been embroiled for generations in shifting tribal allegiances and bitter territorial disputes. The vast investment required by petroleum companies made political co-operation between the tribes essential. There was little point in drilling for oil if constant skirmishes wrecked the possibility of its safe extraction. In line with British interests, Edward had sought, and found, influence with the young Zayed. Over the years they had become firm friends. Zayed had bestowed on him his nickname, bin Hender. He had become one of them.

They treasured those moments in the desert. In its peace they could talk openly of the changes coming to Zayed's country and his people. In return Edward shared with him the ways of Western business and politics. Zayed was at his most content there, with his retinue, his hunting falcons, his tents, his camels and his God. The desert was the home of tribal business. It was so vast and inhospitable that people were insignificant; it was impossible to be anything other than pragmatic. It was there that awkward land and tribal disputes were settled, news was exchanged and plans were made. Respected for his falconry and equestrian skills, Zayed had become a voice for the tribes. He had spent years journeying across the Bedu territories, meeting tribal chiefs, hearing grievances great and small, and offering guidance as the world around them began to change. With unswerving faith he encouraged peace through consultation and consensus, *sura* and *ijma*.

Zayed's instinct for reform and modernity added to his appeal – at least, to those interested in oil. In the early 1950s he had travelled to Europe and begun to build some of what he had seen there into his own vision for the future. He wished his impoverished people to enjoy a life beyond fishing and date farming. It had been in the desert's silence and stillness that he had first dreamed of a glittering Gulf city on the coast.

As night fell the camp grew busier and men returned with rabbit and *houbara* – bustard – from hunting. The fire had been lit, and while some talked, others brought out meat for roasting and set pots of rice over the coals. At sunset prayers were followed by coffee and when the time came to eat, men huddled round trays of food, tearing at the soft flesh with their fingers and pushing it quietly into their mouths. Afterwards they told tall tales, of falcons pinning bustards out of the sky, camel deals and skulduggery, love and land battles. Behind it all lay Zayed's great dream: that the settled tribes and wandering Bedu alike would build a future of shared plenty.

Neither Edward nor Zayed mentioned the trunk. The quarterly payment from the oil company sat unguarded on the passenger seat of the pick-up, awaiting its rightful turn in the proceedings. When it was eventually stood before Zayed, he acknowledged it with a mere tilt of his head. He did not look at the money inside. As far as Edward knew, no one ever checked the amount. On this occasion, though, he had been instructed to ask for a signed receipt. As the payments had soared, Head Office had demanded paper-work. Zayed roared with laughter when Edward opened the envelope and passed him the piece of paper. 'A receipt! Do they no longer trust you, bin Hender?'

Out on the sands, good faith was seen in a man's eye. An official document meant nothing. Zayed looked at Edward, shrugged and called for a pen. 'If this is how it must be now, I will sign their paper.' At that moment both men knew that the old ways would not do in the advancing era of wealth and commerce.

The following morning as Edward made ready to leave, the receipt in his shirt pocket, Zayed's men brought the tin chest back to the pick-up. Zayed asked Edward to do some-thing for him too: he was to take the money, whatever the sum at his own counting, and deposit it at the bank in Bahrain.

I

The Final Disillusionment

You can't see the whole city from the air, but as the plane sails in over the sea I squint through the window and catch glimpses of a million golden lights shimmering in the night haze. In the distance, red beacons flit on and off atop the great glass super-towers, marking the boundaries of a new skyline on the flat desert terrain. It is sixty years since Edward Henderson first set foot on Abu Dhabi's soil, and thirty-five since my own parents arrived. I wonder what they would have made of this ocean of lights. Would any of the three recognise the old Abu Dhabi in the sprawling metropolis below me? The small fishing community they knew has grown into a city.

As I step down onto the Tarmac, people rush past me onto the shuttle bus. I walk slowly, feeling the first puff of desert warmth on my face and bare arms. Then it's a step up, and we're off to the climate-controlled cool in which people live here.

Inside the spherical terminal building there are people everywhere. My heels tap across the sparkling marble floors as I head for the immigration hall. Frankincense wafts behind two women in flowing black *abayas*, the scent of old Arabia. A robed woman in a wheelchair sits in the doorway of the female-only prayer room and Filipino attendants, with buckets and huge grey mops, wash the floors. Men in immaculate white robes and headdresses, the *kandura* and *ghutra*, slide past. The women are as mysterious as night, floating past in black capes and decorated *shaylah* headscarves. They look untouchable, like idealised human forms, not quite real. Haven't they always said here, 'Say what you like, but dress as others do'? I feel grimy and under-attired as I slink into the 'Other Passports' line and wait my turn.

We are a motley lot. Three exhausted Filipinas, a weary French couple, a Lebanese family with a hyperactive child, and a couple of lone businessmen in short-sleeved shirts stretched over thickening middles. An officer patrols the line. He has round eyes and a neatly trimmed beard – like a plump version of George Michael. His green uniform is pristine, stiff with epaulettes and buttons. For a moment, as he waits to send people to the desk, he looks as though he is about to cry. He calls me over with a flick of his finger. 'Where you coming from?'

'London,' I say, with a quiver in my voice.

'Why you come here?'

'I used to live here. I want to see how much has changed.'

He arches his eyebrows. 'When you were living here?' He makes it sound like an accusation.

'The seventies. I came when I was a small child and I've not been here since the millennium.'

He howls like a dog. 'Whoo-hoo.' The sound echoes off the marble and people in other queues turn to look. 'Many long time. Long time.'

He sings, 'Abu Dhabi very big now. Very cool. You will not know anything from then. All is change.' He directs me to the booth on his right and mutters in Arabic to the immigration officer.

Sitting in his glass booth, in a freshly laundered *kandura*, the man tilts back in his chair and chuckles quietly. Then he begins to list the many improvements that have been made to the city, as if I had come to him for advice. 'So many islands. Lulu Island, you can go there. Emirates Palace, very nice. Corniche, very nice hotels.'

He thumps the stamp on my passport and secures the immigration card inside. '*Insha'Allah*. Go. Enjoy our new city.' He beams.

◆ ◆ ◆

It was my brother Bill who first got me thinking about Abu Dhabi again. I was sitting on a commuter train going into London when he called from a small town in the Australian outback with an unlikely piece of news. 'Get this,' he crowed. 'They're building a bloody Guggenheim in Abu Dhabi. Someone's got his wallet out and been shopping.'

An offshoot of New York's great temple of art? Surely not. When I last saw it, Abu Dhabi was a small town with a few medium-sized mosques, corner groceries, chaotically stocked shopping centres overrun with takeaways, like Maroush, Shakey's Pizza, Snoopy's, Hardee's and Tata, fast-food franchises that never quite delivered the fast-food experience as you expected it. It certainly didn't do high culture.

'Believe!' Bill laughed. 'They're going for it. They've done a deal with the French for the Louvre, too, and they're about to get a Sorbonne. It's like a franchise business. They might even be trying for a Tate. They're going to build on Saadiyat.'

My heart twinged. Saadiyat was a place of coral sand and tufty beach grasses where we had camped regularly. The coast off Abu Dhabi was flecked with islets – Saadiyat,

Reem, Bahrani and endless uncharted little drifts that had risen from the ultramarine seas. We used to go out on the boat most Fridays, following the fishermen, my father in shorts at the helm, my mother's hair and scarves flying behind her in the coastal winds. The intense light bleached the skyline and the sea glinted silver. The fishermen, in wooden dhows, *sanbuks* and small *jalboots*, with outboards strapped to the back, would wave as they passed, as if we were friends. We waved back, part of the same salty fraternity. Idyllic.

Bill was rattling through the plans. Two giant ten-lane bridges were to link Saadiyat to the mainland, fast-tracking people to and from the airport and the city. There were to be culture domes and arts centres, even a museum created in honour of Sheikh Zayed bin Sultan al Nahyan, the founding father of the United Arab Emirates. 'You've got to hand it to them.' Bill sighed. 'The leaders have a vision and they're making it reality.'

'You know how conservative they are. What are they going to put on the walls? There won't be any nudes. It'll be all landscapes, fruit bowls and abstracts.'

'They'll make it work. They'll do whatever it takes so long as they screw Dubai and the rest of them into the ground. Actually, I've read they're already planning a huge Picasso retrospective.'

'Umm. His nudes are almost abstracts – but, still, they can't just buy in art.'

'Twenty-seven billion dollars says they can,' he says.

'A reasonably compelling sum.'

This was a change of direction for Abu Dhabi. Even with the possibility of heavily censored content, the arrival of institutions like the Guggenheim signified a huge shift in intention. Until now, culture had never been a priority; there was the odd high-grade BBC TV import, *The Bold and the Beautiful* daytime soap from the US, Alan Ayckbourn plays at the Intercontinental Hotel, and occasional shows by bands that had fallen on hard times at home but whose members needed to pay their children's school fees. I had seen them all – Aswad, Duran Duran, the Gary Glitter Gang Show. Glitter's arrival, pre-scandal, had set the town buzzing with anticipation. As part of the team who organised the concert, at the Marina Club, a members' beach resort, I remember a grumpy, overweight curmudgeon slouched in his dressing room, complaining about the heat and lack of VIP facilities, then demanding oxygen and a breathing mask.

Now, it seemed, there was to be a huge and expensive attempt to corral high culture and draw it into the mainstream. The question, of course, was whether Abu Dhabi's Culture District could ever become a new Left Bank.

'Funny to think it's all going to be on Saadiyat,' Bill said, almost in a whisper.

The background hiss on the line bloomed to fill the space between us. I knew that something had happened to him out there – he had once started to tell me but had stopped himself, saying it wasn't the right time. I'd almost forgotten about it. Now it seemed wrong to press him, but I wondered if he was about to confess.

◆ ◆ ◆

I had come to the capital of the UAE with my parents in 1974. I was three, the same age as the country. My father had taken a posting to manage Spinneys, a British-owned catering company. Set up in 1948 in Beirut, it had branched into fulfilling the growing needs of oil prospectors in the Gulf. As soon as reserves were confirmed and revenues began to flow, Spinneys had opened a large, air-conditioned supermarket in Abu Dhabi. Reassuringly expensive, seemingly modelled on Fortnum & Mason, it guaranteed the swelling population of expatriates a regular supply of Frank Cooper's marmalade, Gentleman's Relish, Bath Olivers and Worcestershire sauce.

By 1975 change was well under way. The seaside village of a thousand, living in the old *barasti* huts, made from palm fronds, was gone. Between the tyre tracks that crisscrossed the sand, asphalt roads were knitting together to form a well-planned seaside town. With them came new mosques, springing up to serve the tens of thousands settling there, all bound together by a common interest in oil.

The desert still had the upper hand. Everything was shrouded in the fine dust that blew invisibly on the breeze and sand piled up in every doorway. But Abu Dhabi finally had its own currency, the UAE dirham, having ditched the rupee and the Bahraini dinar. It also had an infant bureaucracy, housed in disorderly new ministries, managed by men learning how to administrate a nation state while building businesses on the side. An almost palpable sense of chaos and opportunity hung about the place. It was like California's Sierra Nevada in the days of the gold rush.

My mother was stunned at the disarray that greeted her. A Surrey girl, she had married my father at the age of twenty-two and left England for Kerala, in India, then Kenya. Already used to living with unpredictability, she found herself dumbfounded by the chaos of such an unformed society. She reeled at the inhospitable terrain: her letters home tell of a town barely begun, of endless miles of fawn and white sand stretching in all directions to the horizon. The buildings were the same colour, there was not a green leaf to be seen and the roads, such as they were, trailed into dust at every turn. She dared not think about the people or where she would find friends. At first the locals had seemed remote and mysterious. My father, who had come out months before her, had warned her that the Arab was 'an unknown quantity and the place an enigma'. When she arrived with Bill and me, he was there to meet her from the small terminal building at Abu Dhabi's fledgling airport. As we drove down the single-lane road from the airport to the tip of the island, my father had reminded her not to expect too much. He had turned onto the sandy flat that led to the sea, and pulled up in front of a Portakabin on the beach. 'It's all there was, darling,' he explained apologetically. She concluded that it would be best to take life day by day and make the most of whatever kindnesses came her way. At least the sea offered relief from the sand. Writing home that first morning, as my brother and I slept, she told her parents she had come to nothing at 'Sand-on-Sea'.

My father had taken the job in Abu Dhabi in preference to one in war-torn Sri Lanka. Alive though it was with potential, it was still considered a hardship posting. After several months of cultural immersion in London, during which the most important thing he learned was that understanding Arab taste and habit would be best achieved by watchful patience when he got there, he had set to work pulling into shape the ragbag team of British, Indians, Pakistanis, Palestinians, Syrians and Arabs. Several enthusiastic staff showed their affection for their new boss by flinging their arms around him every time he appeared at the office door. The British were the most troublesome – he hadn't worked with any before, other than his old boss in Cochin – but he felt comfortable enough with everyone else to make it work. London expected nothing less than a bonded brotherhood of locals and foreigners, following the efficient, well-ordered creed of profit and loss.

My earliest memories are of a dishevelled, dusty place as enchanting and mutable as the dunes surrounding it. Despite heat so blinding I would occasionally faint, I became captivated by the commotion of the *souks*, enjoying the attention of shopholders offering sweets, fruit and, sometimes, small pieces of silver. I loved hearing the shuffling squeak of sandals across sand, seeing the vast panoramas of my new world, and the absence of colour: everything was bright and white. Too young to know it then, I understand now that I was drawn to the thoughtfulness of Arab ways. They yearned to make those around them happy – to squeeze my cheeks until they ached – with a passion that was more than just the desire to please. Once they had taken to you, it was for ever.

One of my most vivid early memories is of a drive through the interior during a trip round the Arabian peninsula in the mid-1970s. Our convoy stopped in the palm groves leading to one of the outlying villages of the Buraimi oasis, the fertile area in the east of the Emirate close to Al Ain. Through a light mist I saw men in grey and white robes with thick curved knives in their hands, ringed by mounds of wool and thick white fat. Rivulets of bright red blood ran down the slope away from the village.

My father raised his arms in greeting. The men ran towards us. '*Alhamdulillah, salaam alaikum, Eid Mubarak.* Thanks be to Allah. Peace be upon you. May you enjoy this blessed occasion.' Soon every last villager had trailed over to where the Land Rovers were parked. Slowly they came forward, whispering to each other, ushering us towards the village. It was Eid al Fitr – the end of Ramadan – and we, my father told me, were an auspicious arrival. We ate with them. A few had jackets over their *kandura*. Some were barefoot, while others wore sandals. Their headdresses were tightly wound round their skulls and they looked like the desert brigands I had seen in books. They sat us on thick, woven rugs and gave us tea poured from a Thermos flask. My mother offered them 7 Up from one of the coolers in the car. The slaughtered sheep were roasted on stone-packed fires and a few hours later we ate. The meat was tender. It came with rice and soft dates.

These are earthy memories, impressions of a place where nothing ever happened quite as you imagined it would. The crumbled coral, coppery dust and the kind, yet secretive people merged into an unshakeable feeling. There remains in me a physical sense of having been in that desert place. Though the town was growing up around us, the wilderness was at the edge, never more than a moment away. Outside the town of Abu Dhabi the land was timeless, constantly shifting, covering civilisations, bringing peace and small trials. We left no trace. A sense of our smallness left its mark on us.

For several years I attended a small English-speaking school, the Al Khubairat, not far from where we lived. At ten I was sent back to England, to boarding-school, and my parents were posted to Saudi Arabia, Kuwait and Indonesia. After this hiatus they returned to Abu Dhabi, as many expatriates did, for another decade in the sun. By the time I was at university, I was visiting two or three times a year. After graduation I avoided the recession-bound UK, with its negative equity and grunge-rock obsession, for clear skies, fun and the promise of my first job. I became the subscriptions officer at the Marina Club; I was supposed to recruit new members and run promotions, part of a mixed-nationality team – British, Palestinian, Dutch, Swedish, Filipino and Indian. I saw my role as an opportunity to stage events and shows. Getting publicity wasn't easy and it was difficult to find potential new recruits. But when you're young persistence comes easily, and although the job was frothy and my achievements few, my boss told me my prospects were good: I could rise up the ranks of the parent company. Yet I knew I wouldn't stay. Issues of injustices within this tight-knit, business-minded society attracted indifference. The enormous underclass of migrant labour cushioned life for the wealthy. The labour laws, if they were observed, were draconian, leaving workers without much in the way of rights, and dependent upon the good character of employers. 'I'll tell you what's so great about Abu Dhabi,' a workmate had once said to me. 'I had a set of lined curtains made and hung inside forty-eight hours. I could have had my carpet laid the same day too.' Chilled by such disregard for others, I knew I had to leave. The easy life in the Gulf's shiny capital overwhelmed me.

I chose instead the damp, sunless uncertainty of London and a typing course. Friends told me I was a fool, but in

1993 Abu Dhabi was wrapped up in its own comfort. It had no time to turn a critical eye on itself. Besides, I had seen people with good intentions sink into easy routine, losing their drive, passion and values. One old-timer, who had done extremely well out of Abu Dhabi, referred to it as the Velvet Rut. 'And that,' she warned me, 'is the hardest rut to escape.'

It wasn't that I hadn't enjoyed myself there – far from it. I had spent some of the happiest moments of my life in Abu Dhabi, but, susceptible to the idea of real equality, I always ended up feeling guilty for taking advantage of a system in which people were valued differently, by race as well as profession. The hierarchy was unspoken but ritually observed and enshrined in law. No one attempted to challenge the status quo. No one broke from one stratum to another. Most of us were only guests in someone else's country. There could be no gentle criticism or the suggestion that there might be room for change. More than that, censure of the system, and by association the leadership, was illegal. Prison or deportation faced those who spoke out. Either that, or they were discredited. I understood that people might do better than they would at home, in Peshawar or Goa, but I couldn't rid myself of the awkward sense that I was at liberty while others lived in bondage: they were granted leave every two years to visit their families and forced to surrender their passports to their masters in between.

These were the choices that faced every resident. To stay on would have meant adopting local codes and standards or, at least, refraining from flouting them. From the outside this was a city whose purpose was defined by the creation of wealth and the appearance of success. I knew life would be lived on the surface. There were rich people, and powerful people, but no one outside the ruling classes was celebrated for being an individual, a maverick or a visionary. And yet, when I escaped to London, which was also filled with communities from around the world, I missed Abu Dhabi. The ease had bewitched a part of me. I found myself returning to visit family and friends several times a year. It was only after my parents had retired and left for good that I stopped going.

The intervening years have brought more change than seems possible, even for a city as fast-moving as Abu Dhabi. Unlike Dubai, built on the glitzy, headline-grabbing industries of property, tourism and financial services, each at the whim of international public opinion, Abu Dhabi has quietly grown rich on a more workaday mix of oil, gas, construction, utilities, manufacturing and the processing of chemicals, wood, fibreglass and plastics. It isn't glamorous but robust commercial focus has allowed it to attain great wealth without most people having the slightest idea about where it is even located. Many residents say it is a city that changes its character every few years and now, with the attention being given to tourism and art, it seems to be preparing to shed another skin. I wonder if, in a region that is still vulnerable and unstable, it is leading the way in the creation of an open, artistic, tolerant Islamic state.

I'd read the odd report, and occasionally had emails from friends inviting me to stay if I was passing, but nothing suggested that fundamental change was afoot. Now I wondered if the little backwater I had known three decades ago might be about to come of age. When I was growing up, no one had ever heard of it — it hadn't been half as rich or ambitious — but now it seemed to be casting off its traditionally insular ways to throw itself onto the world stage and into the limelight.

And why not? The Abu Dhabi I had known was home to decisive, if cautious, people, with a down-to-earth faith that singled them out from others in the Middle East, and a persistent, fatalistic nature born of travelling the sands. It was not a culture of intellectual standing, perhaps, but neither was it dogged by the weight of expectation, as other, older, centres in the region were. It had no history of being coveted by one civilisation after another. Left alone, the people had their own traditions and superstitions that dated from a time before Islam when they had worshipped the moon and the stars.

As for the rest of the Gulf, the Kingdom of Saudi Arabia was strait-jacketed by conservatism and still out of reach to non-Muslims, except by personal invitation. Oman, on the poorer, more beautiful south of the Arabian peninsula, was concerned with recasting itself as a holiday haven. Qatar and Bahrain were not making the grand cultural plans Abu Dhabi had in mind. And Dubai, the nineties and early noughties It-girl of the region, was floundering: its property boom had gone bust, and its orgy of consumerism had begun to irk even some Westerners, who wondered how a twenty-four-hour party city could reconcile its mile-long shopping malls, seven-star hotels and indoor snow parks with its Islamic roots. Abu Dhabi was preparing not simply to join the wider cultural fray but to dominate it. It had a plan, a big one.

I began to see references everywhere – in the newspapers, on TV, on the Internet, Frank Gehry proclaiming his vision for the desert city by the sea, and *Fortune* magazine pronouncing it the world's richest city. The ruling al Nahyan family was rumoured to be worth $500 billion. Such riches made Russian energy oligarchs look like the comfortable poor.

It seemed the Culture District wasn't the half of it: the city was on the brink of total transfiguration, from provincial oil town to global centre, bringing the world a Hong Kong for the Middle East. And it was happening. The first wave of museum openings, the Guggenheim and the Abu Dhabi Louvre, was due in 2013.

But all the talk of culture and sport – the Formula One decider was scheduled for 2009 – was still bound up with the bottom line. Money, reputation and who was making how much looked to be of primary importance to Abu Dhabi, on paper at any rate. Even the Cultural District on Saadiyat Island was being developed by a tourist organisation. Was it about ushering in an era of cultural openness or merely getting into the culture business? I would go back and find out for myself. I dug out a few old numbers and started making arrangements. The people I had known when I was growing up would tell me what was happening, whether there was new artistic and media freedom, and I would talk to the men and women driving the engine of change to discover whether in fact this was just another attempt to promote the good name of Abu Dhabi to the world.

Given that Abu Dhabi is a closed monarchy, the motivation of its leaders is not always clear. In 2004 the current ruler, Sheikh Khalifa bin Zayed al Nahyan, succeeded his father, Sheikh Zayed bin Sultan al Nahyan, as leader of both the Emirate of Abu Dhabi and president of the UAE. With his ambitious half-brother, Mohammed bin Zayed al Nahyan, crown prince and deputy supreme commander of the UAE armed forces, he is piloting Abu Dhabi towards a new and defining era. Whether these dynastic guardians of the nation are setting themselves up as twenty-first-century benefactors or simply attempting to preserve their own position, they lead a complicated arrangement of bodies and councils that balances the administration of a modern state with service to tribal groups. In Abu Dhabi the Executive Council, a local cabinet led by the crown prince, controls the ministries and departments, from transport and finance to culture and heritage. Khalifa has a *diwan*, or court, of his own and this, holding the highest office in the Emirates, is counterbalanced by various ancillary assemblies. They include Mohammed's *diwan*, the National Consultative Council, made up of members of Abu Dhabi's prominent families and directly connected to Khalifa's *diwan*, the Supreme Petroleum Council, also headed by Khalifa, the Abu Dhabi Investment Authority, the Municipal Council and the Defence Authority. These bodies are interwoven with the same people, members of the ruling family and other leading clans, with decisions always dependent on a final monarchical vote, or veto. As president of the UAE, Khalifa chooses his prime minister – traditionally the ruler of Dubai – and cabinet, while the forty-strong Federal National Council is only an advisory body to the government. In 2006 twenty of the FNC representatives were voted in after the UAE's first elections. Of the 800,000-strong Emirati population the eligible electorate stood at 6,689, each one chosen by the rulers of the Emirates. The remaining twenty, weighted in favour of Abu Dhabi and Dubai, were also appointed by the rulers. It may be a benign system but it is no less absolute.

I had been sent *Plan Abu Dhabi 2030: Urban Structure Framework Plan*. This blueprint document, produced by the Executive Council, set out a quarter-century of co-ordinated development for the city and its surrounding areas: physically Abu Dhabi should grow into a city that is exemplary within the Arab region and the world. The book states, 'This urban plan provides a strong and comprehensive foundation for the development of the city of Abu Dhabi, in a strategic and co-ordinated way. It will ensure that future generations will continue to enjoy and be inspired by ongoing access to the desert, sea and natural assets that are integral to our national identity, while building a global capital with its own rich cultural heritage.'

It looks like a telephone directory, with page after page of detail on what, when and how the city will transform itself, from building heights and land use across the metropolitan domain to transport schemes and achieving social equilibrium. The government is bankrolling change on a scale never before seen in human history. The timetable is precise. Step by step, Abu Dhabi is to become a terminus for culture and business, a centre for bankers, interior designers and artists, filmmakers and musicians leading the way in new technologies and sustainable living. Built on Arab community values, every aspect, from population, culture, economy, environment and leisure to education, has been plotted like a child's join-the-dots puzzle. There are even plans for a string of satellite cities along the newly built offshore islets, linking green quarters and public spaces, cultural precincts, aerial walkways and highways, tunnels and trams. In other schemes people talk of sky cities, high-rise needles with cloud systems generated from silver-nitrate mist, and *Star Wars*-like spherical cities in the desert. These are the new ideals for living and by 2030 the rulers of Abu Dhabi want 3.5 million people to be enjoying them.

A triumph of ambition over common sense? It reminded me of the Third Reich's plan for the Welthauptstadt Germania, the marble-clad vision of Berlin that would have sunk the city into the marshy ground it stood on, had it ever been built. More benignly, perhaps, it resembles the United States' establishment of a new permanent capital on the Potomac river (the thirty-second location suggested and the only one grudgingly agreed on by northern and southern states) in its bid to mark the nation's arrival.

While the Caterpillars and ballast freighters broke ground on home soil, Abu Dhabi had also begun its expansion outwards, buying up strategic assets around the world to ensure its people are protected when the oil runs dry. Sheikh Mansour bin Zayed al Nahyan, another of Khalifa's half-brothers, was emerging into the public eye as a model investor. Media coverage showed advisers coming to buy Manchester City Football Club for a couple of hundred million, and the tabloids were splashed with chirpy head-lines: 'Abu Dhabi Doo', 'Trillion-dollar Wealth of New Manchester City Owner' and 'How I Learned to Love Sheikh Mansour'. He invested the considerably higher sum of £3.5 billion in Barclays Bank for a huge stake in its equity.

Elsewhere Abu Dhabi's sovereign wealth funds have bought into foreign businesses and institutions. The Abu Dhabi Investment Authority, with solvency close to $1,000 billion, has taken slices in Citigroup, the Chrysler Building and a constantly expanding property portfolio across London, Paris, Milan, New York and Los Angeles. With more than $1 trillion now invested abroad Abu Dhabi, known for its reluctance to reveal details of its wealth, has shown strategic intent: by plugging holes in the Western economies, it is writing Abu Dhabi into the big picture.

Sheikh Mansour has pulled back the curtain on the private wealth of the royals. The purchase of his stake in Barclays gave the public a first glimpse of the relationship between the ruling family and their money. It has shaken the tradition of understatement, a characteristic of Islamic humility and the Abu Dhabian tradition of circumspection. On the world stage, with the media free to comment as they please, journalists and bloggers are debating what the buy-in meant. There were certain to be strings attached. It was the Abu Dhabian way. Business meant deeds done and favours returned, no questions asked.

Everything always used to run on *wasta*, the influence one had over others, and *baksheesh*, the backhanders that made the system flow with willingness and goodwill. My parents received gifts regularly from staff returning after bi-annual leave to Egypt, Syria, Jordan, India and Sri Lanka. They appreciated there had to be a little give-and-take – on the advice of a colleague my father had taken an expensive gold Rolex, bought by the company, to a sheikh with whom they were seeking to curry favour. My mother was lavished with free produce and never a *fil* accepted in payment. Where the general oiling of the wheels and outright bribery and blackmail began and ended, no one was ever sure. Indebtedness was the custom. Could urban planners and big foreign-investment deals ever really unpick such old habits?

What was certain was that Abu Dhabi's ambition would put pressure on its cosy provincial ways. It was not whether the urban planning of 2030 was achievable but whether the government was ready to permit its society the kind of freedoms necessary to allow artistic culture to flourish. It was all very well buying up cultural equity but what did the government intend to do with it? It seemed a risky undertaking for such a small country, without experience of or passion for the arts, marked by well-known limitations on free speech, religious conservatism and social prudence. Creative expression had never attracted much attention. It was not easy to imagine a Renoir, a Tracey Emin or even a Dickens, all chroniclers of social truth, carving out a career in Abu Dhabi. The highest-profile artists were those who painted straightforward portraits of the royal family, prize falcons and horses.

As for the rest of the world, what kind of values could it expect Abu Dhabi to bring with it? Were the ways of the desert coming west, or was a new hybrid personality reflecting a multicultural city?

◆ ◆ ◆

I leave Customs with my bland grey wheelie suitcase. Diminutive Asian men scurry around, nodding, eager to pull it along for me. 'Taxi, madam. Take bag, madam.'

'Hotel. Only best places.'

I'd forgotten how people trail others here, women trailing men, servants trailing their masters, the young trailing the experienced. With the Indians trailing me, it's like being back in the old *souk*.

A taxi veers across the road and screams to a halt in front of me. The door flings open and a Pakistani man, in *salwar khameez*, jumps out, lifts my case into the open boot and guides me towards the door in one fluid movement.

'*Marhaba*, downtown, please,' I say, struggling to recall the peculiar blend of English, Arabic and Urdu that is essential for getting around town, 'near the Corniche. An apartment, *yani*. I will show you.' I reach for the seat buckle and he shoots onto the wide, straight highway of neon that runs into the city.

He grins at me in the rear-view mirror with huge yellow tombstone teeth. His eyes are wide and shining. Unusually long, his hair has been stained red and curls over his Nehru collar. 'Yes, yes. We go town now. We go there. Ha-ha. First time in Abu Dhabi?' he shouts, over a tape of frenzied devotional music.

'I used to live here.'

'I am Irfan.' He looks round at me while I gaze straight ahead. 'I show you the city. I give you my card. You need taxi, you call me.'

'Thanks. Your taxi smells nice.' It reeks of some sea-breezish scent.

He giggles loudly, high-pitched, like a girl. 'Yes, yes. You want to try it?'

'No, I'm fine. Thank you.'

'Please, look, look. I have many perfumes. I don't know why. I love perfume.' He pulls four glass bottles from the

25

glove compartment and hands one to me. 'Try one, try one.' Perfume fills the car. I will him to keep his eyes on the road.

It is hard to see the scrub beyond the spheres of light as we bowl along. The many lanes of traffic have been fenced off and lined with evenly planted rows of palms. They used to do this to stop sand drifts from building up on the road. Porsche Cayennes, Range Rovers, Nissan Patrols and blacked-out Mercedes weave erratically between each other like giant slalom skiers. Foolhardy beige-and-white taxis hunt each other down with their horns. Almost every vehicle is immaculate, glinting, predatory beneath the streetlights. Against the palms this gully of asphalt takes on a futuristic air – it's like hurtling into someone else's science-fiction vision.

As we cross the Maqta Bridge to Abu Dhabi Island, Irfan points at the immense floodlit white marble and gold exterior of Sheikh Zayed's mosque, a new structure that I have heard is one of the world's largest. 'You are Muslim?'

'No.'

'Ah, it is very beautiful mosque. Holy place. Zayed buried there.' Irfan nods to me. 'Inside.' Sheikh Zayed, who ruled Abu Dhabi from 1966 until 2004, wanted to create a stadium of faith for his God. It took ten years and 2 billion dirhams to build, and he died before it was completed.

'Fifty thousand men can go inside,' Irfan says. 'Many, many coming for prayers. Largest Persian carpet in the world. You should go.'

'Me?'

'Yes, yes. Christians can go and look. Women can go and look. Everyone can see inside it. In Abu Dhabi it is

OK. They want you to know about it.'

It looks like a huge wafting cloud of Paradise, millions of tonnes of marble and gold, bringing Qur'ānic wisdom to the people of the city. Countless domes and minarets rise into the night sky. The equivalent of the dramatic church spires and cathedrals built across Europe during the Renaissance – or perhaps the Vanderbilts' Grand Central Station or the Twin Towers – this mosque is an icon for the world.

We hit the downtown traffic. Zayed may have passed away, but on the streets he is still very much alive. Images of him, revered as the father of the city, are everywhere. His people cannot quite let go, it seems, and he reigns on, credited with taking the poor, forgotten sheikhdom and caretaking its growth into a peaceful, powerful nation state. Vast awnings for property and telecoms companies hang from high-rises, radiating slogans in nonsensical English: 'Add Life to Life', 'The Reflection of Nature in Your World', 'Living the Art of Life'. Images of the old Arabia, camels, coffee pots and smiling captains on dhows, wink hopefully between them. It's difficult to tell what chasm exists between advertising and reality. The whole place is even more brightly lit close up than it was from the sky. A couple of decades ago, all this neon would have crashed the struggling power grid.

'I show you city. No extra cost. Just twenty dirhams.'

'Why not? Let's do it,' I say.

He smiles and loops round along the eastern stretch of the Corniche. 'Look, there, big development.' He flicks his fingers and gestures into the distance. The Al Raha Beach construction project has reclaimed 5 million square metres of coastline to create a beachfront suburb in the Abu Dhabi-Dubai highway. 'Big houses for super-duper rich mans. Maybe I will live there.' He cackles.

'How many are they building?'

'Many, many thousands houses.'

'We used to go to the mangroves,' I say. 'They were full of shells and crabs.'

He looks at me in the mirror as if I'm mad. On a nearby billboard a man in loose white shirt and trousers balances a child on his knee with an apartment complex behind him. It's an idea of living but not an actual life. Ahead of us traffic inches along.

'Is there an accident?'

'No, no, traffic terrible, always terrible. Many, many cars in Abu Dhabi and nowhere to park. The man has a car, the woman has a car. The man has another car and another car. His children have car too. A different car for every day. Too much. Always terrible driving. All local comes out at night. Likes to drive around. You like to go out. Many, many nightclub, all hotel have nightclub. Hilton on beach. Boom boom. Crazy-time party.' He giggles again. 'But I no go here. I have no money for nightclub.'

We creep into a mosaiced underpass. I feel I should know this place but I don't. Cranes are still moving; lifts run up and down the half-built skyscrapers as men work through the night. A pair of long-necked winches arc across the night sky. Buildings are patterned with Arab motifs, arches, latticework and turquoise glass. The lines follow the curves of the Islamic crescent moon. It makes the skyline of the late 1990s seem Lilliputian.

Sheikh Zayed had kept the pace of change under control.

Before his death there had been a brake on development, a kind of natural sympathy with what was deemed appropriate. The next generation of decision-makers observe no such limits. In the four years following Zayed's death there has been more construction than there was in the previous forty. For Khalifa and Mohammed nothing is too audacious or expensive. The country is rich enough – 420,000 citizens with an average net worth of $17 million each. And a whole lot more oil money goes undisclosed. My father used to say the sudden arrival of money was like everyone in rural Cornwall winning the lottery overnight. Barely two generations on, families who scarcely scraped a living from fishing, camel-rearing, date-farming and goat-herding have become sophisticated consumers of the very finest and most expensive lifestyle the world has to offer.

'Abu Dhabi Mall, Marina Mall, many malls and shops,' Irfan sings, waving both arms indiscriminately as we stop and start in the middle lane. 'Everything here. Designer perfume!'

'We've got malls like this at home. I'd rather go down to the *souk*. That's my kind of shopping.'

'Ha! No more *souk*. Old *souk* all gone. You will see.' He sniggers. 'Everything from old gone now. New centre coming.'

On the corner of Hamdan Street I finally see something I recognise: the Automatic restaurant where we used to hang out. It bears a sign that reads, 'Established 1976.' Outside, the same fake grass and cheap plastic umbrellas welcome customers. A young chef in the window shaves strips of chicken into pockets of flat Arabic bread with the sleight of hand usually reserved for magicians. He wraps up several such sandwiches, *shawarma*, in seconds. We turn off the main drag and creep through the back-streets. Labourers from Pakistan and Bangladesh squat silently by the roadside in overalls, eating and staring; a Filipina girl in capri pants and a T-shirt runs across the grass and trips over a coil of hosepipe; Indian shopkeepers slouch against bales of cloth inside a line of fabric stores. Oddments of English jump out from the signs: 'We Have Oversize for Big and Tall People', 'Titanic Electric', 'Ready Made Garment Apparel Shop' and 'Lucky 1st Chance Love Flowers'.

◆ ◆ ◆

My disorientation on returning brings Wilfred Thesiger to mind. The explorer spent years protecting and serving his companions in the harsh conditions of the Arabian peninsula during the 1940s and early 1950s, writing *Arabian Sands* as a homage to the nobility of those people who guided him across the desert. But when he returned to the Gulf in 1977 he almost died of fright at the pace of the modernisation that had consumed the place and its people. His shock soon turned to angry reproach.

Thesiger was the last of the adventurers in the old British tradition. In many ways he was a self-declared anachronism. Britain was losing its influence as the dominant world power and Thesiger, a child of empire, born at the British Legation in Addis Ababa and unapologetically privileged, represented the last of that tiny élite of British Arabists to be seduced by the romance of the desert and the wild barbarism of its people. There was quite a group – T. E. Lawrence, Wilfred and Anne Blunt, Charles Doughty – and Thesiger was the final outsider to be afforded time to live in the world of the charismatic masters of the sands. He turned his back on the advantages that followed an education at Eton and Oxford for the precarious world of the Arabian peninsula. Like T. E. Lawrence before him, Thesiger embraced the austere, disciplined way of life that the desert demanded. To someone familiar with the cold and forbidding regimen of a British boarding-school, it promised fresh terrain and superior trials. Enforced endurance befitted the man he wanted to become, and he loved the sands more for the conditions in which they forced him to live than their beauty. 'The everyday hardships and danger, the ever-present hunger and thirst, the weariness of long marches: these provided the challenges of Bedu life against which I sought to match myself, and were the basis of the comradeship which united us.' The Bedu belief that satisfaction in any task was in inverse proportion to the effort required was, he said, the most strikingly beautiful expression of humanity there was. 'Among no other people,' he wrote, 'have I ever felt the same sense of personal inferiority.'

What he got in return were men who would become his great love, a people whose strength of character matched his. They took on Thesiger as one of their own, naming him Mubarak bin London, teaching him the codes and intimacies of the desert brotherhood, about the tribes, the lore, how to greet others with broad overarm waves and the tossing of sand into the air, how to hunt with falcons, where to spot the tracks of a hare. And while he was among them, the Rashid considered him a member of their tribe. When he spoke of Zayed's prowess in the desert as a hunter and falconer, he did so as a Bedu. All he ever wanted was to be at one with them, to starve when they starved, to rejoice when they rejoiced, to retain their confidence in return for his own dependence.

The poignancy of Thesiger's writings and photographs comes from his appreciation that the 'barbaric splendour' of the Bedu way of life would not last more than another few years. With the Second World War at an end, prospectors from Britain, America and France courted the leaders of the desert tribes on the Arabian peninsula. Having successfully tapped reserves in Iraq, Bahrain, Kuwait and Saudi Arabia, these oilmen were eager to search territories further south. Geologists were convinced that the thick seam running south from Iraq would yield as far down as Abu Dhabi. Indistinguishable from their diplomatic counterparts, these men were the heralds of change. When Thesiger left Arabia, from the sandy airstrip in Sharjah in the autumn of 1950, he knew he was going into exile from the place he had come to know as home.

During that ill-fated trip in 1977 he was barely able to contain his resentment. *His* Arabia had disappeared and he wanted it back. Blaming oil and the car for the destruction of his beautiful wilderness, his preface to a reprint of *Arabian Sands* was peppered with bile about the fate of the people he had believed the most virtuous on earth. The barefoot Bedu had become lazy, content to ride around in saloon cars. He wondered where the patience, wit and resourcefulness that had defined them had gone. The men had grown fat on rich food. The women were left with little to occupy themselves now that their role had been taken over by cheap labour from the Indian sub-continent. And surrounding the fallen people, a wash of fawning expatriates were drunk on their newly acquired status. Like a lover betrayed, he declaimed this new Abu Dhabi as 'the final disillusionment'.

Thesiger's bitterness arose from his childlike expectation that the Bedu would want the life he would have chosen for them. Yet he was not unconnected with their modernisation. It was after meeting Locust Control Officer O. B. Lean, who was looking for a man to collect information on locust movements and breeding grounds, that he was given the opportunity to travel through the southern part of Arabia. It was an alluring offer, and with the protection of his tribal companions he became only the third outsider to have crossed the Empty Quarter, the deserts that ballooned out from the south-west of Abu Dhabi's territory into Oman and Saudi Arabia. It was a great irony that his data and maps were later used to help oil prospectors navigate the featureless terrain.

In my suitcase I have a small book sponsored by the oil giant BP about the final trip Thesiger made to Abu Dhabi in 1990. Few copies were printed. As an old man of eighty, in failing health, he made one last trip back with the blessing of Sheikh Zayed to attend an exhibition of his photographs. Meticulously turned out in suit and tie, he was welcomed as a returning hero. Sheikh Zayed stepped forward to thank him for giving his people an image of themselves that would otherwise have been forgotten. To the urbanised young, the pictures were a revelation, a shocking glimpse of the gulf between their fathers' and grandfathers' lives and the present. The portraits of lean young Arab men – in robes, and ammunition belts with Khanjar daggers and guns wedged into them, their hair long over their shoulders, black eyes, handsome and high-cheekboned – testified to a distant, forgotten and dramatic world. They looked like mythical warriors, legends that time should have treasured, not discarded.

The book chronicles the final reunion between Thesiger and two tribesmen he had travelled with, bin Ghabaisha and bin Kabina. These once vital young men were white-haired and shrunken, content in the sunset of their lives, with children and grandchildren to carry forward their achievements. There is a snapshot of the three men standing at Birkat al Mauz, a picturesque village in the interior of Oman, like three elderly tourists at the gates of history.

In his twilight years, Thesiger conceded that change had always been inevitable. Though he chose to live in solitude and without electricity in a small house in Kenya, he accepted that life in the modern world had been a welcome advance for most Arabs. He called modern Abu Dhabi a place of dignity and beauty. Given the choice of whether to rise out of disease and extreme hardship, his treasured race had run for the prize and never looked back. Herbs or hospitals? Cars or camels? There was no contest.

◆ ◆ ◆

Irfan floors the accelerator as we escape another set of lights. I am thrown back in my seat and his speedometer hits 120 kilometres per hour. '*Mafi, mafi. Sway, sway.* No, no. Slow, slow,' I shout. I've seen the YouTube footage of the world's biggest car crash – two hundred vehicles mangled on the highway between Abu Dhabi and Dubai.

'Ha! You don't want go fast? You are scared!'

I grit my teeth. 'No, it's OK, you can go fast.' This city demands surrender. You have to fall in with the unpredictable pace of things. Momentarily overwhelmed with terror and exhilaration, I feel an unexpected wave of affection for the place.

2

Write the Bad News in Sand

Before dawn the muezzin begins calling the faithful to prayer. Drifting into my dreams, connecting and disconnecting, the call from the minaret next to my apartment block is joined by another, further away, then another and another. Within a minute, the air is alive with prayer calls from mosques across the city. Tannoys mounted at the top of the minarets throw their cries over the rooftops. Driven to the edge of distortion, they have a near-celestial air, catching the spirit of the city like a distant echo through time.

I sweep back the curtain. Twenty floors up, a rush of vertigo turns my stomach. Below, the lights of looming cranes are losing their shimmer as the sky brightens on the horizon and the city begins to wake. I can see a strip of the Corniche through a gap between two high-rise buildings and just make out the pit where the bustling *souk* once stood. They have razed it to the ground. A cluster of skyscrapers with a space-age bazaar on the ground will take its place. Such wanton destruction of their own heritage cannot be called progress – all that atmosphere: the smell of frankincense, the thrilling chaos of traders and customers bartering, the flip-flop of rubber sandals across sand, the angle of my mother's head when she was being respectful but firm as she bargained, and the hands touching my brother's yellow hair as we passed. All these memories of

36

growing up, strange but exciting, surface. As day dawns it's clear that the town I knew so well has been expertly over-laid with a brighter, glossier mantle.

I decide to buy breakfast from one of the street bakeries.

Behind Khalifa Street the day has already begun. Passing the entrance of the small mosque, whose fervent muezzin had woken me, I peer in. A group of men glower back. I escape into the first shop I come to, M. K. Nahandran and Co. General Stores. It is a tiny treasure trove, supplying the inhabitants of the thirty-storey apartment block above it with an unlikely assortment of goods: sesame snacks, choco-late, Arabic bread, milk, *laban* yoghurt drink, cream, over-ripe fruit, juices, gum, novelty lighters, Pez sweets and boxes of state-government soap from Madras. The shop-keeper eyes me from his perch behind mounds of Indian sweets piled high at the checkout. I pull snacks from the overstuffed shelves.

'Excuse. Where you stay?' He opens his arms and his wide smile cracks his face. 'Which number block?'

I make a nondescript gesture at nowhere in particular. 'Er, close. One near here.'

'OK. You call next time, you tell me where and we bring you whatever you want – anytime, twenty-four/seven. No problem.' He wobbles his head and hands me a colourful card with the shop numbers emblazoned on both sides.

I have developed a very Western suspicion of everyone's motives. The ever-present scrutiny of CCTV cameras, the fear of being robbed, spied upon, defrauded of my iden-tity, mugged and God knows what else is ingrained in me. But of course, here I won't need to worry. If things are as they used to be, nothing bad is likely to happen to me. Asian shopkeepers and migrant labourers, sweepers and cleaners rarely committed crimes. As the BA representative said when I left my laptop on the plane, 'No one will take it. It's not worth it. They're searched coming in and out of work every day. Maybe if it was a diamond and they could swallow it, they'd give it a go.'

The ever-present risk of deportation or an indeterminate spell in prison had always been enough to deter even the most hardened career criminal. Justice and punishment was a shadowy netherworld that human-rights groups had long tried to expose. Calls for change in the conditions and treatment of detainees had fallen on deaf ears. My father still winced at the mere mention of Abu Dhabi's jail: 'It was a bloody hellhole. You didn't want to end up there. It was a dreadful place even to visit. One night would have been punishment enough. No windows, everyone in a cage together. Meals unrecognisable as food.' He once had to negotiate the release of several of his staff: they had been arrested on suspicion of running a substantial illegal alcohol racket.

But for labourers and domestic staff without local connections or a benefactor, imprisonment, without representation, was a catastrophe.

Western expatriates, of course, enjoyed the protective cushion. The safety of their lives in Abu Dhabi was too convenient for many to question. The Gulf was essentially crime-free. Or so they'd have had you believe.

But the Abu Dhabi I once knew was a secretive place. Plenty happened, but you never heard about it – at least, not through the media or official channels. To know anything you had to keep your ear to the ground. Even public information was passed from person to person, and some hair-raising rumour was always doing the rounds: traffic accidents, rapes, frauds, smuggling, disgruntled labourers rioting in their single-sex shanty-towns, children snatched in Pakistan to be used as camel jockeys by the racing syndicates. Up in Dubai a French teenage boy was kidnapped and raped, then almost prosecuted for engaging in unlawful homosexual activity. And there were persistent whispers of a well-known business mogul torturing anyone who double-crossed him in business deals. Justice was not always as we knew it. One story that stuck with me was of a sheikh's son who ran over and killed a French child. Within days news came that the family were back in France, rich as Croesus. *Wasta* and *baksheesh*, local connections and bribery, ensured immunity for the lucky few. Cash was scattered about, dazzling people into silence. When publicity was unavoidable local criminals were protected by the use of initials: 'When MHAZ and KABS attempted to flee the scene of the accident they were swiftly apprehended by the vice chief of the Khalidiya police.'

Many of the people I've spoken to tell me things are changing, and that there is a mood of openness sweeping the city. There is even a new newspaper, the *National*, dedicated to reflecting a more realistic view of Abu Dhabi society. Coverage is no longer confined to the lives of the ruling classes: they are encouraging ordinary Abu Dhabians to tell their story.

The thinking is that even the older newspapers, *Al Ittihad*, *Gulf News* and the *Khaleej Times*, might be spurred on to greater candour. I've heard they have newly operational back-copy departments, too. It seems that Abu Dhabi is taking its history, and the real lives of its people, seriously for the first time.

Is this a sign of a fundamental change of attitude? Not everybody is sure. A journalist working at the *National* has told me that, although there is new intent to catalogue the past, old habits die hard. 'Good luck getting access,' he said. 'It'll be a miracle if you find anything. Let me know if you need help and we'll see what we can do. But don't hold your breath. We don't often get anywhere ourselves.'

The first draft of history is written by journalists. So how was society chronicled in the early years of the UAE? Was everything swept under the carpet, or did Abu Dhabians choose simply to deal with news in their own self-preserving way? There is an Arabic saying, 'Write the bad news in sand; write the good news in marble.' Was everything but the good news deliberately cast aside? Are they now ready to let the facts speak for themselves?

When I think of my childhood in the mid-1970s I always return to one event. It has stayed with me above all others, reverberating into adulthood. It had more widely felt repercussions, too, affecting how people behaved and viewed the place, and marking a watershed in relationships between the various social groups that made up Abu Dhabi society. An English girl disappeared from the sand in front of her house. One moment she had been out playing and the next was gone. No one had seen her vanish and nothing had been left behind. There were no footprints or tracks, no articles of clothing or ransom notes. An investigation rumbled on for a few months. No one was charged and the girl was never found. Instead there was speculation and hushed talk at drinks parties or barbecues, and over dinner-tables. It was in the aftermath, as I childishly reflected on how a person might disappear so completely, that I saw how messy the adult world could be. The event could not be conveniently and neatly resolved. Fault-lines broke out along the borders of race, class and money, and the finger of suspicion was always pointed at any group that wasn't one's own, usually lower down the social order; Baluchis – the warrior people from the vast province of Baluchistan, which spread across Iran, Pakistan and Afghanistan – Pakistanis and non-Emirati Arabs bore the brunt of it. It didn't prevent anyone coming to Abu Dhabi and it didn't stop those who were there wanting to stay, but things changed.

Back then, I didn't understand how fear had tightened its grip so quickly. With time, the scant facts became hazier still, and the story soon collapsed into myth, a cautionary tale to alarm newcomers to Abu Dhabi. Some people scratched on for news, of course. The girl had been at my school. Her brother attended the nursery my mother ran with a friend and a good number of people were convinced that she must know more than she let on because of her contact with the family. Some even pretended they knew the family, mining her for information. They were always disappointed.

Now, all these years on, were things really as inconclusive as I remember? Had it all been shared in whispers and rumours, or had the story been sympathetically and sensitively handled in the media? Strangely, no one can recall. Despite the warning from my contact at the *National*, I decide to go and find the archives. I know there is still no public right of access to information, no codes outlining what may be seen and by whom. No one is obliged to help you. Nevertheless, the past is a good place to start.

◆ ◆ ◆

Out on Khalifa Street, I pass the squatting errand boys, my knapsack laden with water bottles, nuts, dates and a box of carbolic soap bought out of curiosity. After the quaint, *souk*-like interior of the Indian shop, the spires of concrete and glass on the main streets ahead seem almost make-believe, like the Emerald City in *The Wizard of Oz*. These gleaming towers are the images I have seen in brochures and coffee-table books. It is this development that has informed the descriptions of those who champion the city. But this five-star façade of marble atriums and high-rise luxury masks a street universe of ragtag bazaars and alleyways. These *barrios* still hold the essence of an older Abu Dhabi, lined with chipped paving-stones, dilapidated apartments, faded and ripped posters, municipal scrawling on walls and lampposts, schools, houses and associations. They appear to the casual onlooker like streets of the sub-continent. There is noise and commotion, shabby copy centres, money-changers, tailors and snack bars that have never concerned themselves with the small print of a health-and-safety code. Indian cobblers squat in ragged *dishdashes*, making a living from passing street trade, while the narrow streets teem with cars and minibuses, packed with migrant workers, driving feverishly about. Baluchis, Indians, Bangladeshis and Filipinos live beneath the grandeur, like paupers in the grounds of a medieval castle.

I had been told that it is now against the law to string laundry in view of the street, yet balconies everywhere are threaded with lines of drying robes, vests and dresses. Air-conditioning units on outside walls act as posts for the bright nylon lines. The body of the old *souk* may have gone but its soul has claimed this lower world. This is the real engine of the city, with people who have built it brick by brick, girder by girder. Abu Dhabi is a 'first world, fourth world' kind of place. Yet the two seem to exist so closely together that I wonder if, in character, they aren't really one and the same.

The Cultural Foundation, the low-slung centre of arts for the nation, doesn't stand out among the skyscrapers that surround it. There are more people going in and out of the nearby Marks & Spencer. Meandering through the shady cloisters of its vast exterior, past the decorative *mabkhara* crucible, burning oil-soaked nuggets of *oud*, wood, it is a welcoming place, vast and scholarly. The rich scent of spices drifts through the air as I make my way down to the library. There is a reassuring feel of people diligently attempting to preserve knowledge. But, then, the Abu Dhabians do civic buildings well, blending the clean lines of modern architecture with Islamic motifs, the infinitely repeating geometric designs that draw on mathematics and astronomy.

A woman in a black *abaya* sitting at a makeshift table in the atrium raises her eyes from her mobile phone. '*Marhaba.*' Her face is flawless inside her black *shaylah* and her brown eyes hold me to the spot. Resting motionless on the tabletop, her hands are as smooth as alabaster – the skin has never seen the sun. With her plump lips painted a theatrical glossy plum she looks like one of the dark-eyed models from Robert Palmer's 'Addicted to Love'.

'*Marhaba*,' I reply. ' I have been told you keep old newspapers here.'

She raises a single perfectly manicured claret fingernail, indicating that I should go upstairs.

As a child I had watched the women in black huddled in groups like tight-budded flowers as they made turns through the pandemonium of the *souk*. Hennaed fingers flicked away dust and flies and fingered items dismissively. I listened to them whisper, laughing and arguing behind their *niqabs*, the cloth and metallic-looking masks once widely used by women in the UAE. The billowing, black shroud seemed such an odd choice for the climate. Men used to chuckle as they explained that the white robes they wore were to keep out the glare of the summer sun. In six metres of sooty cloth, the women must have felt as though they were inside an oven.

Black was merely a woman's public garb. Beneath it there might be vibrant silk, satin and stylised *khowar*, embroidery in intricate silver and gold thread, and heavy, elaborate jewellery. Until the 1960s it had been the tradition for some tribeswomen of the interior to wear their entire wealth in their ears and round their necks and wrists. But the little girls, in their green and scarlet, pink and flame-tree orange, who played in the streets have been succeeded by another generation who wear skirts and trousers, and walk to and from school, studying so that they might one day be lawyers, sociologists and doctors. The woman before me, as clean-lined as a Russian doll, no longer has to cover her face with a *burka*. Her *abaya* is a nod to her culture and her religion but it is not designed, necessarily, to hide her from life.

Footsteps echo around the acres of polished marble on the floors and walls as I walk the length of the building. A small set of stalls is designed to look like a market next to the café on the first floor. I buy a bottle of Masafi, the bottled water everyone drinks, and a small sponge cake. The stalls are filled with goat-hair rugs and striped tribal cushions, traditional metal coffee pots (made in China, I notice) and Omani bracelets fashioned into novelty ashtrays. The first-floor reading room is quiet, and a group of visitors on the stairs whisper as they ascend. Glossy monthly magazines stand face out on the shelves, like a newsagent's display. *Oil and Gas Journal, Middle-East Economic Digest, Gulf Business, Pipeline Magazine* and other petroleum and gas publications. Where are the people's stories? It is as if the only thing that ever happened worth talking about was the discovery of oil.

An older, tired-looking woman, with purple bags beneath her eyes, approaches. I ask her where I might find the newspaper archive. 'Maybe the library. Ground floor. Also, you try the National Arsheev Centre.' She takes a strip of paper and writes the number in English digits for me. 'You call. Maybe they help.'

'Isn't this the National Archive?'

'No, no. It has moved. I think it is outside now. I don't know.' She smiles at me apologetically. It is Thursday, and in less than an hour the weekend begins. What I can't get done before then will have to wait until next week.

◆ ◆ ◆

It isn't until I am ambling aimlessly through the back-streets off Khalidiya Street that I realise I have seen hardly any sand. Small piles frill construction sites and the odd unpaved patch of hard scrubland, but there is nothing like the flat expanse of old. Abu Dhabi used to be covered with sand. Wind and dust were the twin pillars of life. You were forever shaking it from your shoes and clothes. Now I am skidding from block to block over polished walkways, tiled shopping atriums, asphalted streets and concrete pavements, all of it brushed smooth and immaculate.

The municipal authorities clearly consider sand to be the enemy but I'm fond of it. It's hard not to admire its opportunism and determination as it whips round windows and doors. When my father first arrived, there were always odd-job boys hanging around the supermarket entrance with their brooms. Their job was to clear the sand drifts that blew in along the steps of the new self-service emporium. It was a Sisyphean task. No sooner had they cleared one than it was time to move to another. The doorways were inspected every day, and woe betide the worker who did not keep them sandless.

I spot a small patch along an alleyway between two commercial blocks, take off my shoes and dance across it. The ground gives way under each step and squeaking sand runs through my toes. It is dry and warm, filled with the sensations of childhood.

3
Father of the Gazelle

Since it is the weekend, I decide to get out of town and head into the hinterland. When I was a child, we often ventured out into the desert during the Eid holidays. We would pack our four-wheel-drive GMC Jimmy with Coleman boxes full of ice and food, with a carefully planned menu for cooking on an open fire, and camp as we made our way up the peninsula, through Dubai and the other Emirates, Sharjah, Ajman, Umm al Quwain and Ras al Khaimah. Other times we visited Al Ain and the Hajar mountains, or Fujairah on the rugged east coast. It was difficult to obtain visas, but with effort and *wasta* my father even got us into the unspoilt Sultanate of Oman.

I take out the old map I had found inside a trunk of possessions and papers at my parents' home and plot a triangle, the same rough passage that Abu Dhabi's people used to follow from the coast to the mountains flanking Al Ain and the south-western deserts at the edge of the Empty Quarter, and the Liwa, a sprawl of oases that marks the start of the great ocean of dunes to the south-west. This is where the Bani Yas, the tribal confederation whose people founded Abu Dhabi, sprang from.

◆　◆　◆

Pastoral people drifted back and forth across Arabia more than nine thousand years ago, when the land was more fertile and the climate temperate. Even after this bountiful idyll had ended, in the third millennium BC, and the temperature warmed to today's searing heat, people continued to come. Migrating waves spread up from southern Arabia to settle the Buraimi oasis, the site of modern Al Ain in the fertile shadows of the Hajar, cultivating enough land to support a permanent community. Later, herdsmen of the Bani Yas inched down from Nejd, the large plains at the centre of modern Saudi Arabia, towards the Dhafrah areas in the south-west of Abu Dhabi, in search of grazing land. They settled around the Liwa crescent of oases. It is from them that many of today's tribes are descended.

For these people, and the last waves of hopefuls migrating northwards, the prospects were not auspicious. In a barren terrain, they were forced to eke a living grazing livestock and breeding camels, bringing settled people what they didn't have. Those by the sea traded dried fish to the interior or became pearlers. In the hinterland, people kept animals and grew dates, fruits and grains, selling the dates and stacks of kindling wood to those on the coast where vegetation was scarce. Some raided far-off villages for livestock, camels and people, who could be traded as slaves to anyone who would buy them. The Bedu tribes provided their camels as beasts of burden to those coming to and from Buraimi and the Liwa, and led caravans across the dunes with the turn of every season. Since goods required transporting across the terrain and families always travelled in groups, hoping that their large numbers would intimidate bandits, the camel trains became indispensable.

Over the generations, the settled and the nomadic seemed to change places as fortunes waxed and waned, and tribes learned to work for mutual benefit. Wandering was a necessity: even settled people moved with the seasons to accommodate the climate and the shifting opportunities to make ends meet. They dispersed for winter and spring to the desert with their camels, or the coast, fishing and preparing for the gruelling pearling season, then gathered for the summer in the Liwa or Buraimi oases, where the water was fresh and there was shade, dry air, and dates and other crops to harvest. These people, around seventy thousand of them, lived opportunistically, suspended in the present. Pearls were exchanged for cloth, tallow for candles, soap and foodstuffs, tools and, from the eighteenth century, antiquated firearms, brought in from Basrah and East Africa, India and towns on the Persian coast. Along with his camel, a rifle was the most treasured possession for any tribesman. At sea they followed the stars and the sun; in the sands they read the ground for signs of life. A carpet of brilliant flowers signified that the wadis on higher ground were flowing. The *houbara*, flying south, brought winter cool and the chance to use tamed falcons in the hunt. Superstition and desert folklore attributed aphrodisiac qualities to its meat. Men hunted it until the migration dwindled to almost nothing in the 1960s and the annual ritual, despite the *houbara*'s protected status, moved to Pakistan. On the ground some used salukis for hare coursing, and arrows or guns for the Arabian gazelle. Killing wild creatures was preferable to sacrificing valuable domestic livestock. Since no one knew if there would be food and water the next day, the future was not worth speculating about. 'A drop of dew is as Paradise for a palm tree,' or so the saying went.

From the crescent of oases around the Liwa, the forty or so allied tribes that came to form the Bani Yas expanded their *dar*, territory, through strategic arrangements with independent houses, such as the Manasir and the Awamir, to boost fighting numbers and keep a watchful eye over land. They were not a hardened warrior people. In tough terrain the rooting out of enemies was only done through force of circumstance. War usually took the form of *ghazu*, raiding. Tribesmen would swoop on an enemy village or encampment and snatch camels, goats and people before escaping back into the anonymity of the desert. Smaller clans were happy to enjoy the protection of belonging to a larger, formidable group, and over the generations they created the loose alliance that drew them together to see off opponents from hostile quarters, such as Qatar and Muscat.

Diverse in spirit and skill, the many tribes supported each other to maintain supremacy, or at least independence, through times of conflict and celebration. The Rumaithat settled on the coast, dedicating themselves to fishing and pearling. The Mazari were a traditional Bedu group, the Qubaisat tribesman the incarnation of the versatile desert wanderer and the Hawami always closely connected to the villages of the Liwa. Along with the Mazari and several others the Al Bu Falah spent winters in the desert grazing their camels. Many of the Al Bu Falah also passed summers on the coast pearling. When the Dhawahir, experienced date cultivators from Buraimi, came under their control in the nineteenth century, a settled element was added to the tribal population.

Every sub-tribe fell under the authority of its ruling sheikh, whose decision was final and whose view pre-eminent. The chieftain was a one-man government; arbitrating family disputes, declaring war on other tribes, levying taxes from the pearlers, negotiating trade terms, receiving foreign dignitaries and instilling a sense of loyalty and orthodoxy among his people. He had the power to bring peace and new trade, or foster treachery and bloodshed. Although in theory there was no one above him and his power was absolute, he was in fact held in check: if he did not listen to his people and judge matters of tax, war and the division of food with prudence and wisdom, he would lose their loyalty to another tribe or master. Thus the sheikhdoms bound themselves into tight, self-serving hierarchies in which everyone's needs were considered. Down the centuries there was never any need to change this mutually satisfying framework of governance.

◆ ◆ ◆

When I mention going to the Liwa, Safwan, a local friend from the old days, offers to go with me. 'You cannot go alone.'

When I first began working at the Marina Club he was a member of a tight little gang who roamed the city. We often spent hours driving around, picking people up, until everyone was on board, then journeying off to a bar or a club, or to a party at someone's villa. Usually, the best bit was getting there.

When he was nineteen Safwan left to study in the US and it was more than a decade before he returned to Abu Dhabi. We had lost touch until he found me through

Facebook, and we picked up as if we had left off the week before. When I told him I was coming back he said we should meet up. Now he says he will drive me out into the desert to see the dunes.

'There is a festival down in the Liwa now.'

'You're kidding? In the middle of the desert?'

'Yup. Everyone goes to hang out and get away from the city. They do dune racing and stunt stuff, and guys bring their falcons. You should come. I've got a new SUV. *Yallah*. Let's go see the Liwa.'

Safwan is from an ordinary down-to-earth family. Despite the talk of billionaires, plenty of Abu Dhabians are not rich. Comfortable, yes, and catered for by their government, but not in the league of the royals and other notable families. In the old days he had teetered on the edges of a circle that included some of the wealthiest kids in town. Strikingly handsome, in an angular way, he straightened his hair every night until it hung stiffly round his face *à la* Axl Rose, and wore pristine band T-shirts: Guns N' Roses, Metallica, Motorhead or Iron Maiden. His love of heavy metal and rock was real enough but he was too groomed to pass for a rocker. He was shy, as well: he often had a crush on someone but was too gentlemanly to overstep the mark.

When he appears in the hotel lobby he's unrecognisable. He's in national dress and has filled out a little. The nervous boy with rock-kid hair and rings through his ears is now a self-assured man. He carries himself with the graceful economy of movement men here seem to perfect when they hit their mid-twenties. It's good to see him. He is, he says, home to stay. 'I've done the Grand Tour and there's a lot of good shit going on here now. It's cool.'

He's had a BMW X3 for a few weeks and it still smells new. Strapped in, we high-tail it through amber lights to the bottom of the island and over the bridge to the mainland, but getting to the wilderness is harder than it used to be. Cars stream through the semi-industrial sprawl of fenced warehouses, the out-of-town Carrefour and occasional manufacturing plants. I wonder if the journey will turn out to be a few hundred kilometres of commercial suburb.

He nods at the vista. 'But this is progress, no? What can I say? People here, they love to build things.' He speaks English with an American accent, but a hint of Arab inflection softens the intonation.

'Yeah, and I can't wait to get out. I've been dreaming about sand. I was beginning to wonder if there was any left. Did you pave the whole place?'

He wags a finger at me. 'They're obsessed with tiling, right? Like we don't know how to walk on sand. People did it for thousands of years, and they didn't need fences and hotels. They were busy reading camel shit!'

I fiddle with the radio looking for a station.

'Hey, no Arabic stations! I don't like the whining.'

With air-con efficient enough to bring out goose-bumps, we follow the signs that will take us south. Thirty years ago, coming this far had felt like passing over the lip of the known world. We'd eat round a campfire and sleep under the speckled canopy of stars. In the cold, dewy mornings I would shake out my shoes for scorpions. Occasionally we'd awake in the night to find our sleeping-bags alive with wriggling desert mice that had come seeking warmth. Even to an outsider's eyes the wilderness revealed itself to be less featureless than I could have imagined. We broke down the 'sameness' into small horizons, observing infinitesimal differences between this spine of rubble and that line of trees. And although we couldn't have claimed to travel like the old adventurers, we got to know it in our own way.

Now, with Safwan's crazy Arabian driving, the land flies past. Mirages pull us along the heat-rippled highway. The speed limit is 120 kilometres per hour but we're doing upward of 160. 'What happens if you get pulled?' I ask.

'They'll never stop us,' he answers.

Dusty orange lorries, carrying fresh water and industrial parts, blow their horns at each other as they thunder past. Traffic thins as vehicles siphon off to Tarif and Ruwais. In the back of a Nissan pick-up, two camels sit cross-legged, watching the world race by through their double lashes.

It is reported that traffic accidents cause one in five deaths, which makes Abu Dhabi, statistically, among the most dangerous cities on earth to drive. Only cancer is a bigger killer. It used to be mainly rollovers and smashes on unlit, sandy roads but now nearly half the death toll is made up of unfortunate pedestrians, jaywalkers and passengers. Until recently there were no real penalties for traffic offences. 'Now,' says Safwan, 'they have a black-mark system and a lot of speed cameras. I'll show you the radar boxes. But what's a road for if not speed?'

The highway is less pristine outside the city, populated with a slipstream of dusty, ferocious workers tending the verges. They stand with Arab scarves wound round their faces against the dust, and gloves on their hands. Through slits their dark eyes scan the world.

'People used to travel down by boat. They moored up at Ruwais and carried on by camel. Took 'em days.'

'Not any more. It's almost a shame.'

'Don't get touristy on me. Too many people like the fantasy of that old stuff.'

He spoke in a way that conjured up Abu Dhabian pragmatism. 'Come on, why would you ride a damn camel when there are SUVs? We like this new stuff. I don't need a tent with fleas. I love the space out here, but when I need to get out of the city I like doing it in a car.'

Every so often, out of the horizon, a run of shanty shops appears. The state petroleum company, ADNOC – Abu Dhabi National Oil Company – has stations right across the desert. A trucker's rest stop, a dilapidated motor-spares store and a gathering of men under a faded tarpaulin cover are banked in the shadows of a crest of sand. We pull in and park outside the tiny white mosque that sits to the side of a restaurant. A neat row of sandals lines the mat. It's the midday call to prayer. The muezzin's cry from the loudspeaker on the minaret escapes into the desert.

Two men stand outside, cleaning their hands with their wrists and their feet with their ankles, performing the ablutions necessary to enter the mosque and connect with God. I watch them go in and think of the fasting faithful during Ramadan, wilting on shop counters and petrol forecourts, too exhausted to move. 'That's dedication, five times each day.'

'Not so much. God is inside them all the time.'

'But how do you stay focused in such a busy life?'

'The conflict begins within oneself,' Safwan is reverential for a moment, 'or the responsibility. Anyway, I don't think of it as conflict. Family is at the heart of it. We care about our loved ones and our community. These are the thoughts behind Islam and it's keeping that in mind. The rest is just stuff.' He shrugs. The trappings of his life may represent a secular, Western world but he doesn't have to lose himself to a temporal outlook. 'I talk to Allah. On days when I'm not sure, I implore Him. Am I doing the right thing? I ask, and I wait for the answer.'

'Us infidels call that conscience.'

Abu Dhabi has satisfied the faithful with lavish public funding of many hundreds of mosques at home and across the Islamic world. In Pakistan, they are given to communities where the sheikhs hunt, and in Izzariya, on the West Bank, Sheikh Khalifa is dedicating a huge mosque to the Palestinian people. A necessary element of the Emiratis' portrayal of themselves as dutiful Arabs and Muslims by serving the needs of the wider brotherhood, this generosity extends to overseas aid for Islamic communities too. The Abu Dhabi Development Fund has given billions: aid and troops to assist the Bosnian Muslim population during the Balkan crisis of the 1990s, construction of the Marib Dam for the Yemenis, help to displaced Kuwaitis after the 1990 invasion by Iraq, and now to the Iraqis as they rebuild their country. The money demonstrates Abu Dhabi's unceasing devotion to the Islamic way. Yet at home the government stands by its constitutional pledge to discourage proselytising while tolerance of other faiths is a central pillar of the national outlook: St Joseph's Catholic Church was consecrated in 1965, the Anglican St Andrews in 1968, and Christian holy days are respected. Although there are no temples, Hindus and Buddhists are able to worship as they please at home. And the Tabah Foundation, established to foster a contemporary Islamic dialogue, worked in 2006 to alleviate tensions after the inflammatory response to the Danish newspaper cartoon of the Prophet Muhammad and subsequent demonstrations.

Abu Dhabi's acceptance of other faiths is in stark contrast to the Kingdom of Saudi Arabia's denial of public expression to any religion other than Islam.

'Zayed was tolerant. It's a very Abu Dhabian perspective on religion.'

'His tolerance, you mean?'

'Yes. He believed Islam to be peaceful. And the Bedu said, "We have no king but God." All men were just men – you know what I mean?'

Perhaps the Bedu had it right. Tolerance – or the expert illusion of it – was necessary for survival. When numbers were small, they needed diplomacy to keep encroachers from all sides out of their *dar*. The tribes had to acknowledge the differing needs of their own people and of other clans whose assistance they relied upon. Statesmanship and dialogue were crucial to survival. Expedience, too. And it suits them still. With big, bellicose neighbours, radical elements at the sidelines and Western countries crawling across the region after commercial gain, the rulers have more of a balancing act to perform than ever.

◆ ◆ ◆

The Bedu do not call the great desert across the south-east of Arabia the Empty Quarter, or Rub' al Khali. To them it is al Rimal, the Sands. There are many words for the openness and emptiness of their terrain, and experience has taught them the pitfalls of the mountainous dunes, the distinctive haze of the *sabhka* salt flats, the gravel plains and mountains of the Hajar.

The road we are on, though, is lined with streetlights. It is an eerie, post-apocalyptic panorama, a savage white emptiness trimmed by a line of lamps. I squint behind my sunglasses. Little wonder that women here attempted to protect their eyes from the glare by wearing thick streaks of dark kohl. A line of wild camels, a hundred or so, saunter over pale orange dunes that have begun to rise out of the plains like ripples on a calm sea.

We pass a sign for the Forestry Commission. 'Believe it.' Safwan registered my bewilderment. 'It's weird. It was like he was obsessed. Zayed planted millions of trees out here. He said if he planted enough the climate would change.' He roars with laughter. 'You wait.' We ride on and over a crest of dunes and there it is: a vast strip of palms and ghaf trees stretching to one side of the road, hundreds of thousands, with roots long enough to leach out subterranean water. They are clinging on, alive but not quite thriving. 'No one waters them now. Not since Zayed passed. They'll leave them to die. But, hey, it was a sweet idea.'

They won't last long. This is heat so fierce dates used to be plucked early from the palm so they would not shrivel and die.

We rise over a large crest and then, as if out of nothing, Mizaira'a, the heart of the string of settlements that make up the Liwa, appears. It nestles in a dip at the base of a huge rise of sand. There are stoplights and junctions, and a marble slab that is the Abu Dhabi Islamic Bank. Older-style dwellings made of mud brick flank the new town.

There is a dilapidated strip mall, general stores, a KFC, dark expanses of lush greenery and strips of sand for boys to kick about in, schools and municipal buildings, dark, sketchy-looking palms. The town appears cupped in some giant hidden hand. But what was remote even in the 1970s – there was no asphalted road until 1978 – is now a pit-stop town of about thirty thousand. We hit a small traffic jam. 'You hungry?'

'Yes, kind of.'

'We'll go to the Liwa Hotel and get some food, yeah?' He swings the car round and heads up a long, arcing track that rises onto the outcrop of rock overlooking the dunes.

The Liwa Hotel feels a little like the hotel in *The Shining*, grand, largely empty, perched on the edge of hundreds of thousands of miles of rolling desert. It is fully staffed but guests and human activity are scarce. A waiter advises us not to sit outside, on account of the flies, so we take a table in the air-conditioned restaurant next to a group of young Russian cabin crew and two local men in crisp *kandura*, their sandals slipped off their feet. A European woman strides past in an *abaya*. Her head is bare and the kohl around her eyes has turned them a livid green. On the Russian table there is an occasional giggle and the absurdly loud ringtones of Arab songs over the genteel clink of glasses and porcelain. 'It's popular at weekends. Expats drive out, play a little tennis and sleep. Us Arabs like to get down here and reconnect with our roots.' He smiles.

Even with burger joints and streetlights, the town feels cut off from the city world of Abu Dhabi Island. Acres of palms settle beneath steep dunes where people have made their homes and small-holdings. Some have camels and goats in traditional palm-frond pens. There may be no *bait sharar*, 'houses of hair', any more, for the nomadic herders but many family compounds are the old colour of wet sand, with Arabic doors, delicate stars and Islamic motifs painted across the walls. Still, how many live in the old way? Perhaps not even 5 per cent of Abu Dhabians.

Afterwards we drive into the sand. In front of us the emptiness shimmers. It is the beginning of the Rub' al Khali, the Empty Quarter, almost a million square miles of sand, billowing like a great golden blanket as far as the eye can see, the largest expanse of dunes on earth. There is no escape out here.

The Bedu, those dwellers on open land, lived side by side with their expansive, omnipresent God, privileged enough simply to be. As we sink barefoot into the slopes it is impossible to pretend we are significant. Women in robes once sat on camel trains, sliding down the steepest sands, as they journeyed to the coast. Outside the cool leather interior of the car, there is nothing but the purest, most unself-conscious part of ourselves. The desert eases time and geography into one, and who does not dream of sailing along the sharp edge of the natural world, leaving buildings and ambition behind? It deserves to stay as it is, one of the last great uninhabited spaces in the world.

◆ ◆ ◆

I wonder how much most Abu Dhabians know of their history. Nothing of what preceded the feverish hunt for oil was taught when I was at school here. I learned history and folklore from my mother. She made it her business to swot up on the past and drum into us the history of our hosts until our eyes glazed.

In 1762 the Al Bu Falah family discovered Abu Dhabi Island. A group of huntsmen had been sent by their chieftain, Sheikh Diyab bin 'Isa, in search of food for the tribe. Following tracks, they spotted a single gazelle over a golden dune and began to stalk her, following her through dusk into night and on into the next day. It was the start of a long journey that drew them north to where the golden sands and scrub yielded to the glistening white salt flats and the translucent coral waters of the Gulf.

By the sea they lost her. A thick coastal mist blew in and wrapped her in its vellum haze. The hunters were ready to turn back when the mist began to burn off and they spied her again, across the water, her silhouette clear enough for them to follow. With their robes and scarves trailing in the shallows, they crossed the causeway to the island. After scrambling over breeze-blown ridges, they reached the spot where the gazelle had been and found a spring trickling up from beneath the scrub. It was water, brackish but fresh.

When the huntsmen returned with this news, Diyab bin 'Isa named the island Abu Dhabi, Father of the Gazelle. The Al Bu Falah returned to protect their find and in 1793 they made the island their permanent home. They built an imposing coralstone fort, Qasr al Hosn, close to the spring, which became the ruler's palace until the ascent of Sheikh Zayed in 1966. Today's ruling family, the al Nahyans, are descended directly from those first settlers.

There are few gazelles left. A few inbred communities are fostered in conservation programmes, along with oryx, but the days of legion, roaming herds are over. These days, they are found on mugs, tea-towels, stamps and the currency. Every twenty-five *fil* coin carries an impression of the original gazelle – which was probably eaten – a small reminder of how it all began.

4
The End of Empire

The rites of empire had been woven into the dealings between the British and the people of the Arabian peninsula many generations before the discovery of oil. But Britain had not been the first to try to corral the tribes of the Gulf. The land is peppered with the signs of the Mesopotamian, Persian and Assyrian empires and even early Christian communities. Islamic envoys came in the seventh century, when the religion was young and its converts in the first throes of spreading their message. When the tribes did not immediately take to the new faith, the Islamists forced their way in. After receiving word of Muhammad's death, the people around Dibba, a large town in the north of the peninsula, rose up against the voice of the prophet hoping for a return to their old ways, a blend of their animistic gods and spirits, the stars and moon, with strands of Judaism and Christianity woven in. But it was not to be.

Abu Bakr, the zealous expansionist who succeeded the Prophet Muhammad as first caliph, sent an army from Mecca, recruiting believers on the way to crush uprisings in Dibba and elsewhere in the region. Many thousands of tribesmen were slain; their graves still circle the outskirts of the town. In the years following, the caliph used the port of Julfar, on the northern strip of the peninsula, close to present-day Ras al Khaimah, as a launch point for the conversion of Persia and territories further east. He stamped Islam's influence and authority upon the Arabian peninsula, pressing his new religion into every port, town and island until the faith began to flourish.

In the fifteenth century, the Portuguese began their assault when Vasco da Gama discovered a shorter route to the East around the Cape of Good Hope. Lusting for supremacy over the Ottomans, they established a stronghold that ran from Hormuz across the waters and down through the lower Gulf. The empire did not last, but their buildings, and the memory of bloodshed and cruelty, lived on. A good number of forts and castles in the region date from this time.

The British secured a maritime presence when the East India Company helped the Persians expel the Portuguese from Hormuz in 1622. They set up trading posts at Bandar Abbas, Lingah and Bushire in Persia and Basrah, now in southern Iraq, and began to use the waters of the Arabian Gulf as a trade route.

The stakes rose in the late eighteenth century: Anglo-French relations soured when Britain objected to the colonial ambitions of their European rivals amid accusations of piracy. Having quelled Portuguese power, the British were not about to stand by and allow the swaggering French to take over their imperial trade route to the sub-continent. India was the jewel in the crown of empire and the East India Company the heart of its economic success. The Gulf was one of India's imperial frontiers: safe passage around the Strait of Hormuz and the Gulf peninsula was the key to continued prosperity at home, as well as the expansion of its domain.

By the end of the eighteenth century the British were

poised to wrestle for dominance, not only against the French but with the Ottomans, Persians and anyone else who came in the way of establishing vital sea routes. None had succeeded in curbing the pirates who controlled the coast or, perhaps, the most fearsome obstacle of them all: the Qawasim. This territorial tribe from Julfar, several hundred miles north of Abu Dhabi Island, ruled the coastal waters with a nine-hundred-strong fleet. Their territory spanned the northern part of the Arabian peninsula and a string of towns along the Persian coast at the mouth of the Gulf. Once known for their fine trading prowess, the Qawasim had turned to piracy as a means of raising funds when their commercial fortunes began to wane. By the early nineteenth century no one was safe. Whether Omani, British, French or Persian, vessels had every chance of being attacked by the plundering, pillaging and looting buccaneers. Even small-time trade and fishing expeditions by the nearby tribes were fair game. Transferring the tradition of *ghazu*, raiding, to the seas, the Qawasim drew most of their bounty from flotillas of valuable spices, jewels and ivory. Those spared the pillaging, and costly ransom of prisoners, were levied in return for safe passage through their waters. All who were foolhardy enough to lay chase found themselves outrun by the wild buccaneers, who, knowing the coastline like no other, disappeared into one of the many coves and *khors*, inlets, that dotted the peninsula.

Seemingly invincible, the Qawasim were doubly irritating to the British for their embrace of Wahhabism, the Islamic religious sect spawned in Nejd on the central plains of Arabia, whose adherents wished to prise Islam back from the clutches of the decadent Ottomans. With their strict interpretation of Islamic texts, the Qur'ān and *hadiths*, the sayings of Muhammad, Wahhabists declared all non-Muslims heathens and infidels. The Qawasim had not forgotten the Portuguese reign of terror: it had instilled a fear of all European Christians. Rivalry on the waters no longer stemmed from simple commercial necessity but was inflamed by religious dogma. Despite the unchecked hostility, the British feared the possibility of a clandestine union between these brigands and the Omanis, who historically had claimed sovereignty over the Qawasim: such an arrangement might lead to the denial of port access along the coast of Oman on the southern stretch of the Gulf. The government in London decided action was needed: the empire was at stake. After several furtive, partial attempts to subdue the confederation in the first two decades of the nineteenth century, in 1819 Britain sent a large fleet under the leadership of Sir William Grant Keir. The British armada sailed in on the December tide and devastated the entire Qawasim fleet at the port of Ras al Khaimah. Sailing on to Umm al Quwain and Ajman, they burned boats there too. Only Dubai and Abu Dhabi, untainted by piracy, were spared. As the fires raged, the first peace treaty was signed and, with others following, the Strait of Hormuz all but belonged to the British.

With the debilitated Qawasim confined to tiny fishing-craft, the British set about making peace with the stunned sheikhdoms up and down the coast. Sir William Grant Keir refused to acknowledge the authority of the sheikh of the Qawasim, Sultan bin Saqr, over additional tribes in his dominion. He concluded separate agreements with the sheikhs of Ajman and Umm al Quwain, unseating the Qawasim for good by making them independent, then, as the other sheikhs signed, he looked for a tribe with whom he could build a mutually gratifying relationship. Since most had lost a great deal on the lawless seas the arrival of a foreign guarantor who might temper rivalries and safeguard waters was greeted with some relief. He encouraged the ambitious Bani Yas in Abu Dhabi to step forward. As a mark of colonial respect, British East India Company officers conferred upon their new allies a three-gun salute.

The series of truces struck between the British and the remaining tribes culminated in the Perpetual Maritime Truce of May 1853. In signing the agreement the sheikhs made peace with each other for the first time. The truce also acknowledged the 1833 division of the Bani Yas tribe, when the al Makhtoum family, of the al Bu Falasah sub-tribe, established themselves as rulers of Dubai, leaving the rest behind. This ended the era of piracy and gave the once-perilous seaboard the name it would bear to outsiders until the establishment of the UAE in 1971: the Trucial Sheikhdoms, or States.

Though the subdued tribes occupied both the interior and the sea routes, it was pearls as well as trade that kept British and other foreign interest centred on the coast; pearls had been traded to faraway empires for thousands of years. The Egyptians, the Greeks and the Romans had all prized them. Renaissance Europeans treasured them as a symbol of global dominance, exotica and authority. From the time of the Medici to the end of the British Raj, these jewels of the sea adorned crowns, orbs and the finery of the aristocracy across the kingdoms and principalities of Europe. It was the same in the East. From China to India, pearls were highly sought-after. For the tribes on the Trucial coast pearling offered the greatest opportunity to change personal fortunes. Successful divers became merchants and were able to buy date groves in the fertile grounds of the Buraimi oasis, allowing the already settled land dwellers to manage them while they continued the nomadic tradition as over-lords.

Having secured the trade route, the British showed no interest in colonising the people of the Trucial coast. Unlike in other parts of their empire, they did not establish schools, hospitals or anything that would knit together a perma-nent society. There was no transference of knowledge or sense of obligation to social progression. Commercial success was their only concern. Internal affairs remained under the jurisdiction of the tribes, and what the British didn't see didn't bother them. But with flourishing trade, and the advent of the telegraph, steam-ships and a postal service, other foreign powers grew antagonistic towards Queen Victoria's acquisitive empire. There were a number of small incursions into British territory: the Persians attempted to annex Qatar and Bahrain, the Ottomans sent warships, and in the early 1890s Russian and German ships arrived in Trucial waters. However, it was French actions that tipped the balance once more when arms dealers were reported on the coast in 1891, charming the sheikhs and selling weapons to the tribes. With France and Russia sallying into the region, Major Talbot, the British Political Resident, moved swiftly to secure Britain's interest in its protectorate. The sheikhs would be asked to maintain a relationship with the British, and only the British.

With several decades of Pax Britannica successfully behind them, the belt of fraternity between Her Majesty's

Government and the sheikhdoms was tightened a notch. In an exclusive agreement drawn up in 1892, the 'treaty of protectorate', Britain took on all foreign relations for the coast, which meant support against aggressors on both sea and land. The Trucial sheikhs swore to forgo any contract with another foreign power, and not to sell or mortgage any part of their territory, 'in their generation and their heirs', to anyone but the British.

The timing proved fortuitous. The twentieth century brought with it the thirst for oil, and after success elsewhere in the region, it was simply a matter of time before concessions to search Trucial territory were granted. Preparations made through the 1930s were halted by the Second World War but towards the end of the 1940s geologists returned and in 1950 the first drilling rig was spudded in, at Ras al Sadr. This was the start of the search that would eventually reveal reserves beneath the sands around Bu Hasa and Murban-Bab and offshore at Umm al Shayf. Overnight the Trucial territories gained fresh strategic importance. This time it was the land rather than the sea that mattered, and the challenge came from a new set of commercial foes.

During the interwar period the British had been called upon several times to make good the promise of the 1892 treaty. They rebutted claims from Saudi Arabia, Iraq, Iran and America, whose commercial lawyers were consulting with the founder of the modern Kingdom of Saudi Arabia, Abdul Aziz ibn Saud, on securing the long-disputed territory around the Buraimi oasis for themselves. The House of Saud, after permitting the Standard Oil Company of California to prospect in 1933, struck oil in Dammam in

1938. The small British-Indian naval force, which had kept the peace along the Gulf for the previous century, was rapidly expanded. The Trucial Oman Scouts, formed in 1951, became a large, expertly trained and disciplined force, commanded by British officers stationed in Oman, Sharjah and Bahrain. By 1968, three years before Britain's permanent withdrawal from the Gulf, more than nine thousand soldiers were garrisoned there.

It was with the announcement by the prime minister, Harold Wilson, in January 1968, that the British would withdraw from the region at the end of 1971 that the fight for survival really began. But for Britain's Labour government neither the cost nor the ideology of empire, nor the expenditure on defence, could be justified. The sudden timetable for withdrawal came as a shock, both to diplomats with long-standing ties to the Trucial States, and to its people. As a protectorate the sheikhdoms had never enjoyed full colony status, yet since the war the British government had belatedly begun to involve itself in Trucial society. After upgrading political representation on the Trucial coast in the 1950s, they established the Trucial States Development Fund in 1965. Using funds to drive modernisation, the Foreign Office worked in consultation with the rulers, pushing for education of the Trucial people to equip them with technical skills they believed would be required for the sheikhdoms' entry into the industrial world. Feasibility studies were conducted during the 1950s and 1960s and hydrological, soil, road and transport surveys laid the ground for modernisation. Against such initiatives withdrawal looked more like betrayal than the granting of freedom; it strained hard-won Arab trust. Abu Dhabi's Sheikh Zayed feared the vulnerability of his people to larger regional powers, as well as interested parties from further afield: the British presence and latterday years of instruction had provided a buffer of safety. He offered them many millions of dirhams each year to maintain a presence in Abu Dhabi, but Whitehall's decision was final; and with the British population shifting its focus to the home economy, the nation's military and political presence overseas contracted. Besides, the Arab world was alive with nationalism. Cairo Radio had been broadcasting to the region since the advent of battery-operated radios in 1963, bringing the first real news to the sheikhdoms of what was happening beyond their shores, and broadcasting the words of President Nasser to his Muslim brothers: he called on Arabs everywhere to take their place in the fight against colonialism and reclaim their countries from imperial forces. After the Aden emergency in 1963, and subsequent conflict that led to the British pullout a year earlier than planned in 1967, independence was the only possible future.

The journey towards the inception of the UAE had, perhaps, been inevitable since the end of the Second World War. Zayed was far-sighted enough to recognise that for his tribes to survive they must outmanoeuvre their more powerful neighbours with cunning and the kind of unity never before seen. Yet inter-tribe feuds – some generations old – rumbled on amid predictions from outside commentators that the tribal structure was 'pre-disposed to resist federation'.

Zayed travelled the peninsula counselling each of the sheikhdoms at a series of summits. With the prospect of British withdrawal providing impetus to his vision, he asked each to join him in establishing a federation: knowing that concessions were necessary, he gave way to Dubai on the thorny issue of overlapping boundary claims around Khor Ghanada that had erupted into war between the two states in the late 1940s, and struck an agreement with Sheikh Rashid bin Said al Maktoum, Dubai's ruler, in February 1968. The British government, despite its commitment to leaving, exerted pressure through political agents and visiting representatives in support of a federation, and Zayed continued to sell the sheikhs a vision of a strong, independent nation able to repel its greedy, oil-hungry neighbours.

It was a powerful ideal. Bahrain, Qatar and the Trucial States came together in the months that followed, finding agreement in principle, though not over the practicalities of union. By the start of 1971, with the reality of withdrawal looming, there was still no formal agreement. Already modernised as a result of oil, Bahrain, which had been the first Gulf state to make a strike in 1932, declared it would go it alone, and Qatar followed suit shortly afterwards. Other than Abu Dhabi and Dubai, none of the states had much in the way of oil reserves and, therefore, lacked the same chance of exceptional wealth. Zayed vowed that, in return for solidarity, he would share the profits and bring comfort and wealth to all his Trucial brothers. Four of the remaining five Sheikhdoms – Sharjah, Umm al Quwain, Fujairah and Ajman – pledged agreement to a union, and Zayed was appointed president. The morning after the British terminated the protection treaties, on 2 December 1971, the new country, the United Arab Emirates, came into being.

A few months later the shape of the UAE was set when Ras al Khaimah joined, having failed to find international support for its own independence. The leading tribes of the region, the Bani Yas, the al Ali, the al Sharqi, the Nuaim, the al Qasimi, had put their centuries-old differences behind them and taken control of the south-eastern Arabian peninsula.

The formation of the UAE dumbfounded the cynics, who believed that the tribal system, based on absolute allegiance to one leader, would not be flexible enough to sustain it. But Zayed had believed the tribes would see the sense of holding together. 'Our experiment arose from a desire to increase the ties that bind us, as well as from the conviction . . . that they were part of one family, and that they must gather together under one leadership. I am not imposing change on anyone. That is tyranny. All of us have our opinions, and these opinions can change. Sometimes we put all opinions together, and then extract from them a single point of view. This is our democracy.'

The Trucial States were, perhaps, unusual in choosing monarchy when the region, from Iraq to Egypt, was swelling with young republics. But its *de facto* orthodoxy allowed for progress and Zayed, always committed to Arab unity, held the reins of absolute power with dutiful humility.

◆ ◆ ◆

Immediately, trade in the UAE's new capital, Abu Dhabi, took off. With the canopy of military policing lifted, foreign corporations were free to make overtures to the ruler and his counsellors. Although Britain had lost the virtual monopoly it had held, many of its businesses – in catering, desalination, shipping, water purification, energy and utilities – were still closely aligned to the new leadership. With large quantities of oil assured, the opportunities for future trade increased. The British might not have brought the Anglo-Saxon lifestyle to the region but in Zayed they had a fan. During his visits to London and Paris in the early 1950s, he had been inspired by the way in which people lived and dreamed of bringing it to his people in the form of schools, hospitals and a comfortable quality of life. The British way was to be admired, aped, even, ensuring that two centuries of entwined history would not be forgotten.

None the less, British policy encouraged a slow erosion of influence. Abu Dhabians might once have favoured the British, but Harold Wilson's alliance with the Israeli government of Golda Meir upset many Arabs, whose allegiance was to the Palestinian cause. It resulted in a boycott of British goods and even a small anti-British demonstration along Abu Dhabi's streets. With the Emiratis under no obligation to choose British products, manufacturers found they were hit by international competitors. Then, in the autumn of 1980, the Conservative prime minister Margaret Thatcher announced plans to cut tertiary-education grants to students from Commonwealth countries and former protectorates, and British universities were suddenly among the most expensive in the world for foreign students. Britain was no longer the preferred destination for the thousands of Middle Eastern teenagers who left home each year seeking a degree. Thatcher's policy was politically justifiable: this was a time of upheaval in the education system, high unemployment and social unrest in Britain, and patronage of overseas students was indefensible in the market-driven economy the Tories championed. The changes went ahead despite the warnings of opposition leader Neil Kinnock, the British Council and the Foreign Office that Britain would lose abroad what it needed to keep above all else: its influence.

Thatcher's conceit lay in believing that the brightest and best would still choose to come. Instead, gifted students from territories of the former empire went elsewhere, most often to the USA's Ivy League institutions that offered modern courses in marketing and engineering. In one stroke of Thatcher's pen, Britain's sway was ended.

Given the choice, perhaps Abu Dhabians would always have come to prefer America's ideology of disposability: Betty Crocker, Pop-Tarts, Kraft Cheez Whiz, Dairy Queen, huge cruising cars and walk-in refrigerators. America was a young country, built on the efforts of the pioneers who had tamed the land to establish their nation state. Abu Dhabi, leading its own frontier culture, perhaps found a mirror in the determination of those early settlers struggling to subdue the Nebraskan plains, struggling on in the belief that God would provide good crops after frosts and disease. Its own clansmen had cultivated just enough of the desert to sustain life. When oil relieved them of their hard existence, they rushed, with absolute dedication, at a new age of plenty. They made a life where convenience is king.

5
Grande Dame

The winter months in Abu Dhabi are the most comfortable time of year. Temperatures hover in the high twenties, and on the coast the humidity is not as drenching as it is in summer. Children play football on the grassy strips at the edges of residential streets and in the municipal parks, while the Corniche fills with people out walking. But not 2008. This year the usual January showers have turned into an uninterrupted week-long deluge. In a country where rainfall is almost non-existent, such a downpour is a once-in-a-generation event. With rain gushing down during official visits by Presidents Bush and Sarkozy, I am told by everyone old enough to remember that these are the heaviest rains since 1982. At an official function given for the French premier, the tent had split, soaking half of the guests in a surge of water.

Last evening I'd had dinner with some old friends of my parents, Anne and Dick Hornby. It had turned into quite a night, and today Anne insists on driving me uptown to my morning appointment. 'You'll never get a taxi in this.' She laughs. 'There won't be any golf today, and I'm happy to miss my bridge.'

Anne and Dick have been in Abu Dhabi since the early 1990s. Dick is a naturalist with an environmental agency and a team of crusaders who grow busier each year, counting trees, selecting marine and soil samples, tramping the length and breadth of the Emirate and reporting on the potential impact of the many thousands of new building projects under way on once untouched offshore islands. Dick's love of the natural world is evident from the time he has spent as a volunteer for Emirates Natural History Group. On the subject of birds, gazelles and other indigenous mammals, he is almost unstoppable. And despite what he leaves unsaid about the irreversible changes he has witnessed I can see how the passion of a few has laid the rich foundation of scientific knowledge about the country's biodiversity.

Anne, a bright and lively redhead, had been a senior nurse with the NHS in Britain. Now she is an accomplished golfer with several bridge fours each week. 'You have to work hard to fill your days sometimes,' she had said, the previous evening, as we sat in her lounge, drinking large expatriate measures of gin and tonic. But her excess of time allows for generosity, and I'm relieved that she has come to my aid.

We plough through another lake, which sends arcs of spray into the air. The wipers struggle while huge rain-drops burst on the windscreen. I can barely make out the red tail-lights of the car in front.

Among the many young graduates coming out to boost numbers in IT and property, Anne and Dick could almost be considered old-timers, but there is still a handful of true expatriate elders. I am on my way to visit one: Jocelyn Henderson, wife of the late Edward Henderson, diplomat, oilman, friend of the Arabs. Edward and Jocelyn were among the first British settlers in modern Abu Dhabi.

Jocelyn has lived through the end of empire, the birth

of the UAE and the dawning of the age of comfort and privilege. My mother called her 'old Gulf'. When she and Edward had arrived, Abu Dhabi was fit for only the most adventurous and intrepid. There were no hotels, no running water, no schools or roads, just sand tracks, travel by dhow between Dubai and Abu Dhabi, and shanty homes. Only the ruler's palace at the old fort was a secure structure. But Edward had felt at home, and within a year of joining him Jocelyn had made her own mark, helping to establish the first Anglican Church community and library.

Anne corners onto Karama Street where the downtown skyline yields to large estates and high-walled compounds. At the fountain roundabout I see the familiar low wall marking the entrance to Sheikh Zayed's royal stables. 'We'll be in time,' Anne says, as we pull up to the security barrier. She looks excited at the prospect of popping in on the Grande Dame for tea. When I told her where I was going her eyebrows had shot up in surprise. 'I know she's a distinguished figure now,' I said, 'but she was our neighbour when I was growing up.'

The young uniformed guard peers at us from his sentry box. He evidently doesn't want to come out in the rain. The barrier rises, and we curve slowly into the tranquil terrain of plane trees and imperial privilege. Past the disused stable block, the horse boxes and the overgrown schooling rings, an understated row of bungalows appears between swaying jacaranda trees. We park outside one, the faded, old-fashioned sort of property you see in films about the days of empire: whitewashed, long and flat with a shaded veranda running the length of it, with bougainvillaea and frangipani trees. The only concession to the modern world is a swimming-pool. It's one of the last vintage buildings in the city.

A dog barks behind the door – Bertie, her spaniel. He must be old now. I can hear someone shuffling across the floor, accompanied by the tell-tale thud of a walking-stick. The bolt is drawn back slowly and the door opens. We stand for a moment in front of each other. She is frail and stooped, a widow in her eighties. Her light brown hair, once at her shoulders, is cut short. She is dressed simply and elegantly, and her eyes burn with the same fierce intelligence that, as a child, I had mistaken for sternness. 'Hello, Joanna.' She smiles. 'It has been a long time, hasn't it?'

I step into the hallway, Anne following. 'What time shall I come back?' she says, after an exchange of pleasantries.

'We shall call you,' says Jocelyn, inching up the corridor. And that is that.

I shrug my shoulders at Anne, who smiles and mouths, 'Good luck.'

The house is a shrine to an Arabian life. Framed photographs of a city and people from another time cover the walls. Images of track-marked desert sand with majestic tribesmen clambering on trucks or pointing their rifles at the sky hang next to portraits of Edward, Zayed and the Henderson family. One picture has caught Edward and Zayed in the middle of an animated exchange. Both men look young and happy.

A colourful painting titled *Henderson's Folly* hangs in the hallway. It portrays the first house to be constructed for a foreigner on the island. Edward had chosen the spot because it was the landing point for the dhows that took him to Dubai. Back in the 1950s that was still the quickest and least hazardous way to travel between the two towns. Behind the sofa a Perspex block containing Edward's MBE sits on a console table.

'It's a special place,' I say.

'Well, I think so. People call it a grace-and-favour dwelling but it's my home and, I'm led to believe, always will be. Do sit.'

Sheikh Zayed assured Jocelyn she could remain at the stables as long as she wished. When he died, Crown Prince Mohammed renewed this promise. 'After Edward died, my staying on was never in question. Some, like my sister, assumed I would be on the first plane home. It never once crossed their minds that I might not want to leave.' Her eyes flash and she wobbles her stick at me. 'Besides, I really don't like the weather in England. A wretched climate.' She shudders, settling herself on one of the sofas arranged round a large, low table. 'Tea or coffee?'

'Tea would be perfect.'

'English tea?'

'Why not? You can't beat it, can you?'

'Well, I don't know about that.'

The rain drums on the corrugated-iron roof. Above the orchestral din Jocelyn calls for Lucky, her houseboy. He pads out of the kitchen and stands by her side. 'Tea, Lucky, and bring a little something for Bertie.' She turns to me. 'Bertie does so like a biscuit. I'm afraid he's horribly spoilt and more than a little overweight.' She brushes the dog's stout little body with a finger and eyes the rain spraying through the veranda doorway. 'Now, where shall we begin?'

◆ ◆ ◆

Jocelyn came to the Gulf in 1967 after marrying Edward. He had considered it his home since 1948. Once destined for a military career, he had resigned his commission in the Arab Legion over the British decision to hand Palestine to the Israelis: 'It wasn't ours to give.' Instead he went to work for the Petroleum Development Trucial Coast Ltd., a subsidiary of the Iraq Petroleum Company. With trade opening up, Edward's detailed knowledge of the region and its people proved invaluable to the men exploring the empty tracts of desert in the lower Gulf.

After several years' brokering promises on behalf of the company, his success drew him to the attention of the diplomatic service, into which he eventually transferred. But these early deals between tribes had brought stability to a region whose leaders were embroiled in ever-shifting allegiances and cantankerous land disputes. For the investors in the West it was imperative that they had the co-operation of the tribes. Edward, in line with British interests, found himself drawing closer to the young Sheikh Zayed and his brother, Shakhbut, then still the ruler. 'Zayed was still in his brother's shadow, but Edward saw his potential early on. He liked Zayed. He thought him not only affable and intelligent but a natural statesman. From their earliest meetings, when Zayed was the young governor of the eastern province of Abu Dhabi, based in Al Ain, Edward saw how his authority extended far beyond his own people. He was a figure of trust, especially to the smaller Bedu tribes, who frequently needed assistance in settling their own grievances and navigating the commercial minefield.'

Zayed was broadminded, looking beyond his own experience of governance to help shape his leadership and authority. He communed with Bedu elders and other leaders, asking their views for representation at council. During hunting expeditions, he learned what they wanted and made it his business to help them. All men called him Zayed, and nothing more.

Despite his friend's faith and humility before God, Edward sensed a steely conviction in him. Zayed, in turn, trusted Edward like no other infidel. They had forged their friendship in turbulent times, working together to repel the Saudis from disputed territory around the Buraimi oasis in the mid 1950s: reviving old claims to the land, the Saudis had taken the audacious step of installing a representative there in 1952, who attracted attention and support by bringing food to the starving population. By October 1955, with tensions continuing to rise, a military clash looked unavoidable. The Saudi king had Aramco oilmen behind him, drawing old documents together to prove the legitimacy of his claim to Buraimi. And he brought in troops to see the claim through. Edward managed to avoid confrontation by undertaking quiet, face-saving negotiations and moving the Saudi troops from inside Abu Dhabi lines with a guarantee of safety as they withdrew. With the relationship between Saudi Arabia and Abu Dhabi severely damaged, Edward led the search for a solution through arbitration. It was this that led to the establishment of the Documentation Centre for Historical Research, which attempted to bring together papers that showed the provenance of disputed territories.

'I don't think it would be going too far to say they were true friends,' Jocelyn says, between sips of tea. 'They saw eye to eye on so many things and they trusted one another.

That was the real key. They were very similar characters. It was always Edward who would be called on to drive out to the desert when there was something to discuss. Zayed spent much of his time out there, in the silence. It was where he thought best.

'There were times, of course, when their bond was tested, but I think he enjoyed seeing Edward whatever the occasion.' She sits up in her chair and fixes me with a penetrating stare. 'Edward didn't hold with this romantic notion of the desert at all. The desert wasn't a friend. It was terribly dangerous if you didn't know what you were doing. We kept everything we might need if the truck broke down or there was a dust storm – fuel, ropes, water, tyres, all those things. The heat was suffocating. I had a lovely white linen dress. To stop the sweat from my hands soiling it I would lay a towel across my lap and spread my fingers perfectly still across it. I tried not to move at all as we bounced along.'

It is clear that Jocelyn has acquired something of the Arab way: an unshakeable calm, the delicate sense of propriety that some might misinterpret as starched middle-class formality.

'Well, I suppose I might have taken up one or two of their ways. I certainly built strong friendships with the women. Edward wanted me to get to know Zayed's wife. Of course, there was something useful in that but I believe he wanted me to find the rewards he had. The fact is that I could easily meet the women. And few of us socialised with them at that time. To most they were considered a closed order. And they had such different lives. We appeared to live marvellously, with our aeroplanes and so forth. Little wonder they wanted it for themselves.' She blinks slowly, remembering. 'The women were invisible, really. As I recall, the Japanese wanted to make a film of Edward's life, based on his book, but they said they couldn't because there were no women in it. I got to know them better than most. Some had a great deal of influence.'

Jocelyn's first solo visit to Al Ain came with an invitation to see the sheikha's newly completed villa. She'd flown up in a small Dakota with Edward, who had journeyed on into the interior leaving her there. 'Villa proved something of an overstatement.' Jocelyn chuckles. 'I got there and it turned out to be little more than a block of grey concrete set away from the *souk* and the old walled fort.' It was nevertheless the sheikha's pride and joy. Amid the palm *barasti* and mud-brick houses of the village it stood out as a beacon of aspiration.

'When the sheikha came out from behind the curtain that divided the room into the sleeping and reception areas, she took my hand and proudly showed me round the house room by room. I remember being amazed at seeing a proper bathroom. It was large, with gold-plated taps and porcelain basins. I admit I was envious. Such luxury seemed miraculous. But later she confided that it was all for show. There was no running water in the house and everyone washed out of doors in the courtyard, just as they had always done. Even once the money came and people began to install huge American-style ranch kitchens, most people continued to cook outside in the old-fashioned way. Such extraordinary effort, just to look the part.'

'Appliances and cars were like falcons,' I say. People had added them to the old symbols of status and wealth – pedigree birds, weaponry and camels.

'Exactly that. It was rather lovely. They didn't let me out of their sight for a minute. When the sheikha gestured for me to sit on her rugs, Nadia, her daughter, knelt silently at my side while many bowls of dates and other fruits were brought through. She peeled a banana and fed it to me by hand. When I had finished, she opened another. I ate it and then another came and another. What could I do? I had to take what was offered. The poor girl looked so very pleased with herself. I had barely finished one and she would start peeling another. I thought I would burst.'

And all the time, behind the lengths of richly woven cotton hanging from the ceiling came the rustlings of children and servants, padding quietly about on the other side. 'Occasionally I saw bright cloths and drapes. I even saw her young son, Khalifa. It occurred to me then that one was really never alone there. Out of sight, perhaps, but never alone.'

Over the years the two women spent time together in easy silence. The sheikha radiated a peaceful charm. Centuries of living in the heat have produced a people able to convey a great deal from the slightest movement: with no more than a blink or a tilt of the head a teacup was refilled or a plate restocked. 'I think we rubbed along rather well, actually. There were many moments of humour between us, about our husbands, and she was always pleased to see me because I brought toffees.'

Lucky arrives with a second tray of tea. 'Will you be baking today, Lucky?' she asks.

'Oh, yes, madam.' He nods. 'A carrot cake for the bishop's visit, no?'

Jocelyn stayed on to mature with the city. 'It has changed

a great deal but I do still go down to town,' she says. 'There are lunches in the Brasserie at the Millennium with a group of us old-timers and the weekly trip to Spinneys with Lucky.' She laughs at the thought of them ambling round the aisles, selecting the week's groceries. 'And I have church functions to attend. There is no lack of things to do.'

'Do you still feel British, or is this home now?' I ask.

'Well, yes, I suppose so. Britain was the country we stood on behalf of. When Edward jumped ship to the Foreign Office he had to complete a great many forms for the bureaucrats. The Civil Service asked applicants if they were married. And they covered the spouse with just one question. Is she representational? I think we were always aware of that.'

'You were an ambassador for Queen and country.'

'Quite. You were expected to get on and never to make a fuss. It wasn't like today when people fly home every few months. You found your place among the people here but you knew where you had come from. What's more, you always respected that difference.'

The royal family's loyalty to Jocelyn and Edward has not wavered. After Jocelyn broke her hip, members of the family came to see her every afternoon in hospital. When she fell in Mushrif Park, walking Bertie, the labourer who helped her to her feet was taken in for questioning twice, to make sure he had not caused the accident. Such steadfastness comes from a time when those on both sides bent to each other's ways with the open-minded enthusiasm reserved for the genuinely new.

Jocelyn insists on driving me to the taxi rank in her white leather-seated Mercedes, then returns to the compound.

There are no taxis waiting, of course – no one in this part of town needs them: this is the grand end of Abu Dhabi, home of sheikhs and sheikhas, dignitaries, merchants and diplomats, living in rambling family compounds around courtyards and gardens, with drivers on call day and night. We are a long way from the skyscrapers and the cheek-by-jowl homes of those who live close to them. I'm happy to sit under the shelter and wait.

6

I Against My Brother

Time is easily filled in Abu Dhabi. Things just happen. It's not serendipity but a peculiar relaxation of the brain, a letting go that, in often tightly controlled lives, feels counter-intuitive. It allows opportunity to find you. The Arabs call it *insha'Allah*, God's will.

Such fatalism is often mistaken for lack of interest and passivity. To the Arabs it is more the understanding of oneself as a humble soul in the all-powerful hands of Allah. If the outcome is pre-ordained it should not be resisted amid a flurry of wasted actions and empty promises.

In practice, *insha'Allah* is a great proviso. It allows people to let others down gently without embarrassment on either side. *Insha'Allah* means never having to reject anyone. Whatever life's disappointments, it is God's will if things do not run as you might have wished. If a message does not get through or a deal goes sour, so be it. Likewise, if the people you wish to see are able to accommodate you, that, too, is Allah's will.

Vague as it can be, *insha'Allah* is infused with optimism. In surrendering to a higher order, there is always the possibility that things might turn in your favour. There will always be another time, another moment.

I wake to my phone ringing. The sun, already high, blazes round the edges of the curtains, blinding me as I fumble for the handset. It's Dick Hornby. He's out on Reem Island. There's a lecture at the Cultural Foundation on tribal history tonight. Would I like to go? In fact, I'd been hoping to meet my contact at the *National* and ask where the archives had been moved to but he had been called to an embassy function. Plan B had fallen through, too – meeting an Englishman raised in Al Ain alongside some of the sheikhs – so I was free. *Insha'Allah* in action.

The talk is by Peter Hellyer, a respected society figure. For many years, he edited *Emirates News* and now has a consultative role on the National Media Council, the controversial body that helps shape and censor the print and TV industries. Away from the media he founded the Abu Dhabi Islands Archaeological Survey, now part of the Abu Dhabi Authority for Culture and Heritage, and is best known as a specialist on the natural history and archaeology of the region. He arrived in the late 1970s when little had been catalogued, and is one of the few outsiders to have worked themselves into a position of influence.

A cuddly, moustachioed man in jumper and slacks, he stands on the stage of the lecture hall at the Cultural Foundation. In a city of such meticulous formality, where dress codes still count, his relaxed appearance is a statement of authority. He speaks for ninety minutes without pause on the ancient origins of the tribes, their in-fighting, and how they have arrived in the modern age with so many of the old tribal ways and distinctions intact. The club members make notes and nod at every insightful point. He peers up at his audience, all expatriates, and warns, 'If you're looking to live and work here – and succeed – take the time to find out from which tribes your colleagues and principals come. Are they Bani Yas, or Manasir or Awamir? Are they Bani Qitab? Were they a settled or seafaring people, or Bedu? You will fail if you attempt to bring together once-feuding tribes or clans. It is still a closed world, with a history of allegiances forged long ago out of defeat and butchery.'

It is sobering stuff. I had picked up some through years of watching my father navigate his way through the old allegiances and rivalries that drove competition in business. Even the al Nahyan family are fragmented into distinct factions. The six Western-educated sons of Sheikha Fatima bint Mubarak, Zayed's favoured fifth wife, of whom Crown Prince Mohammed is the eldest, are the rising power-block to beat these days. The president, Khalifa, who has no full-blood brothers, maintains long-standing allegiance to the Bani Mohammed bin Khalifa branch of the family. This, and other strategic marital alliances, contain and balance the axis of power in a complex family structure. Tribal history in the UAE has an almost arcane power which persists, albeit beneath the surface. Ambition, competition and the desire for supremacy are at the hidden heart of the Abu Dhabian psyche. And everything is done in the family name. They no longer murder the competition; instead victory takes place in the ministries and boardrooms and at the camel track. An Arab saying sums it up: 'I against my brother, I and my brother against our cousin, my brother and our cousin against the neighbours, all of us against the foreigner.' In the past, warring clans would take up arms against a common enemy, only to draw swords against each other again when that enemy had been slain. Skulduggery and chicanery were as much the backbone of life as hospitality and kindness. This is still an honour society, in which the shame of a slight requires vengeance. The honour code, *sharaf*, translates awkwardly into the modern age. To more secular societies, espousing self-determinism and equality, the idea that the *ird* – or honour – of a woman, whose life was valued historically at half that of a man, embodies the good repute of the family is burdensome and unjust. But Abu Dhabians set great store on social orthodoxy, impressing a collective sense of responsibility on each member of a clan to behave appropriately. People do all they can to avoid bringing family or tribe into disgrace. Their society relies on trust, as it did when during long periods of absence one tribe tended another's herds, their date palms or their boats at the coast; a group's good name was crucial to its survival.

The other side of honour is ambition. The al Nahyan's history includes more grisly murder and bloody aspiration than the houses of York and Lancaster in the run-up to the reign of Henry VII. At certain moments in the past, to become leader of the Bani Yas was to be handed a death sentence. In the last twenty generations, over half have been murdered by vying brothers, sons and uncles. In the years after the long rule of Sheikh Zayed bin Khalifa – the first of the two Zayeds, known as Zayed the Great – between 1855 and 1909, the region entered its most intense period of fratricide.

After Zayed the Great's eldest son refused the rulership it passed to the sheikh's second son, Tahnoon. After reigning for three years Tahnoon died suddenly and was succeeded by Hamdan, the fourth son, who ruled for just a decade. When the pearl industry slid into recession and European wealth was diverted to armaments for the First World War, his younger brothers, Sultan and Saqr, murdered him because he would not, or could not, pay them the expected stipend for their loyalty. Sultan became ruler but was soon murdered by Saqr, leaving his eight-year-old son, Zayed, to be spirited into hiding under the protection of his uncle. It was Khalifa, the eldest, who stepped forward to break the run of blood-shed. Still unwilling to rule, he had Saqr killed, reputedly by a slave of Sultan who had witnessed his master's murder, then persuaded the eldest of Sultan's sons, Shakhbut, to return from exile and assume leadership, promising that the killing would end. Shakhbut returned in 1928 and reigned for almost forty years before his brother, Zayed, claimed the throne.

This catalogue of betrayal and disloyalty is largely absent from accounts of Abu Dhabian history. As Hellyer skirts diplomatically round the savagery, I watch the audience sit forward. The fiendish side of tribal ambition is engrossing. At one point, Hellyer ponders aloud whether he should be talking about it in public. I wonder why the authorities would consider sharing these stories dangerous and disloyal. The English monarchs and American presidents who were plotted against, deposed, exiled, discredited or assassinated is a match for anything the al Nahyans can offer. Flick through Shakespeare, and you will find the ignobility of Richard II and the brutish whim of the Tudors. Across the world the story is the same. In London this murkier side of history is celebrated in tourist delights such as the Tower, the London Dungeon and the Jack the Ripper walk, as the Bedu once celebrated their mythology with tales of desert perils and mysteries. The Abu Dhabian monarchy is twitchy – but surely the tales are of a time from which they have been freed.

Hellyer's account of tribal skirmishing contrasts with Thesiger's idea of the noble Arab or Jocelyn's stories of bonhomie under endless desert skies. Zayed was capable of making the swift, irrevocable decisions required of desert leadership: he deposed his brother Shakhbut (with the support of a family coterie and the British) to gain control.

Shakhbut steered his people through the bleakest times they had ever known – famine, starvation, the Second World War and the depression that accompanied the final decimation of the pearling industry. Once cheap and perfectly formed cultured pearls from Japan came on the market in the 1930s Gulf pearl fishing disappeared.

However, history has all but obscured Shakhbut's contribution. These days, if he is mentioned at all, it is as a man with his head in the sand. He believed that in drawing on the outside world the essence of the Bedu way of life would be lost, and that their strength of spirit would be subsumed by new ideas and material goods. He could not argue against education, medicine, brick homes and cars, but he knew they would not come without profound cultural cost. His people had managed for generations with camels, dates and palm leaves: in an instant the old assets had become worthless. However, the prospect that children might not die needlessly, that herbs, charms, bloodletting and prayer would no longer be God's cure for sickness, that they would see the end of the unceasing search for water and food was too inviting for most to resist.

Shakhbut had not started out that way: far from resisting modernity, in 1939 he had granted the first oil concessions. After he had heard of the discovery of reserves in Iraq,

Bahrain and Saudi Arabia, and the wealth they were bringing, his greatest hope was that his windswept state might find its own fortune beneath the ground. He prayed five times each day that prospectors would discover oil. It was a long time coming. Immediately after the Second World War prospectors returned to Abu Dhabi to select sites in the desert and run tests, but it was not until 1950 that drilling began, and 1958 when a strike was made offshore at Umm al Shayf. Onshore, at Bab, it was 1960.

Shakhbut had prayed for oil, but when the scale of the vast reserves became known he began to turn his back on progress and the riches it brought. He looked on wealth with suspicion, and only reluctantly agreed to let his palace be wired for electricity. In the early 1960s the first desalination plant was built, then a post office and telephone system established, but these were piecemeal developments. Where Shakhbut could resist progress, stockpiling money in case of emergency instead, he did. In 1961 he placed a ban on all construction.

Alarmed by his attitude, the British tried to inspire him: they invited him to tour London, Paris and New York, but the trip only served to convince him that Western life was fractured, uncivilised and godless. New York, he said, was the most barbaric city of all, where 'people lived as ants, or swallows in the cliffs, with no sun on the streets'. His Achilles heel was the motor-car and he spent most of his trip eyeing the array of vehicles on the streets. 'Keep the cars going,' he told the Americans, knowing their need was his fortune. Back home he owned a splendid yellow Cadillac that he drove in the desert, cruising alongside visiting dignitaries and his fellow sheikhs. But even this was an object of fantasy: when it broke down he abandoned it and used a rickety Land Rover. Eventually he returned to the camel, only reluctantly travelling by car: 'I did all my travels by camel in the old days, but now I have to go by car because if the ruler went by camel people would think it peculiar.'

It was Shakhbut's strange relationship with money that most enraged his critics. As the oil revenues began to flow Abu Dhabians looked for money to invest in starting their own businesses. Many had enjoyed employment with the oil companies – seasonal work as watchmen, guides and labourers was well paid and regular. 'Shakhbut was so staggered by the reality of all the revenue coming in that he couldn't bring himself to spend any, even on his people,' Jocelyn Henderson had said. He insisted that the oil revenues were delivered to him personally in cash, and Edward frequently had to arrange for trunks of money to be flown from the banks in Bahrain. Shakhbut had no faith in balance sheets and liked to be shown that the money existed. For years it was stuffed inside mattresses at the palace, and eventually transferred to the palace dungeon. Only when insects and rats had destroyed the trunks and started on the cash did he agree to entrust it to a bank.

In the early 1960s diplomatic correspondence sent to London bristled with indignation. 'The Sheikh's mind resembles a revolving door. Since Abu Dhabi has virtually no water (a glass costs about the same as a glass of gin) there is a desperate need for modern equipment to distil seawater. But the Sheikh has three times shifted the location of a proposed new distillation plant and may well shift it three or thirty times more.'

Arab entrepreneurs were equally frustrated, complaining

about the lack of pay for months of work. The people of Abu Dhabi, labouring for a relative pittance, knew that wealth was being stockpiled but saw none of it, while their cousins in Bahrain were driving expensive cars and living in purpose-built, air-conditioned villas. Until a real working town was established, ordinary people were destined to remain in the dark ages.

Shakhbut's recalcitrance at surrendering the old order was driven by a deep suspicion of the British. He believed their contracts and commercial enterprises were skewed to favour their own interests. When the first shipment of 33,000 tonnes of oil left the newly built offshore refinery on Das Island in July 1962, he demanded control of his 20 per cent stake so he could fix a market price for it. Attempts to explain that trading did not work this way only made him more obstreperous. Firmly of the belief that someone was out to swindle him, he sought counsel from other nations and even tried to set up an alternative sale for his share. But Her Majesty's Government called on the terms of the treaty of protectorate to control visa applications and prevent foreign businesses, hopeful of building ties with the sheikhs, from entering the territory.

Representatives, though, had been making headway with Zayed. As Shakhbut became more unpredictable, his younger brother met with the oilmen. Knowledge of the interior allowed him to play a practical role, guiding prospecting geologists to some of the remoter locations. And the tribes already trusted him. His fresh ambition and attraction to twentieth-century convention cemented the belief that, for the good of the nation, Shakhbut must be asked to stand down.

A year and a half later, at the end of 1963, when oil began to leave Jebel Dhanna, the first onshore terminal, it was obvious that Shakhbut could not retain power for much longer. His proclamations of the ruinous effects of modernity were falling on increasingly deaf and resentful ears. His impoverished people wanted more. By 1966, all patience had run out.

The British, while maintaining a position of non-interference, supported moves within the al Nahyan clan to effect a change of leadership. It was not without precedent: in 1923 Britain forced the abdication of Sheikh Isa bin Ali al Khalifa of Bahrain in favour of his son, and in 1948, the ruler of Ras al Khaimah had been deposed with their tacit approval for a more advantageous appointment. On 4 August 1966 the al Nahyan family told British representatives of their decision to ask Shakhbut to stand aside in favour of Zayed. With all sides hoping to avoid bloodshed the British stepped in to stage-manage the moment.

It was two days afterwards, on 6 August 1966, that Shakhbut was arrested at his palace by British representatives – the decorated commander of the Trucial Oman Scouts, Freddy de Butts, and Deputy Political Resident Glen Balfour-Paul – supported by two squadrons of Trucial Oman Scouts. He was driven to the airstrip and escorted up the steps of a waiting plane. The only reputed moment of resistance came when one of his daughters stepped in with a gun but she was overpowered and the plane left as planned, flying Shakhbut into exile in Bahrain.

Many say that Shakhbut accepted his brother's vision. Perhaps he was glad to be relieved of responsibility. At any rate, he was not long deemed a threat and after several years in Bahrain and Beirut, he returned to the UAE to settle in Al Ain. He had been born in the oasis, and in the late 1980s, he would die there. Each year he and Zayed met at the British Embassy and exchanged news and pleasantries. There are photos of them standing, drinks in hand, beside the ambassador at the Queen's birthday celebration. If Shakhbut still believed his brother's ideas spelled the destruction of their people there was no hint of it in his face.

There was never any choice for Zayed: Abu Dhabi was among the poorest places on earth, the most arid of all the Trucial States, and the world wanted oil. Zayed knew that if he and his people did not work with outsiders they would be driven out altogether. Pugnacious neighbours in Saudi Arabia and Iran and oil-hungry industrial nations would chase their own gain whether Zayed wanted them to or not. If he could bring the tribes together, he saw that prosperity and stability were Abu Dhabi's for the taking. By opening his country to oil he gave his people a destiny. He took the Bedu from the desert to the world.

7
And Then There Was Oil

My father always said that when change came to Abu Dhabi it hit far harder than anyone expected. 'After Zayed took power the town exploded overnight. Most people couldn't wait to rush at modern life – they'd waited long enough with Shakhbut doing nothing and countless foreign outfits were circling for a piece of the action.'

Zayed, whom Political Agent Sir Archie Lamb described as the man with the wind of heaven blowing through his *bisht*, cloak, had his people behind him. Shrewd, he was committed to shielding his people from exploitation. He renewed the oil contracts, squeezing higher percentages and better rates than those agreed by Shakhbut, and decreed that every foreign business should take a local partner, who would receive 49 per cent of the profits. 'Often for doing almost nothing,' my father chuckled, 'but it gave all those who were interested the chance to involve themselves and learn. And it got money churning back into their system. It was one hell of a business model.

'He enjoyed the benefits of his position, the women and the high life, but he never let his people get sidelined. In the first days of exploration the locals were used as labourers, but I was never under any illusions about who was boss. The local guy was top dog.'

Zayed wanted to safeguard Abu Dhabi's future. As a

child, he had witnessed the collapse of the pearling industry, which had proved to him the danger of relying on an economy that was at the mercy of foreign commercial interest. With the advent of the Japanese cultured pearl, Abu Dhabi's livelihood had drained away. Zayed never wished to see such a depression again.

Every man received a leg-up onto the ladder of perpetual income with cash and property. As the old *barasti* huts were pulled down to make way for modern houses, the owners were recompensed with cash and at least three pieces of building land, for a home, a shop and an industrial site. In the Liwa and other interior villages, families were allocated farmland and machinery. Zayed wanted his people to come up with ideas and show initiative. Every business scheme bubbled with the potential for productivity, skill development and the novelty of adventure.

With free water, gas, electricity and no taxes, Abu Dhabian citizenship became a byword for privilege. For the first time in its history there was enough wealth to lift everyone out of subsistence.

The seeds of transformation had been sown with PDTC Ltd's search for oil. Gradually, the people required to build the industry arrived, bringing the skills and services to realise their mutual ambition. Offshore, new marine concessionaries, the International Marine Oil Company, and from 1954 Abu Dhabi Marine Areas Ltd, selected Das Island, a ragged teardrop of land 140 kilometres north of Abu Dhabi, as the best site from which to co-ordinate the marine search. Barren, sitting beside a channel of naturally deep water, it was big enough to manage the rush of prospectors and, eventually, to house a refinery. Divers arrived to pull samples of dolomite, sandstone and shale from the seabed and run seismic tests. The French arm of the oil consortium sent Jacques Cousteau.

On the mainland, geologists explored the desert hinterland, looking for surface indications of subterranean oil around Murban and Bu Hasa. Working from their makeshift tents, the early teams were small, including scientists, oil executives, doctors, caterers and Bedu guides, but once they were certain of large enough cavities beneath the ground the operation expanded. Planes landing on *sabhka* (salt flat) airstrips brought engineers, construction workers and more caterers. Ships carried the parts for rig assembly, steel rods, hulls and A-frames, and lorries hauled them across the desert. Caterpillar diggers and rollers flattened the sand for pre-fab homes, a row of real toilets on the beachfront and tented camps, and the first migrant Indian labourers came to help Abu Dhabians put together the machinery and pipelines for extraction and storage. When oil was struck and the numbers grew, so did the desire for home comforts. Houses were built for wives and families, while boxes of Ovaltine, Lifebuoy soap and Johnnie Walker Black Label whisky boosted morale in the arid heat.

By the late 1960s PDTC had been renamed the Abu Dhabi Petroleum Company (ADPC) and the town was full of men pitching products and services. Even the nefarious 'umbrella merchants', as arms dealers were euphemistically known, were attempting to ingratiate themselves with the population. There were still only two places to stay: the Beach Hotel and the Al Ain Palace, known affectionately to all as the 'Ally Pally'. Since neither could accommodate even half of the oil and construction men wanting rooms, the lights were always on at the bar, and spirits flowed. Depending on flight times, nights were sometimes split into sleeping shifts. In those early years, it was common to see bleary-eyed men in suits wrestling with suitcases at four in the morning as the next crew of sleepers were shuttled in from the airport.

Anxious though he was to convert his dream of a glittering city into reality, Zayed also wanted to retain the humility that came with faith and respect for the Qur'ān: the UAE should thrive through commerce, but on their journey into the twentieth century his people must not be waylaid by the Western vices of drinking, gambling and directionless secularism. Foreigners' ways were permitted – alcohol was sold in licensed bars, and churches lined the Corniche – but he looked to incomers to respect his people and help them to preserve their dignity and principles. Businesses, even long-standing ones like Spinneys, were scrutinised for their integrity.

'My partners, well, we didn't even speak the same language,' said my father, 'but it didn't matter. You saw straight through to the soul of a person without the distraction of all the chitter-chatter. The conversations were in pidgin. They did the best they could; we slowed down and spoke in simple sentences. And when detail was essential, we had Sami Suleiman, our sales manager, to interpret. The point is, everyone wanted things to work, so they did.

'It was thrilling. Everything was half formed. The town was a building site and no one had any idea how things would go from one month to the next. Half the time there was no fresh water, and cargo ships were stuck out at sea, queuing up for miles to have their freight lightered off.

They couldn't get in because it was too shallow, and Mina Zayed, the port, which had opened only in 1969 wasn't big enough to accommodate most of the ships. Some were out there for months at a time. But there was oil, and these people who had been living off the sea and in tents since time immemorial started to twig that they were going to become spectacularly rich. And they wanted a bit of everything. It gave the place a heady atmosphere.'

Three decades on, Abu Dhabi is still a building site. Cranes and steel pillars are just part of the landscape. Zayed envisioned an ocean boulevard, with flowers, leaves, lush palms and ribbons of lights, and the work that started in the 1960s has never quite come to an end. The tides that dragged sand up and down the coast, opening creeks and shifting shallows, have been subdued with a breakwater. Millions of tonnes of rock blasted from the vast quarries high in the Hajar mountains, above Al Ain and Ras al Khaimah, created a new barrier for the town. Labourers dug trenches, laid cable and erected huge steel poles. At the turn of the 1970s the Corniche was looped with lights, their bright trail throwing shadows out into the nothingness of the Arabian Gulf and the desert.

When I was growing up, the skyline was like a piece of rolling news. We saw villas, apartment blocks and the first high-rise offices go up in weeks. Half of the town was filled with concrete-mixers and steel rods wedged into the ground. Sand came in huge trucks from the desert, and smart developers laid deep foundations for four- and eight-storey blocks so that later, when demand rose for higher, safer buildings, they could knock them down and push skywards. Wide boulevards grew out of the sand; roads covered every track.

Leisure clubs and hotel beaches opened, nothing one day, manned and bustling the next. The desert was being tamed.

Now the Corniche has shifted almost a kilometre out to sea. The beach is a six-lane highway with a terraced pedestrian waterfront, edged with manicured strips of grass. Belts of green gleam as sprinklers drench them in the peachy light of early morning, and glass-sided buildings reflect the first rays of the scorching sun as it lifts over the horizon. The sandy-coloured Hilton Hotel and the Corniche clock tower, once the bold icons of the town, belong to a different, romantic Arabia, one of sweeping dunes and changing winds, not of buildings burning upwards into the sky.

The human cost and confusion is shown in odd, small ways. In the early 1990s an island, Lulu – meaning pearl – was laid over a coral bank a couple of hundred metres out from the Corniche. My father, forgetting it had found its way onto the map, crashed straight into it on his way back to Abu Dhabi Island from a day out around the islands. 'Shit! I forgot they'd built that,' he muttered, as the boat flew up the sand and beached itself, almost knocking us out.

Such rapid, transformative growth has led to environmental disturbance. While I was staying with Dick Hornby I asked him about the impact on natural flora and fauna. He muttered a little about the few remaining gazelles' grazing land having been broken up by pipelines, but didn't want to say more; in some ways it's self-evident, and his role is to guide those who will listen on what is vital and achievable. It is not a lost cause: 'Things regenerate,' he says. 'If you give them enough time, most ecosystems revive themselves.' Others are more vocal. 'I'd like to think I was

contributing to helping the environment, not destroying it,'
says one environmental consultant. Certainly in the short-
term, the government is enjoying the goodwill that comes
from appearing to adopt an environmentally sensitive
outlook. Notional preservation programmes are in place
throughout the country and heartening stories in the press
profile nesting and migrating flocks of tern, tree-planting
schemes and *houbara* breeding. But the people of Abu
Dhabi, and of the UAE in general, use more energy per
capita than anyone else on earth. Water is being drained
from the gulf for electricity, irrigation, industrial and
domestic use, marine life is drenched in pollution, and
noxious, warming gases are sent into the atmosphere as
commercial interests extract and produce oil for the
demanding world market and the residents' power-profligate
lifestyle, which depends on huge vehicles and icy air-
conditioning. It is all at a rate that exceeds the planet's
ability to replenish itself and yet, less than half a century
ago, the villagers used the beach as a communal bathroom,
waiting for the tide to dispose of the waste in its gentle,
natural cycle. Now whatever is saved is nothing compared
to the wildlife and habitat being lost.

My father saw the devastation in the 1970s. In the early
1960s he flew over the Arabian Gulf for the first time on
his way to Kerala. The plane refuelled at the desert airstrip
in Bahrain, a stop on the Imperial Airways route east, and
was making its way southwards along the Arabian Gulf.
Hundreds of miles of luminous coral reefs, swirling like
bright shreds of ribbon beneath the water, bloomed out of
the turquoise below. They were like a submarine Milky
Way. A decade later, flying along the same stretch to Das

Island, he had looked through the window of the old military C-119 Flying Boxcar and his heart had sunk. Grey shadows remained where the coral had been. The ocean was no longer pure aquamarine but in places a dense, darker blue where dredgers had scored deep submarine thoroughfares for ships and tankers. These workhorses were everywhere, tirelessly churning up the ocean floor, leaving swirls of 50-million-year-old trilobites, worms, crustacea and other fossils to be washed in with the tides of silt.

On Das the scrubby beaches that had been the undisturbed dominion of the greenback turtles were breakwatered with huge slabs of concrete. The refinery resembled a bright steel intestine, a maze of pipes and cylinders, roadways, walkways and cathedral towers spreading down one side of the island. Amid wide columns of smoke, a thousand waste flares burned day and night, lighting the sky with ethanol, as millions of barrels of crude oil from undersea reserves were filtered and pumped into tankers that lay in long chains. The greenback turtles that had first laid their eggs there thousands of years before could be seen paddling furiously out to sea.

8

The Unseen Hand

I find myself following a routine. I wake, wash and dress, then wander down to the bakery at the back of the block for warm pitta bread, and to the corner shop next door. Kassim, my new best friend, waves at me from behind his checkout. '*Salaam*, Miss.'

'*Salaam.*' I loiter round the racks at either side of the multicoloured beaded curtain that leads into his Aladdin's cave. There are a great many more newspapers and magazines than there were a decade ago, Arabic, English, German and French. Familiar titles and faces are presented in Arabic-friendly editions. Hollywood style dominates. The covers of *OK!* and *Hello!*, and the UAE version, *Ahlan!*, look as though they have had an Arab makeover: Angelina Jolie, Antonio Banderas, George Clooney, the Beckhams and a few Arab stars attract passers-by – 'Queen Rania Launches Campaign for Women's Rights', 'The Beckhams in Dubai', Brad Pitt with Jolie and their rainbow family. Pitt looks more substantial and manly than I've seen him before, as if he's gained three stone and grown a second chin. Here, a little bulk equates to status, power and provision. Keira Knightley's blank, doe-eyed symmetry has been airbrushed a shade or two duskier on the inside cover of *Vogue*, and her eyes seem darker. She looks half Arab.

I pick it up and flick through the accessory ads: Chanel,

Gucci, Chopard diamonds, Theo Fennell, Asprey, Tiffany. More handbags than I have ever laid eyes on, plenty of expensive dresses and shoes, all of which are available at flagship concessions in the glass-fronted shopping malls. It's as it is at home. The only things missing are the scrawny, half-naked models and the occasional slipped nipple.

When I was growing up, the pages of imported women's magazines were scored with clumsy lines of black marker pen. Women in bikinis, in depilatory ads and the famous Piz Buin campaign, with bottom cheeks at various stages of tan, were daubed with impenetrable black ink. Occasionally the censors would miss a flash of shoulder or thigh. As girls becoming fashion aware, we would piece together what the original beneath must look like from the edge of a bra strap or a bead.

The way they doctored magazines was nothing compared to what was left on the cutting-room floor of scheduled TV shows. Even now I'm sometimes surprised that I can watch a film or TV drama and actually follow the plot. *Charlie's Angels, The Six Million Dollar Man* and blockbuster movies like *The Andromeda Strain* and *The Towering Inferno* were spliced and re-edited in the name of decency. Watching television was frequently an exercise in decryption. Dialogue would jump suddenly, mid-sentence. Two characters moving towards a romantic clinch would spring apart and be sitting at a lunch table or making an angry exit. Countless plot revelations were snipped out with intimate bedroom scenes. The censorship did not extend to violence: the more shootings, stabbings, beatings and explosions, the better.

Sometimes, when there was enough humidity in the air, we could pick up the TV signal from Dubai or Qatar. My mother would sit behind the Sony portable twiddling the aerial, hoping to find something more edifying. 'They do like their violence, these people,' she wrote in a letter home.

Censorship extended to the borders. Abu Dhabi did not recognise the state of Israel so Israelis or those with an Israeli stamp in their passport were turned away. Yet the directives were inconsistent: I received letters from a friend who had been reluctantly recalled to Israel to do national service because his father was a rabbi in London, but my mother had to cut out the labels of our new Marks & Spencer knickers when we returned after our summer break in England. If the men searching our bags at Customs found them, they were taken to join the mountain of underwear confiscated from expats. Now there is a huge M&S downtown. It's a star retail attraction, packed with eager Arab shoppers. I hear that nowadays an Israeli stamp in a passport is acceptable, though still not an Israeli passport. With Abu Dhabi's history of tightly controlled media – an unmistakable sign that the country was, in practice, autocratic – I am tempted to consider the relaxation around print and retail a sign of progress, rather than commercial expediency.

Except that, despite the appearance of freedom, stiff penalties remain for overstepping the line. Moves towards greater transparency are stalling as fast as they are conceived. The 1980 media laws make it a crime to criticise the leadership or say anything that might blot the country's reputation or economy, and have traditionally been punishable with heavy fines or jail sentences. New draft laws propose replacing prison with a fine of up to a million dirhams. An improvement of sorts, but Human Rights Watch and increasingly outspoken UAE journalists are not convinced by the apparent simplification of laws that remain vague enough to ensure that any number of comments could be regarded as critical. To my suggestion that the *National* seems founded on new principles of freedom, a contact at the National Media Council insisted, 'They are being *allowed* to push the boundary.'

Not knowing what to do about the Internet, the authorities seem content with infantilising people by heavily censoring traffic. The state phone service, Etisalat, blocks both anti-Islamic and Islamic extremist sites, pornography, gay and lesbian rights sites, any critiques of the UAE, such as UAEprison.com, and others focusing on human-rights violations, as well as anything with an Israeli source code. Even Facebook has been known to disappear, so several friends tell me. There are ways round it, of course. Enterprising citizens log into dummy servers that mask the activities of the user. But this only accentuates the general restriction placed on individuals. Like people posing best side forward for a photograph, the establishment prefers to keep a firm grip on how it is seen by the world at large.

Zayed managed to sidestep the uglier questions around censorship by transferring the responsibility for upholding the reputation of the state to the individual. He knew, perhaps, that his people would regulate their own behaviour in the interests of the group. They wouldn't want to let him or their young nation down. For generations, every member of a clan had been responsible for upholding its reputation. Such tight and unshifting allegiance to others grew into the stiff structure of social interaction, with loyalty overriding all else. When scandal threatened, the tribe turned inwards. So long as transgression did not reach the public domain everything could proceed as normal. Unconscious self-regulation allowed Abu Dhabi to look liberal.

The media was as whimsically managed as it was restricted by the censors. Television-programme timings shifted arbitrarily. As a child, I found the news interminable when I was waiting for *He & She* or *Tom and Jerry*: every man who made the official line-up at a state reception or an airport-greeting committee would be named in full. One of the Abu Dhabi Television newsreaders told me how his cameraman sat eating pistachios on the floor by the camera and throwing the empty shells across the shot while he ploughed through the endless headlines.

By the mid-1970s there were several daily papers: *Al Ittihad* (Unity), *Emirates News*, *Gulf Mirror* – a weekly from Bahrain – and, in 1978, the *Gulf News*. There was no tabloid culture. Newspapers were founded on the same protocol and public-relations mix as television: editorial policy ensured that each organ offered public support for the new country's endeavours. The authorities preferred to shelter people from the worst kind of news: urban crime was unsettling to this small, familial culture and there was a fear its incidence would be exaggerated. There might have been more than enough business to fill the papers but much of it was too exposing and embarrassing to be reported by a young, vulnerable country keen to persuade neighbours to take it seriously. There were endless swindles and heists that took advantage of inexperienced locals. Fly-by-night export companies dumped seconds on Abu Dhabi entrepreneurs, and hoax companies traded non-existent goods and absconded with the cash. Lack of commercial experience and naivety over others' motivations left locals at the mercy of criminal self-interest and dishonesty, but they learned to keep these embarrassments quiet.

The politics of the region was counterbalanced by the opening of leisure clubs and new business partnerships with Western companies, Spinneys competitions and raffle winners from hotel gala dinners. Crime was usually only reported once the villain had been apprehended and the exultant police chief could be congratulated for protecting his people.

In the 1960s the idea of a written press was new to Abu Dhabi. To a people who did not read or write there had never been any need for a printed 'voice of the nation'. In the 1930s a prototype news service posted up bulletins of the day in a shop in Al Ain for those who were literate to share with others. But between this and the establishment of *Al Ittihad* in 1969 there was virtually nothing.

I am not sure whether the papers have changed much. They look more contemporary, and seem to be filled with supplements and specials but, alongside the international and regional news, there is still an unchallenging stream of reports about sheikhs meeting other dignitaries and Arab heads of state at protocol receptions. Other stories are an eclectic, passable mix of announcements about investments, ethnic issues and a few general-interest pieces, but there is little analysis or conjecture. As far as crime goes, Emiratis are still not named when they're on the wrong side of the law.

◆ ◆ ◆

The librarian at the Cultural Foundation told me I would find the National Archive at *Al Ittihad*. This Arabic-language newspaper occupies a huge monolith on Eleventh Street. It

is Soviet in scale and appearance, whitewashed and institu-
tional, and almost impenetrable with barriers and sentry boxes
guarding the shaded parking spaces reserved for the VIP élite.

A man at Reception stares down his nose at me. 'I have
come to visit the newspaper archive. The back issues.'

He looks at me blankly. 'What is arsheev?'

'Old newspapers.' I rack my brains for the Arabic. 'From
the seventies to the nineties.' He hands me over to the
stocky young security guard, who takes me on a complete
tour of the building. Between one dead-letter outpost of a
department and the next, we pass unnamed offices, empty
rooms, long-abandoned desks. The storage area he brings
me to is deserted. We move on to a distribution centre.
When he realises that piles of shipping pallets are not what
I'm after, he ducks into a tiny two-person lift. 'We go to
proper store,' he says, motioning upwards.

As we journey up he stares at the floor unable to look
at me directly. He does not want to shame me, or insult
the husband he assumes I have. This displaced sign of
respect never fails to unnerve me.

In a tiny editorial department he asks for someone who
can help. Everyone smiles and nods as if they have met me
before. A woman in a decorative *shaylah* comes forward.
'You look for the arsheev?'

'Yes,' I say. 'I have been told it is here, no?'

'No, no, we have nothing here. Only after 1995. You
must go to Cultural Foundation.'

'But they sent me here.'

'Khalifa, where is the arsheev?' she calls in Arabic.

'You must go to the Cultural Foundation,' shouts a man
from the back.

Lubna, an assistant who has watched me from her desk, calls me over. 'We go. I will ask director. But you are sure it is not Cultural Foundation you should be visiting?'

'No, really. I've been there,' I assure her. 'They have a few magazines about oil, but no newspapers.'

'You are English?'

'Uh-hum.'

'I am from Abu Dhabi.' She is tall in patent-leather court shoes and a turquoise dress. Her *abaya* skims it like a long-line cardigan as she sweeps down the endless corridors and secured doors. The director sits in his office, blockaded behind a huge wooden desk clogged with covered boxes of tissues, penholders, a decorative clock and wedges of coloured folders. He flicks his *ghutra* off his shoulders and comes to the front.

'*Salaam alaikum.*' I offer him my hand. This may be a little more forward than he would like from a woman, but he is good enough to take it limply. Lubna explains what I have come for.

I have rarely seen a more bewildered expression on a man's face. 'Sit,' he says, sinking slowly into his armchair. He is silent for a few seconds. Then, suddenly, his eyes light up. He sends Lubna away and strides several paces in front of me down another corridor to a man who sits behind a desk in the middle of what appears to be a half-vacant warehouse.

This fellow, in grey slacks and a short-sleeved white shirt, looks thrilled at the prospect of a visitor. 'Yes, yes,' he rubs his hands, 'I will help you. I know people at the National Archive.'

'So there is a National Archive?'

'Not really, but there is a place—' He breaks off and disappears for a few minutes, then returns with a cup of tea for me. I sit on a plastic chair, about five metres across the room from him, as he starts making calls. He looks up every so often and smiles. 'Hold on,' he tells me. 'I have spoken to my friend who used to work at an archive. He says he has heard of someone who might help you.'

I just want to know if there is such a place as the National Archive. 'Please, let me have the number.'

He wobbles his head. 'No, no, I must call for you. You must wait.'

◆ ◆ ◆

Waiting. Behind me a clock ticks away the seconds. He gets hotter and more excited as he goes on making calls. An hour and he has nothing, only more names. The number of possible departments, and personnel, seems to expand each time he talks to someone new. 'It is complicated. Government is paying to bring information to one place.' He gives me abrupt fragments every second or third call. It appears that an institution is funding the collation of Abu Dhabi's records. Information and material is being gathered from a variety of sources, like piles of sand, and organised into one centralised system. I wander over to his desk and try nonchalantly to read the numbers upside-down. He looks up at me. 'Someone can help you. She is a woman, but it should be OK. You wait two days, maybe more. She will look through the records. Then you call, please.'

I nod, delighted. He hands me a note. 'Ziyana,' it reads, and underneath, the number in large, angular digits.

'*Shukran*,' I mouth. He sighs. He has lost the battle to do it for me.

Outside, in the startling light of day, my eyes water before I find the sunglasses that have disappeared into the bottom of my bag. I have been sitting in a room with a faulty neon strip and a few ropy wires for so long that I had forgotten how hot it was outside. It is one thirty and Palestinian mothers in *hijabs* are walking their children home from school. The little girls wear trousers and carry Pocahontas and Barbie lunch boxes. Despite the warmth I fold a pashmina round my shoulders for modesty and walk past the Siddiq Qur'ān Memorising Institute, waving to every passing taxi until one glides in to where I stand. '*Marhaba, yani*, Hilton Hotel,' I tell the driver. Since all I have for a day's efforts is a scrappy note, I will go somewhere I used to know and read a few of the papers in my bag.

With its reliance on dockets, chitties and multiple-ledger entry systems, the bureaucracy in Abu Dhabi, unlike the Indian system on which it was doubtless modelled, has not changed. My mother had learned not to go it alone when she first arrived. Desperate for her driving licence and imagining such a young country would have a simple system, she had thought she would be able to take on the Ministry of the Interior with ease. She failed. She was a foreigner and a woman. From her place in the unmoving women's queue, she had peered through the haze of smoke and incense and been unable to understand anything anyone told her. 'Certificates,' one man said, but what kind of certificates neither he nor anyone else could say. As soon as the midday call to prayer came, the place shut down altogether.

It was my father's sales manager, Sami Suleiman, who saved her. The debonair Palestinian, resembling a younger Omar Sharif in his sharply tailored suits, was Spinneys' fixer. He swaggered round town using his *wasta* to call in favours for the necessary medical and ID certificates, then took my mother back to the ministry. When she stepped towards the women's queue, he laughed and steered her away. 'No, no, Sara, nothing happens there. *Insha'Allah*, I have a friend who will help you.' It was a quiet exchange, this passing of favours: '*Shukran, shukran*, my brother, my friend.' Within a minute the paperwork was done. While others had waited years for a licence it had taken my mother ten days. Those without a Sami Suleiman could not hope for success. Now, with Abu Dhabi claiming such sophistication, I am enjoying seeing if it is possible to manage without a Mr Fixit.

◆ ◆ ◆

Hemingway's is part of the cluster of bars to the side of the Hilton complex. A huge plaster relief of the author appears to extrude from the wall of the restaurant above the doors and a menu board listing the conditions for entry: no sandals and no workwear – not that any workman could afford to drink there. The dress codes in Abu Dhabi seem more stringent now than they have ever been: stilettos and designer eyewear are the order of the day. Hemingway's was always fairly relaxed, at least in the daytime. Besides, whatever they say, if you're rich enough and you run with the right sort of crowd, the rules don't apply.

Hemingway's is one of those *faux* south-of-the-border Tex-Mex places, an old-fashioned steer-ranchers' drinking-hole, all American-themed cocktails and nachos. Around the wall there are black-and-white photographs of Hemingway gazing imperiously into the distance, and stills from several films of his novels, *To Have and Have Not*, *The Old Man and the Sea*, *For Whom the Bell Tolls*. Flat-screen TVs are fixed to the walls. An English soccer game is showing while the ceiling fans whir discreetly above. I order a lime and soda and spread out the papers I've been sent, copies of newly declassified MI5 documents on US President Richard Nixon and the 1973 oil crisis, emailed to me by a friend in London. It seems fitting to read them here. It turns out that while my father was doing his best to get in with the desert people in 1974, Nixon had not long let go of plans for an invasion.

When Nixon threw his support behind Israel in the Arab-Israeli Yom Kippur War with Egypt in October 1973, Abu Dhabi aligned itself with other Arab nations and placed sanctions on its oil exports to the US in response to Washington's re-arming of Israeli forces. The Organisation of Petroleum Exporting Countries (OPEC), of which Abu Dhabi was a member, also shrank oil production hoping the American government would back down and meet Arab demands. France and Britain called for Israel to withdraw to pre-1967 borders and found supply more or less un-affected. In the US, where sanctions compounded a surge in oil prices, panic ensued about the long-term stability of the petroleum market. As the price of crude continued to soar, Nixon felt the pressure to do something. For the first time since its formation in 1960 OPEC was flexing its muscles, controlling production, setting prices and sending shockwaves across the developed world. At the pumps petrol quadrupled in price, and the US fell into fuel turmoil. Ordinary Americans were getting up at dead of night to queue for gas and begging for work as industry and transport were forced to a near halt. On the back of Woodward and Bernstein's unpicking of the Watergate scandal, and the inconclusive war in Vietnam, the oil crisis looked as if it might be Nixon's Waterloo. For the first time, the American people were forced to consider fuel-efficient cars, most of which were being made in Japan rather than by their own giants, General Motors, Chrysler and Ford. Affronted by the sudden change in their circumstances, they demanded Nixon's head on a plate. He began to busy himself with ways to guarantee America's oil supply. If he could secure it, he might weather the storm.

From the correspondence and MI5 report, I see that presidential aides were furious at being held, as they saw it, to ransom. Nixon's adviser James Schlesinger, writing to Lord Cromer, the British ambassador in Washington, spits with rage at being dictated to by 'underpopulated, underdeveloped nations'.

The letters set out America's intention to seize oilfields in Saudi Arabia, Kuwait and Abu Dhabi. With a single brigade of troops assigned to each country, they would need no more than fifteen thousand in total. *Ergo*, it would be a breeze. The British assessment of the situation was less rosy: despite Washington's desire to draw the British in, Whitehall rejected the idea of military intervention. Also, Cromer found Schlesinger distasteful: 'Couthness is not Schlesinger's strong point,' he wrote, in a cable to the British PM. 'His remarks bordered on the offensive.' Cromer's view was that invasion was a fanciful idea and, if attempted, would destabilise the region and trigger a war. To Schlesinger, though, 'It was no longer obvious that the US should not use force.' As the mood escalated the Joint Intelligence Committee, steered by Edward Heath's government, drew grim conclusions in their white-paper assessment of the situation. Invasion would almost certainly result in an indefinite continuation of the US oil embargo. There would be a deep US–European rift, the possibility of Soviet intervention through Iraq, and troops stationed on foreign soil for a decade or more.

I pause. The fragments of the white paper seem ominously prescient. While we covet oil, political and commercial interests will remain easily fused, with self-interest driving decision-making. Still, I am astonished that this episode of near-warmongering passed with barely anyone knowing about it. There might have been war, yet there wasn't: without support the US had held back and begun making plans to increase exploration in other areas of the world and push alternative energy sources such as coal and nuclear. By the following spring sanctions had been dropped and the oil flowed once more.

Abu Dhabi might have profited from the peaking prices of crude, but knowing the cost per barrel would again fall, Zayed had found a more prudent way of acquiring influence. Abu Dhabi would make a friend of Washington, gain its protection and, inch by inch, improve its position through trade. Unlike other countries, with their nationalised oil industries, Zayed took a circumspect, alliance-led route to establishing an integrated and productive oil and gas industry. After incorporating the state-owned Abu Dhabi National Oil Company in 1971, he authorised acquisition of a 25 per

cent interest in the two existing foreign-owned oil enterprises, Abu Dhabi Petroleum Company (ADPC) and Abu
Dhabi Marine Areas (ADMA), in 1973. The following year
he increased this holding to 60 per cent, a modest majority
that still allowed the original concessionaries behind ADPC
and ADMA – which included BP, Total, Exxon and Mobil
– to retain large chunks of equity as well as the chance of
long-term opportunity and profit from Abu Dhabi's oil
wealth. In return his country would acquire the finest technology being developed in the West, and retain foreign friends
in high places. After all, power was better used when one
was on the inside. The advantages of this arrangement have
allowed Abu Dhabi's oil industry to flourish more or less
uninterrupted for three decades, and kept intact the circle
of international partners, who have never let anything get
in the way of their share of the country's oil gains.

◆ ◆ ◆

A few people have ducked into the bar for lunch, businessmen on contract work, the odd couple sharing
chimichanga, the spicy Mexican dish. The resident enter-
tainer soundchecks his little stage pod and patrols in his
patent-leather shoes.

'Mind if I sit here? I'm waiting on some friends and
they're gonna be a little while.'

I look up into the face of a weatherbeaten man. He has
white hair cropped short and a neatly trimmed beard. He's
lean for an American, dressed in a crisp cotton shirt and
khaki slacks. The deep lines on his face have formed a sort
of grid pattern. A leathery sixty. There are plenty of tables
available but he seems intent on company.

'Whatcha reading? Something important? I won't pry.'

'Actually, you probably don't want to know what I have here.' I smile, hoping he will leave me to read in peace.

'Can I get you a refill there?' He waves at a passing wait-ress.

Grudgingly admiring his persistence, I tell him about Nixon. He scans some of the text. 'Darn those presidents. And he was one of the worst, being caught by the balls, if you'll excuse my language. But it all worked out the way it was supposed to in the end. He got kicked out and we came here instead. How come you're reading this kinda thing?'

'Oh, someone sent it to me. I grew up here in the seven-ties and now I'm back to see what's changed.'

'Well, that beats me. I came in the mid-eighties.'

'Doing what?'

'Texas oilman.'

It turns out he really knows about oil. His uncle and father were oilmen and, as a child, he saw the fields around Houston fill with nodding donkeys and sink pumps. 'Dad supplied machinery. Now I do the same. I keep ahead of oil extraction. The return ain't what it used to be, but the technology is still moving ahead fast. Every dollar they save on a barrel extracted adds up to billions in profit.' He winks and drops his guard. 'The irony is that we're the only ones who can tell these camel-shaggers what to do about it.' I blanch and he laughs. 'Now, correct me if I'm wrong, but I believe it was you British who coined that particular nomenclature.'

He says the Middle East is more Texas than Texas in many ways. 'We got similar heat, similar dirt and sand. Just the *mullah* and the water is different. And maybe the labour force. The Mexicans do that kind of work at home but I wish I had Indians working for me. They just keep on going.'

'Tell me you look after them,' I say feebly.

'Of course! They're paid enough to keep 'em coming to Abu Dhabi, at any rate. The difference is that they don't get an ounce of respect from the locals even though they built the damn place for 'em. I guess we try and give 'em back a little something. We call Das a "community of nations". Did you know that? It's no roughhouse camp any more. They got stores and movie theatres and some weird cricket club, where you British and the Indian guys like to put on a match. There's a church out there, too. In the bad old days you had men crying out to get back to Abu Dhabi every Sunday so as they could go to church. Now they got a mosque and a hospital. But there's still no liquor for the labourers and no women.'

'It sounds like an open prison,' I joke.

'That's the way it is. Everybody wants the oil, honey. And for those al Nahyans, now they got it, it's like winning the state lottery every day of their lives. They just wanna spend. It was the same in Texas. What you got was men with dandy pools and ice-makers sitting around thinking it was a bad day when they didn't make a million. Once you've got money like that you can't go back. They gotta go forward. They gotta keep protecting what they got.'

9
The Pearly King

At home, I open my email. There's a message from Lara, the assistant to Abdullah Masaood, a discriminating Abu Dhabian for whose business empire my father had worked as an adviser. 'Mr Abdullah is busy today – the Pakistani prime minister is in Abu Dhabi on a state visit. Mr Abdullah will be attending a dignitaries' luncheon. He will, regrettably, be unable to meet with you.'

It's the third time our meeting has been postponed. I'm beginning to wonder if Abdullah doesn't want to see me. I email Lara and agree to yet another date. I'm anxious to meet him: I bring greetings from my parents, but I also want to see the man whose quiet charm has lit my memory of Abu Dhabi and find out what he thinks about the ruling élite's plans for the future of his city. Abdullah is old enough to have been born in the time before electricity, highways or oil and is now one of the few who know how far the people have come and what it has cost them.

My father met him by chance in 1975 when they were boating around Abu Dhabi Island. Abdullah was with his English girlfriend, a young merchant making a name for himself building up the trading company established by his father, Mohammed bin Masaood, back in the 1950s. To my father, Abdullah's confidence in a climate of strict social etiquette was immediately obvious, so when a couple of years later, he was looking for another local partner for Spinneys, it was to Abdullah he turned. Spinneys already had three local partners, assigned by Sheikh Zayed in the late 1960s. Beyond their large minority stake the goatherd, nightwatchman and fisherman were uninterested in how the business was run. For my father, the opportunity to work with Abdullah was the difference between expansion and stagnation. The deal made Abdullah his first fortune and launched the Masaood empire. Franchises and partnerships in car manufacturing, experimental farming, jewellery and travel all followed. Eventually my father became adviser to Abdullah and his brother, and remained so for the rest of his professional life.

Today Abdullah is protected by several tiers of security. The possibility of dropping in on a whim has gone. On the day of my rearranged appointment, I make my way past a loitering watchman, a shambolic-looking sentry, and step out of the lift into a polished marble hallway. A majordomo peers round a half-open door and glares at me. 'I'm invited,' I blurt. 'Mr Abdullah is expecting me. I'm from England. My father . . .' While he goes to check I sit in a reproduction Louis XV salon chair.

He returns and ushers me into a room where Lara greets me and guides me into Abdullah's office. He rises from a pale kidskin armchair and sweeps towards me. '*Salaam alaikum.*' I have not seen Abdullah for several years but he seems more or less unchanged. He kisses my cheeks lightly, my right hand in his.

The floor of his office is lined with ornate wool rugs in tones of cream, pale blue and sand. An enormous director's desk, with gleaming chrome legs, is covered with stacks of books and papers, *Gulf Business*, *Emirates Today*, *Kul Al'Usra*. Awards, plaques, photographs of official occasions, the tokens of a life spent in business are in pride of place. A large photograph of himself as a younger man, in sunglasses, with a treasured falcon on his forearm, hangs on the wall.

Abdullah's way is so relaxing that it is easy to forget his status in Abu Dhabi, as well as his almost unimaginable wealth. He is a respected business entrepreneur, from a family of standing, and now Chairman of the National Consultative Council, the quasi-governmental advisory body that filters the concerns of the people to the *diwan* of the ruler. I remember him as a man who didn't speak much but perhaps he didn't need to. Observation made him successful, my father said. He could captivate people with a nod or a smile, a gesture so small you might not even notice it consciously, but it would command your attention.

Riches have made some younger Abu Dhabians jittery, unpredictable and arrogant. As a teenager I had met some exceedingly wealthy young Emiratis who were unable to muster even the simplest of courtesies to others. With Abdullah, it always seemed that he could give up everything he had in an instant. At receptions or events he would fiddle with his prayer beads while people orbited him, wanting an audience. He would listen politely to their schemes then vanish, like a *djinn*, to the life he lived elsewhere. Often, after a meeting with him he would send some wildly generous gift to our house, but the contrast in wealth meant that what I saw as heirloom objects to be treasured for ever were mere gestures to Abdullah. Most of all I admired his decisiveness. My father tells a story about an ill-fated American delegation from a huge construction corporation who petitioned him to become their local partner. Several rounds of negotiations with underlings had brought both sides close to signing a deal. When the team of young negotiators came to sit with Abdullah in person the meeting should have been a mere formality, but the moment Abdullah set eyes on them he knew the deal would not go ahead. One man had sat down and swung his feet, soles upward, onto the table. Abdullah closed the meeting and left the room without a word. To my father, all he said was, 'It is finished, John.'

Abdullah's family were of the merchant class that had risen through the eighteenth and nineteenth centuries to a position of relative comfort and influence. The taxes they paid in pearls, dates, rice and other crops were a crucial source of income for the rulers in plentiful and hard times. Through the provision of these dues they developed close relationships with their sheikhs, and when oil came they were among the first to benefit. Business concessions were passed to the privileged inner circle of contacts, and pearls were replaced with machinery, food, utilities, property and holidays.

Abdullah gestures towards a suite of white kid chairs arranged in one corner of the room. Against the leather his sateen *kandura* glows silver. To the uninitiated eye one robe might look much the same as another, yet in the pristine finish of the cuffs, with their thick, overstitched cufflink holes, the pressed creases down the arms, there is a hand-tailored elegance and fine detail particular to the people of this city. I have never seen other Arabs as well turned out as they are in Abu Dhabi.

The cloth of his *ghutra* cascades over his shoulders. His immaculate appearance is proof that the practical work-wear of the Bedu has become a modern statement of identity. A similar revolution is taking place in womenswear. Young Emirati designers are sending *abaya* and *shaylah* collections onto the catwalk in crêpes and silks, studded with Swarovski crystals and embroidery. Some tailors are producing branded fakes, bearing CK, Prada, Gucci and Fendi logos. These are not the clothes of desert drudgery: they are designed to distinguish an élite from the foreigners around them.

'How do you find our city after so long away?' His eyes settle on me, watchful, reminding me of the desert maxim 'To be surprised is to die.'

'I don't know what to make of it,' I tell him at last. 'I want to say, "Wow, isn't this amazing," but I'm finding it . . . very intense. There's not much space left.'

He leans forward and presses his fingers together. 'Ah, yes. We move fast now.'

'But you are part of it.'

He rises without a word and glides across the room to pick up two presentation boards from his desk, detailed illustrations of a super-sized beachfront leisure complex he hopes to build in the Tourist Club area. It is a landscaped village of coral-sand beaches and eco-domes before an arc of luxury apartment blocks, hotels and a giant aquarium. It is to become his 'tent', a commercial twist on the fabled Arab hospitality. At the right price, all will be welcome.

'Have you started building?'

'Not yet.' He sighs wistfully. 'We have our land. It is the best location in the city. We are ready to make a beautiful place for people to come. But the plans for the city stop us going ahead. The government wants to put a highway there.'

'Another? How many highways does a city need?'

He shrugs. 'Many, they say. They tell me they need the land for the traffic in twenty years. How is it possible? Ten lanes here, ten lanes there. How many cars? It's crazy. No one knows what the future brings.' He shakes his head. 'People have forgotten the past and now they forget the present. The future is all they think about.'

With oil reserves peaking, surely forward-planning is exactly what Abu Dhabi needs. They must be learning from their neighbours up the coast. Dubai is groaning under the weight of over-expansion and bad debt, the result of lightning property development and over-investment that has left it vulnerable to external economic conditions. Although the Kingdom of Saudi Arabia sits on 25 per cent of the world's oil reserves, it, too, is running at a loss. It has a long-term challenge to make the revenues from oil work more usefully. With an economy based almost entirely on petroleum, it has managed only high unemployment, vast expenses in defence, increased security issues, an exploding population and a public deficit of billions. Any question of development must meet with the conservative, theologically rooted male culture that has traditionally resisted change. Abu Dhabi is not quite in that position, but the expenditure and the plans laid out in the 2030 proposal are more strategic than lavish, intended to help it avoid such misfortune. To the leadership, who do not want their city to be what Washington is to New York, or Canberra to Sydney, but instead a London or a Paris, it is not a case of whether the city will be established as a centre of cultural excellence but that it must.

'I've heard Abu Dhabi is aiming to become the cultural and financial capital of the Middle East,' I say.

He shrugs his shoulders and skims his phone along the coffee-table. When he eventually looks up his eyes are watery. 'Truly I remember when it was only sand here. I see this myself. In 1955 we were sitting with the German delegation come to talk about trade. Just me, a few men and my grandfather. He never knew of electricity but life was good for him. This year, President Bush sends a delegation of four hundred people. For what?' He chuckles. 'Imagine four hundred people in tents and *barasti* on the sand. Eating rabbit!'

This is not nostalgia. The world he is handing on to his children is one his grandfather could never have comprehended.

'Of course we needed roads and houses, schools and hospitals. You know how my father and my grandfather lived? Four months in the desert, four months in the mountains, four months at the sea, with the fish and the pearl. Moving always. We used the plants of the land. We were eating from the land – dates and camel's milk, goats and bread. We had a very simple life. Happy times, when God was with us. Myself, I liked to hunt for the rabbit. We went into the sand and spent the day and the night chasing them. I was a good hunter. I watched for them and got them with my falcon. It is a very good meat, rabbit. A healthy meat. We used everything. Not one thing was wasted. We worked all the day and took enough to live, but we did not ever forget to give thanks.' His tone hardens. 'We thanked God for each thing that we had, food and peace at night. Now, they have plenty and no one give thanks. People are slaves here. They talk and think about the job, the money, but they do not live well. Time is their boss. Before, people were happier.'

'And you? Were you happier?'

'Yes. Everyone was happier. When I was a child I loved my mother and father. I thought I should die without them. And their mothers and fathers felt the same in turn. Now there is no family left. I feel sad people are reaching so high. They will fall.'

He trails off and fiddles with his phone, flipping it open and snapping it shut with his thumb, like modern *mesbaha*, the prayer beads so many used to carry. 'Look, I must show you. My island.' He beckons me to an aerial photograph of a small but perfectly formed paradise. It has its own runway. 'We made it,' he says, so quietly that I have to ask him to repeat it. 'We made it. The island was not there before us.'

They have dredged a new weekend hideaway from the seabed, just as they built the new Corniche and the breakwater. It is a popular thing to do now. Google Earth shows all kinds of new additions to the coastline. One island owner has dredged his initials into the seabed off one side of his island. The channels are so deep and black I wonder if they can be seen from space.

It's easy to imagine this as just another spectacular manifestation of extreme wealth, but it's part of a more universal urge. Abu Dhabians like Abdullah have much in common with the eighteenth- and nineteenth-century British aristocrats who, enriched by trade with Africa, China and South America, created fanciful villages, towers, Grecian follies and lakes – the Buxton Tower, Chesterton Windmill, the

Follies of Mad Jack Fuller, even Virginia Water, with its Leptis Magna ruins. The desire to master nature is a novelty for a race whose culture has been constantly erased by the sand and sea. They have skated on the surface, knowing survival itself is against the odds. And the buildings, the great glass towers and huge marble mosques, are their Pyramids, their Inca temples, their Babylon. The Guggenheim Building, the Louvre and the Emirates Palace Hotel are designed to tell the world that the desert people are here.

'I miss the sea. My grandfather and my great-great-grandfather were from the sea. I have the sea here.' Abdullah touches his chest. 'You know my grandfather was a pearl fisherman. He became the one who sent the boats out with the divers, and then he bought the boats and sold the pearls.'

'A merchant?'

'Yes, a merchant.'

Families like the Masaoods had made a living from the water for as long as anyone could recall, fishing for *hamour*, snapper and barramundi, taking part in the annual odyssey for pearls, the *ghaus al kabir*. In the nineteenth century, under the leadership of Zayed the Great, the pearling tradition flourished, and by the end of the century thousands of men were diving each year. Fleets of white-sailed dhows were hooked together in long chains, voyaging along the arc of the Arabian Gulf to the great pearl bank. While men chanted songs of devotion and distraction, the vessels hovered over the pearl beds and at the word of the *nukhada*, the captain, sinewy men disappeared off the bow in white woven loincloths and leather-sheathed gloves. With their curved pearling knives in hand, wrists attached to long ropes, they scissored through the water, tight bone pegs over their noses. Twenty, thirty, forty feet below lay the oyster beds. It was a hard life, but a practised diver could stay down for two or even three minutes at a time. In the salty shadows their gloved hands would wrench shells from the rocks and drop them into their nets, *diyyin*, until their lungs tightened. Then a sudden jerk on the rope alerted those on the boat and the dizzying rush for the surface began. Bursting up from the deep, divers routinely passed out. They were given a few minutes to recuperate, then sent down again. Symptoms of the bends, ascribed to evil spirits, were cured with words from the Qur'ān, bloodletting and incense.

Abdullah points on a sea chart to where the island is, some way down the coast. 'I also built the house in Fujairah. I go very often, to get away. I love to fish – *hamour, shari*. The *hamour* always go to the same place. It is their habit. In the seventies I had a speargun, but I tired of it a long time ago. That is not fishing.' He waves a hand dismissively. 'Now I fish as I did when I was a child. The old way, with nets sometimes. Really, it is funny to talk of these things. No one here ever asks me about anything like this. But it is my past life. It was amazing. As a child I would fish with my friends in a small boat. I had to crouch because there was no room to turn round. Everywhere ached after a while in a boat like that.'

His phone chirrups on the table and he's into another discussion about the Nissan showroom shipments and a visiting politician who wants to see him. I look at the walls, the pictures of family, his boat, regional maps and small reminders of the old world. Through the opulence of his adult life I glimpse the child, wedged into a tiny *shashah* canoe, Abdullah and his friends rowing across the shallows singing to make the fish come.

I remember talking to Abdullah at a cocktail reception he'd thrown one New Year's Eve, downtown, in a penthouse he owned. There must have been two hundred people there, a mix of Abu Dhabians, Americans, Germans, Palestinians, Egyptians and Norwegians, people with money and their own spheres of influence. He'd decided to pull it together only the day before, but the apartment was heaving. His staff stood one to every eight guests and kept the vintage champagne flowing. After a discussion with an Armenian-American woman, who collected art, and her oil-savvy husband, he told me that one's identity is sharpened by watching strangers flood into your space, not by being a foreigner living somewhere new.

He snaps his phone shut and, for a moment, we are silent. Then I ask Abdullah if he feels that foreign influence has destroyed the Abu Dhabian culture.

'There were not enough of us. We had no expertise. We had to let people come. We could not have made all this happen on our own.'

Abdullah's people have surrendered one set of uncontrollable forces – the desert, the sun and the wind – for another: commerce, the creation of wealth and globalisation. In the desert, God got them through. Faith did not spring from moral righteousness or superiority: theirs was a God of forbearance, carrying them through their life and landing them safely in the hereafter. They had nothing they did not need, and God was with them in every wind-whipped dune, drawing optimism from the depths of their spirit.

Now Abu Dhabians make up barely 20 per cent of the population, and the height of luxury extends far beyond ownership of a date grove. Modernity, imported so quickly, drains traditional familial values. Still, I wonder if there is a people anywhere else in the world with the same pragmatic acceptance of foreigners. Even with the cushion of immense wealth, most nations could not withstand the sheer numbers that have flooded in. Walking down the Corniche, you could be in Kerala or Manila, and in the Hilton jazz bar, Beirut via Paris. Heroes, the dingy basement of the Crowne Plaza, reminds me of a surreal British pub. 'I cannot say how others would have been with this,' Abdullah smiles, 'but it is so.'

He hands me a model of his new executive Lear jet. 'I bought it to fly my family up to Fujairah at the weekend,' he says. 'We are decorating the villa. It is almost done. Very nice.' He allows himself a small smile. 'Yes, we are very happy away from the ugliness.'

Abdullah is a part of his country's development, yet terrified of the fierce change that accompanies it. He has lived by a modern, pioneering credo. His English girlfriend became his wife, and his elder son is married to an American; the family splits their lives between two continents. However audacious it might have been when he married, it is now just another sign of the integration that has swept through his city. They may make up just a fifth of the population, but a new Abu Dhabian is mixing his tribal bloodlines across the world. The younger generation parties in Beirut, dresses in the catwalk collections of Paris, London and Milan, hires Filipina nannies to raise their children, summers on the Riviera and winters in Switzerland, Canada and

Morocco. They wander globally now, rather than across the desert.

'Do you think of this as an Arab place still?' I ask, as I get up to leave.

He hears me but does not answer. 'We are having a lunch with the family soon,' he says. 'We would like you to join us. We will let you know when. You will be there.'

10

The Next Generation

I am the only white person on the Corniche. I know this because I have been wandering up and down for hours, making repeated calls to Ziyana. She is not in and the woman from the phone company tells me several times to try again later. Patience is a necessity here. As far as I can tell, after days of fruitless meetings and telephone calls, the newspaper records for an entire country have disappeared: no one seems able to locate them.

Something exists, though, in the Centre for Documentation and Research. I have met with Frauke Heard-Bey, a well-known historian who has been archiving since 1968. Working for the ruler's representatives in a room at the old fort, Qasr al Hosn, she was one of the few given the task of researching historic documents from the British and German archives that would defend the position of the Trucial States in disputes. 'As the British started moving towards withdrawal and significant stretches of territory were still unresolved, Zayed knew he needed evidence that was legally impossible to contest. Material from the British archives, cut from papers stored mostly in the India Office and the German and Dutch archives, offered perspective as to who had traditionally occupied a region or a settlement.' Most of the history that exists is filtered through foreigners, whose interests were often particular, and whose records, like John Gordon Lorimer's *Gazetteer of the Persian Gulf, Oman and Central Arabia*, were practical. Compiled by the British government in India, the *Gazetteer* was used as 'a convenient and portable handbook' among the British officials hoping to strengthen their influence along the increasingly important Trucial coast. It outlined geography and tribal boundaries, and detailed populations and material goods. Other fragments unearthed in the search included trade receipts for pearls and firearms, and travelogues from naval personnel.

There are newspapers too. Frauke has amassed a large collection: 'I had tin trunks, of the kind Pakistanis use to travel with. We filled them with cuttings from the papers and editions of *Emirates News*. I set up categories to ensure that the cataloguing of papers would continue beyond the seventies.' With a historian's eye she recorded the, often scant, data to form a chronicle of the times before the information age. 'They are being digitised. Teams of technicians are scanning the material.' My face must have lit up. She wagged a finger. 'It is very hard, if not impossible. No one can get in. And I'm not sure how they are storing the pieces as they index them. They bring in new technicians all the time and each one appears to favour a different system. It's haphazard but they are proud to have so many million pieces on computer. Yet unless it is tagged in a way that makes it possible to search for it, then everything is lost.' I have read that even NASA has lost precious images of Earth this way. Still, I am fired by the idea some records may be available.

When Ziyana finally answers the phone the next afternoon I almost whoop for joy. 'Aha,' she says. 'Mrs Joanna.

Yes, I hear about your request. I have been to the records, but we only have back to 1979. Nothing before.'

'Are you sure? I've spoken to Frauke Heard-Bey. She tells me there was a lot of material, papers and a lot of documents stored by subject. And some newspapers.'

'Not here, I am very sorry.'

'Please, can I get to the archive myself? I'm sure that if I could search through what you have I would find what I'm looking for. I can sit anywhere. Or, if not you, is there anyone else at the Centre who could help? Would you be able to look for me if I gave you information?'

'There is nothing public, I am sorry. Why don't you go back to the Cultural Foundation?' Her soft voice is patient, but unyielding. I have come full circle.

After this abject failure to get anywhere, I consider how else I might find anything and decide to spend a day or two catching up with friends while I think about it. I leave messages for a couple, including Michael, the brother of my old American friend Elizabeth, then go out and walk down towards the Sheraton. Warning signs tell me that jaywalking the six hair-raising lanes of the Corniche will earn me a 200-dirham fine, no questions, no excuses. A long black Mercedes rolls along the kerb and lowers its windows. The driver hisses and clicks his tongue at me. Three artfully styled *ghutras* lean towards the open window and begin making *mughazala*, the vulgar, flirtatious overtures men make to women. It's like being in one of those slow-motion videos where overweight men driving tasteless, showy convertibles lick their lips to a Redondo Beach rap soundtrack. But this is Abu Dhabi, and unsolicited attention is part of a woman's day. Some men mutter, others stare, and a good many make rash, occasionally unrepeatable, gestures. It is not threatening but all women are conspicuous enough to live their lives being watched in this way. When I was twenty I couldn't understand why the local women didn't revolt and throw off the *abaya*. Now, stirred equally by amusement and indignation, I understand its role: it is as much an elegant shield against the impropriety of men as it is a statement of feminine piety.

Young men and women are given few opportunities to come together in an ordinary, unobserved way. For men it is often easier to meet and form a bond with a foreign woman than an Emirati but nevertheless the eruptions of inappropriate behaviour from the kids in the car suggest urges they should not express. And from the risqué look of some Facebook profiles, with profile pics of glossy lips wrapped around cherries and perspiring navels, women don't seem to be any less eroticised than in the more permissive societies. In Abu Dhabi, where misconduct is not simply a matter of individual conscience, unseemly behaviour is a more rebellious act than it would be in Europe.

When my mother was bringing us up in Abu Dhabi construction labourers would masturbate openly as she walked to and from Spinneys or down to the *souk*. They would stand on the sand, shuffling about inside their baggy pantaloons. Some would flash at her. 'One just carried on, darling,' she told me, years later, when it had come up in conversation. 'Most of the time they did it in their trousers. Anyway, you didn't want to give it too much attention. It only made it worse.'

I run to avoid the traffic and my phone goes. It's Michael. 'What are you doing? Where d'you wanna meet? We'll come get you. Things are just insane right now.' He and Jon, his minder, are on the way down from Dubai.

'You'll be hours.'

'Nah, forty minutes, we'll be there.'

When I was a child there had been one frayed strip of asphalt through the scrub connecting Dubai with Abu Dhabi. It was a perilous road: drifts of sand blew across it and cars would plough off into the emptiness, tyres blowing out in the heat, while at night camels appeared suddenly in the glare of headlights. The accidents were invariably fatal for someone. You saw crashed or abandoned cars everywhere. Bill and I would ride without seatbelts in the back of our Mercedes, counting the wrecks. We got points for each burnout we passed on our side of the road. The winner was the first to make it to a hundred.

Wreckage and the old road are long gone. A huge eight-lane freeway traverses the wilderness, with metal bollards, white lines, street-lamps and grass verges, fed by elaborate sprinkler systems. It is fenced its entire length, and broken only by underpasses to shepherd the camels safely from one side to the other. For most of the way it is a corridor through buildings, high-rises, free zones and suburbs. Construction runs almost the entire 130 kilometres between the cities. Abu Dhabi and Dubai may be arch rivals but they are slowly joining together. I wonder how long they will remain separate world-class cities. Surely, on this coast-line, there can be room only for one.

Immediately Michael has picked me up we are off on a series of errands. 'I'm runnin' late, hon. Let's stop by the villa, all right?' he asks, in a chipper Dick Van Dyke mockney accent. 'I have to interview a girl about a job. That OK?'

I'm happy to go along with whatever he suggests. When I last saw Michael he was a spindly adolescent running around town with his gang of friends from Choueifat, an international secondary school in Abu Dhabi, showing off his Arabic and getting into fights with angry taxi drivers. Now he is turned out in southern European, Arab-lite apparel. Shirt, pressed jeans, square-toed leather loafers and gelled hair that waves back from his forehead. He is squeaky clean, as assiduous about his personal hygiene as the locals.

He is back after a spell in LA, working in film production and starring in the American version of the *Big Brother* reality-TV show, and intent on bringing a little film glamour to the UAE capital. In the leather seat of his four-by-four, he rests his left wrist on the steering-wheel while the right hand fiddles blindly with his new iPhone. Driving while making calls is not discouraged here.

'This is my favourite city in the world. It's where I grew up. It's what I know.' He pauses. 'And the movie studio is going to be something else. It's more than I could have hoped for in the US. I'm here because it feels like home now.'

Michael has been given the chance to do something he never would have been able to do in America. Abu Dhabi suits the man whose favourite films and books are the epic legends and swashbuckling fantasies of our time. *The Count of Monte Cristo, Lord of the Rings, The Clash of the Titans.* 'It just happened.' He laughs. 'I ran into a guy from school in a Hollywood nightclub of all places and drunkenly confessed that I wanted to set up a film studio. He asked what it would do. I told him it should make movies and television shows, lead animation and production tech-niques. Big ideas, ahead of their time, filled with inven-tiveness and creativity. And he just said, "OK, let's do it." That's how they do things.' He shrugs. 'Right?'

Barely two years on, Timesands, one of the the largest film studios in the Middle East, is operational. The friend's wealthy father bankrolls the project, and Michael puts in the creative vision on the understanding that the invest-ment will realise a profit at some point.

'Why not in Dubai? Wouldn't that have made better sense? The entertainment industry's already established there.'

'Come on.' He smashes the heel of his hand on the steering-wheel. 'I hate Dubai. Never put me in Dubai. It's a car crash of a town.'

'Really? But they do media, don't they?'

'No way. They just want the razzmatazz. It's glitz, expense and celebrity. I want to make real films. You know what I like about Abu Dhabi? That it has waited. They want to do it differently. Something classy.'

Abu Dhabi is by far the richer city. If a handful of its sheikhs wanted to persuade Posh and Becks to buy here and Kylie to come and sing, they could throw more money at them than anyone else on earth. But they haven't. In attempting to create an intellectual and cultural capital, their ambitions are more serious and long-term. Michael tells me that the first NYU overseas campus will open in 2010. 'It's like a New York-Vegas schism.' He peers over his Ray-Bans at me. Then his mobile rings and he motions with a finger for quiet. '*Marhaba, habibti* . . .' he coos. His business partner is calling with details of a journalist from *Vanity Fair* who wants to bang the drum for the studio.

The mobile flashes again. 'Texts. Jon.' He passes the phone to his minder and waits for them to be read out to him. They are from a rich, bored sheikha. 'Ha! She wants my script,' he says, tight-lipped. 'Can't do that. My reputation.'

Michael is consumed by the studio. With thoughts of Ziyana fresh in my mind I wonder how much artistic freedom he will be allowed to make the kind of films he dreams of. Quite apart from the censors poring over every new TV show and publication, it is the circumspection Ziyana showed that makes Abu Dhabi the peaceful autocracy it is. People have learned to sidestep awkward moments and subjects. Bad news is ignored in a collective act of forgetting. Censorship angers no one because people are fed by the state or, if they are foreign, by their sponsors. Above everything else people in Abu Dhabi want money. The creation of wealth is an obsession. Freedom of expression is a luxury that most cannot allow to take precedence.

'We tell people we have no agenda, no politics, no religion,' Michael says. 'It's entertainment.'

'You're brave.'

'No offending anyone either. You can make a joke inoffensive. You can get rid of the punchy bits.'

But what are you left with? Something that isn't a joke.

Still, Michael grew up in Abu Dhabi. He knows the culture and has accepted it as it is. Men and women may appear flamboyant and *outré*, but they are rooted in a heterosexual, male-decision-making society. 'Not so much now. The time is right. The will is there to change things. They want it to happen. They want great work, with personality. Besides, in the Middle East, this is a first. There's nothing like what we're doing anywhere else.' He beams, and we roar away into the traffic.

He is adamant that his studio will better Studio City in Dubai, and show more grasp of programming and content than Rotana Media in Saudi Arabia. 'We're going to do real films. Big feature films. And all kinds of other content, too.'

'Like what?'

'Films for some of the construction projects out here.'

'Ads?'

'No, films for their internal audiences.'

I ask him if he has watched *Poet of Millions*, the Gulf talent show in which Emiratis compete with descriptive *nabati* poems they have penned themselves on their history and way of life. It has now been commissioned in several other Arab states, including Egypt and Beirut. The production company's greatest pride is in creating a hit that showcases the Bedu's four-hundred-year-old literary tradition, and hones talent, without a hint of sex. Michael hasn't seen it, but he says, 'Yeah, that's what I mean. There's a whole thing out here that hasn't been tapped. They want fun, you know.'

'Why you, though?'

'Come on, it has to be someone like me. Local guys don't stay in the job. They tire quickly. Most are so freakin' wealthy they don't really want a job, even if it's a big one on the board of some oil company with a lot of profile. So many live beyond salary. These guys need people who need money to make things happen for them.'

Michael sees himself leading the creative charge. It's not just a wish. It's a plan.

We pick up the girl he's interviewing from outside her aunt's house a couple of streets away. They shake hands, lean in to kiss twice and then, for good measure, add a third, covering all bases. She is Iranian, educated in America and living in Abu Dhabi. He is an American, educated in Abu Dhabi and Europe. I listen to them from the back seat. They are part of the city's shift in focus. In deciding to settle here they have made themselves part of a new world, even if they don't yet know it. They are not representatives of a thrusting empire; they have not been sent by a corporation or the military. They are setting up businesses and cruising on the strength of their ideas. When I look at them I can tell the country is opening up. The skill set is deepening, as physical construction extends into cultural collateral. Expatriates used to come for building and oil. Then there were estate agents and IT experts. Now the lifestyle industries, film, advertising and PR, are joining them.

Michael and his interviewee are the children of a third culture. The almost-Arab society that grows in Abu Dhabi is neither a replica of far-off homelands nor the same culture the locals once enjoyed. It is a hybrid, second-order civilisation, foggy and foreign, yet familiar enough. Michael may speak pure Californian but he is a synthesis of influences, styles and cultures. From the moment his San Franciscan parents hit Europe in the 1970s he learned to exchange one set of rules for another. Now he slips between cliques and social chapters, taking tea, playing cards for hours during Eid, declining an invitation without saying 'no'. Michael, like a great many of the displaced, is a dilettante and an adventurer, a complex composite in a city that is turning out to be the same.

As we drive into Spinneys – Michael and his potential colleague are going to the Mugg & Bean coffee shop – he turns to me: 'Hey, I forgot to tell you. Elizabeth's about to get on a plane. She's coming back. She'll be here tomorrow.'

Elizabeth Donnellan, my great friend when I was in my early twenties, is flying into Dubai the following day. She, too, it seems, has been drawn back. I'm not surprised. It's an entirely Abu Dhabi kind of coincidence.

◆ ◆ ◆

I began adulthood with Elizabeth. I had left university and, in my first job, was on the lookout for friends. We were new together, steering each other through the *haut monde* of a wealthy élite who subsidised the rest of us. Theirs was a strange nocturnal life. Elizabeth, I discovered early on, had her ear close to the ground: in just a few weeks she had manoeuvred herself to the centre of a royal scene, taking me with her.

My days were spent working in the Marina Club, poring over membership lists, trying to convince extended family members to join when a cousin or an uncle had been accepted. The Marina was a kind of Cheers for its members; not quite trendy or ostentatious enough for the young crowd, it was held in real affection by regulars, one of whom, Rashid, would totter up the marble corridor to the bar with his precious falcon on his arm. The Swedish fitness instructor, Marita, would often be called to hold the bird while he played pool. Once he brought with him a tiny gazelle. Marita had told him it couldn't stay, but he seemed so anguished at leaving it outside that she relented. The next day he had invited her to a barbecue: 'You must come. We're roasting the gazelle. He will be delicious.'

By night I glimpsed a world of people who lived without restrictions. The local teen-élite had been born beyond police or state control, immunity ensured by their extreme wealth, and answering to no one. It was a struggle to understand them: their sense of time and of what life meant were utterly distorted. There was no work ethic or driving ambition. Neither was God in the frame. I couldn't keep up, but for a while Elizabeth and I were in the midst of it, as free as the company we kept allowed us to be.

I wonder if she ever thinks about *that* party, one of the first nights we ever went out together, or of the morning afterwards when she reeled out of the car, so troubled by the film we had seen that she vomited on the sand.

◆　◆　◆

Elizabeth was nineteen, I was twenty-one, and we had been introduced by her mother, a journalist on the first locally produced magazine for women, *Emirates Woman*. She had grabbed me from the tedium of a dinner and whispered, 'Can you get away? Let's go party.' Before I knew it I was in my car, with her directing me off the Corniche towards a large new block. Elizabeth was full of the confidence that sets certain teenagers apart. With wavy flaxen hair and the kind of pert all-American face that adorns fifties Coca-Cola billboards, the Abu Dhabians loved her beauty. I found it easy to like her because there was substance beneath the exterior. She spoke five languages and made me laugh.

We stepped from the lift into a large, empty penthouse. 'This can't be it,' I said. And then I glimpsed a panther on the balcony. I felt no fear – or surprise, even: with the blazing lights of the Corniche beyond, a big cat on the prowl seemed almost ordinary. Its head lolling rhythmically from side to side, it passed beneath the beam of a spotlight, focusing intently on the lights of the city beyond the window. For a moment I wondered if it was really there. It was only when it shifted pace and found its way towards the French windows where we were standing that I wanted to run away. I could see the crisp brown markings and the fine fur of its underbelly. As it came to the door, the world receded. It padded into the room, stopped behind the sofa, and yawned widely, revealing immaculate fangs. Flicking its tail over one hip, it moved further into the room. I groped for Elizabeth's arm but she had stepped away and was peering about for our host.

He floated into view from the far corner, his bare feet silent on the black marble floor. His hands were outstretched and he wore a diamond-studded Rolex Cellini at the cuff of his crisp, freshly laundered white *kandura*. '*Marhaba*. Good evening, ladies.' He planted three delicate kisses on my cheeks and patted his hair, which had been gelled back into jagged spikes. 'I've got a few things to do and we're waiting for some friends. Then we can get going, OK?'

Elizabeth checked her watch. 'Oh, cool, the party's some-where else. Sounds great, darlin'. Joanna, this is Khalid. The party's wherever he is.'

Khalid ignored this shameless flattery. 'Just grab your-self a drink and kick back, yeah?' He was the perfect Arab youth, beneath the dense, dark stubble around his jaw, not quite nineteen.

Since he hadn't appeared to notice the cat, I jabbed a

finger in its direction. 'That?' He sneered. 'She's beautiful but, man, is she dumb.'

'Does she hunt?' I asked, naively imagining she had a purpose alongside the priceless falcons and salukis that were taken to hunt in the scrublands of northern Pakistan for the now traditional winter retreats among the wealthy.

'She couldn't kill a chicken. She's a house cat.'

He clapped his hands and barked across the room in Arabic. '*Habibti!* She's supposed to do tricks.' He clicked his fingers and the cat sank to the ground on her haunches, her tail curved neatly around her paws. Her eyes were sleepy; she looked drugged.

He lost interest before she had started her trick and walked towards the TV. He stabbed the remote and the huge screen was filled with gaudy colours. A badly dubbed voice, gabbling in Russian or maybe Polish, blasted out from large cylindrical speakers to either side. The picture wobbled and the soundtrack blurred, as if the tape had been stretched. A sub-standard pirate copy. He threw the remote at the sofa, scooped up a leather soccer ball from the floor and flicked it into the air, then bounced it, lobbed it over his shoulder at a basketball net fixed to a doorframe on the other side of the room and meandered back to us.

'*Bravissimo.*' Elizabeth threw her freckled arms into the air and clapped like a cheerleader. Even her accent, a dizzying blend of American, Italian, French and English, was pure theatre. But the winsome clapping fell a long way short. Khalid had the uninterested countenance that only huge amounts of money can bring. He probably wafted from one air-conditioned environment to another without ever landing. But Elizabeth did not see this.

'How well do you know him?' I whispered.

She tapped a Marlboro Light out of its soft pack. 'Umm, well, I've been here a couple of times. Mom is *thrilled* I'm meeting these guys. He's very generous and *soooo* cute. Definitely one of the nice ones, don't you think?'

How wholesome could a man with a panther be? I felt uncomfortable; we were in a place where there was nothing to contain her exuberance. She leaned on my shoulder. 'He knows a guy I think you'll like. He'll be at the party later. He's *gorgeous.*'

A diminutive Indian in a blue housecoat and white satin gloves bowed to one side of us. 'What you will want for drinking, please?'

'Two-vodka-tonics-lots-of-ice.' Elizabeth rattled it out.

'Whisky.' Khalid raised an arm. 'And give one to Nina, she needs to wake.'

'Yes, sir.' The Indian bowed and withdrew.

Elizabeth took my arm and dragged me to the other side of the vast living room.

'Where are we going? Who's Nina?'

'Sssh, I'll show you,' she hissed. We walked through a marble arch that divided the room towards yet another arrangement of leather sofas. A girl was curled up, asleep, on the black cushions of a gold Louis XV-style *chaise-longue*. The polished marble walls and low lights cast dim shadows across her heart-shaped face, made up with a thick layer of foundation. Heavy crescents of kohl lined her eyelids and her hair, dyed black, fell in waves round her face, blending with the velvet as she lay there. Despite an artful attempt at exotic Eastern *jamaal*, the vulnerable bloom of an English schoolgirl glimmered through.

'That's Nina. You can see why he likes *her*. She's so pri-dee.'

'That's his girlfriend?'

'Yup, if you can call her that.'

'She doesn't look well.'

'Jetlag. She's just flown in from Brunei.' She looked directly at me. 'Nina's the daughter of some British family. It wouldn't look good if it got out that she was, you know, being done by an Arab. Well, you know, it's supposed to be a secret but everyone knows.' She sucked her bottom lip. 'The point is, he likes the—'

Something darted from the shadows and she yelped as a gazelle clipped nervously into the room. Its slight frame trembled as it edged along the wall, watching us, never blinking.

'*Jeeesus.*' Elizabeth stifled a giggle as she released my arm. 'It's a freakin' deer. Shall we tell the panther dinner is served?'

'Poor thing looks terrified.'

'Attagirl.' She pressed on with an elaborate account of Nina and her Prince Charming. How they had met at Annabel's one weekend when she was in London on an exeat, under age but in possession of Dad's credit card, and Khalid was there too. He had sent champagne to her table and waited while she looked about to find the generous admirer. After the club closed he had got his chauffeur to drive them around London until the sun came up. 'It's romantic, don't you think? And she adores him so I guess it's all OK. They don't see much of each other, only when she stops off on her way to Brunei or when she's going back to school. She dumps her ticket and he buys another through his own travel agent. I don't think her parents have any idea.'

The long black jersey she was wearing seemed to have been wound around her like a cocoon. 'She looks very young.'

'Fifteen. She's doing her exams.'

Our conversation was cut off mid-flow by the arrival of yet another exotic creature, a bird-like Filipina who appeared through the door that the gazelle had used as an exit. She was wearing a spaghetti-strap top and a pelmet skirt. 'Hey, my honeys,' she crowed, with a wide grin.

Elizabeth straightened to her full five foot ten and waved her away with an exaggerated flick of the wrist. 'Euuuch.' She wrinkled her nose at the call girl. 'Check. It. *Out.* There goes the tone.'

◆ ◆ ◆

At that time, I was more or less ignorant about sex as a profession, and filled with misleading, schoolgirlish ideas about what was required to succeed. It wasn't until later that year when I met Alyona, an astonishingly self-assured woman who had come from a small town in the Lithuanian countryside to set herself up as a mistress, that I discovered how, for any lady attempting prostitution, daring was the only option.

After the raising of the Iron Curtain, planeloads of flawless, cream-skinned beauties had flooded the desert states of the UAE and ended the long-held dominance of the Indian dancing girls and Filipina sex workers. The girls from the former Soviet empire were ruthless. They did not care whom they displaced or how they did it. Aware of the power they held among Arab clientele, these night butterflies pitched themselves accordingly, demanding fancy apartments, cars, fine jewellery and bags of real money.

One sleek mansion block, situated downtown close to the Zafar Tower, which was itself a haunt for men who wished to recline at the feet of the dancers, had been leased entirely by Arabs for these girls. Like a latter-day harem, its jewels hidden behind chrome and glass, it was a long way from the glum Communist austerity most had fled. But though it featured a state-of-the-art quartz-encrusted glass front entrance and a spectacular marbled foyer, few visitors were inclined to enter or leave the building through the front. Instead, anyone looking at the workman's entrance would see men in white *kandura* slipping out of the block into blacked-out Mercedes and purring away.

The Filipinas slowly dispersed. Some were taken into service as housemaids. Others were sent home to their villages. Alyona, whose gravity-defying figure and unblemished porcelain skin was wrapped in an endless array of tight black jeans, satin shirts and jewellery, had shrugged off the guilt. 'There are not so many Filipinas now. Even the guys with two, three wives, even the old ones, want sex with gorgeous European woman. But will not last. One day men here will want other kind of girl and we will be ones going home.' She paused. 'Maybe sad Filipinas should go to Russia.'

During the late summer of 1992 I met Alyona a couple of times, first on the yacht of a mutual friend and later at Le Meridien. She showed me how the pick-up was done. She swept in and slid her perfect round bottom onto a prominently placed barstool. The barman had her drink in front of her without a word being exchanged. She wrapped her twinkling fingernails round the icy tumbler of vodka-tonic, tossed her hair until it was spread across her shoulders and turned sideways so that her long legs twisted to the ground. That she was the mistress of a tycoon did not stop her looking around. 'You cannot leave future in the hands of one man. There is always chance I meet someone richer.'

When I had talked of love, she had slapped my thigh. 'Come on! You kid me? What I need that for? I find love anywhere. One question to know only: what is he worth? The rest not matter. I look at all man. If he good-looking, then is OK – but so what? If there dust on shoe, forget it. Also, only diamond Rolex, Patek Philippe, Vacheron OK. Anything else, no good. I always know which man have real money. No other reason why to be here.'

◆ ◆ ◆

I almost gasped with relief as an immaculate gloved hand set more drinks on the table. As I drained my glass, I caught sight of the panther sitting just inside the balcony door. Its tail brushed the floor. From the opposite side of the penthouse tiny hoofs skittered on the marble.

I took one of Elizabeth's Marlboro Lights and thought of the white Mazda marooned outside on the sand. 'When d'you think we'll go? I mean, if Nina's still asleep . . .'

Elizabeth sank deeper into the sofa. 'Come on, relax.'

A bell chimed, the gold-plated lift doors opened and three young men stepped out, in 501s and neatly tucked-in Ralph Lauren polo shirts. A haze of Hugo Boss aftershave drifted in their wake. 'Khalid! Waz!'

'*Salaam.*' Shouts from the white corridor heralded the appearance of another man from the bedroom corridor. An enormous, hirsute creature, naked beneath the strip of towel stretched round his huge brown stomach, strode into the living room. His hair was oiled back into a curly pigtail. He had come straight from the shower. 'I been busy, my friends.' He produced a used condom from behind his back.

'Don't stare,' Elizabeth whispered, pointing to one of the others, 'but he's got a club foot.'

'Listen, guys. I'm going to get tidied up. Relax for a minute and check this out.' He changed the tape in the video-player, throwing the remote into the air for one of the others to catch. 'It better be good. Cost me ten thousand bucks.'

The video began, the screen fuzz yielding eventually to an image. Out of the black a landless horizon appeared. There were no credits or music, just the sound of the wind rushing into a camcorder microphone. The hand holding the camera panned over a sea that spread out on all sides. It was an unremarkable sequence, a home video with a bombastic American voiceover. 'It was a classic case,' the deep voice said, 'of being in the wrong place at the wrong time.'

The film was taking place on what looked like a mid-sized Bayliner crammed with semi-naked boys and girls in their early twenties. They were holding bottles of beer and horsing around. It was a singles boat party of the kind that happens around the world in warm, sunny places. Elizabeth and I couldn't hear what was being said, but it seemed that the whisperings of a small group of kids had resulted in a bet. A brown-haired girl in a red bikini laughed, waved and flung herself overboard. Two skis were thrown in after her, into which she drunkenly began to wedge her feet. Even without the handicap of intoxication she was clearly a novice, and between her awkward grapple with the tow-rope and her struggle to keep both skis together she was barely ready when the boat picked up through the water. Giggling uncontrollably, she managed somehow to stand. The camera turned with the boat as it weaved back through its own wake. The girl bent her knees and bumped across the waves. Boys off-screen shouted and hollered at her until, with one hand on the rope, she pulled the halter-neck strap of her bikini top over her head and wiggled her hips. Both red triangles dropped to her waist and she thrust her breasts forward. The crowd on the boat cheered her on.

She attempted to undo the bows on her bikini pants but lost her balance. Squealing, she hit the water and lost her skis. While she floundered, grabbing one ski and pulling herself vainly towards the second, the boat looped back towards her. She didn't notice it as she paddled forwards until it was too late. When she finally looked up her face froze. She panicked, waving her arms, trying to get the attention of the boat's driver. The wobbling camera found her eyes. Her confused face filled the screen. Splashes of water appeared across the camera lens and the boat cut right through the place where she had been.

The engine choked, the hull jolted and the boat ground on through the water. Images of bare feet and sandals could be seen as the camera was carried to the back of the boat. A mess of seawater and bloody froth churned at the stern. She was in the water, blood pumping from her open chest. The girls on the boat were screaming and the camera zoomed into the water. Drunk and confused, two men in sports shirts and deck shorts dragged her onto the boat. She was split in two, but alive, her body splayed on the fibreglass gunwale, blood draining out of her.

'She's gonna fucking die,' someone shrieked.

And the voice of the cameraman: 'Abso-fuckin'-lutely.'

The girl knew it too: she looked so disappointed.

Elizabeth exhaled and, with shaking fingers, tapped another cigarette out of the packet. 'Jeez, what was that about?'

I pushed the iced rim of my glass to my lips, looking for protection. The entire sequence had taken fifteen minutes and not one of the people in the room was saying anything about it. The three men were now ignoring the television, circling the floor behind us, clinking glasses and singing fragments of Falco's 'It's My Life' to each other in heavily accented English. Waz emerged from his room and pulled a white T-shirt over his head.

'Waz,' Elizabeth called, 'what the hell? You are *so* unbelievably weird.'

'You girls happy?' He whooped as he disappeared back towards his bedroom without waiting for a reply.

'He's such a creep, that guy. But Khalid loves him. So we all have to love him.' She was trembling as she waved to the Indian hovering outside the porthole of the swing doorway to the kitchens. 'Hi, can you get us two more vodka-tonics? Really, really strong ones, OK?'

The video was now showing a scene that looked as gruesome and disturbing as the last. I glanced at Elizabeth and tried to focus on her, but couldn't help seeing what was on the screen. Another home video, shaky and occasionally fuzzy: two people cowering on a sofa, a man and a woman in a windowless basement. There was the sound of a drill from the other side of the door – and then the houseboy was presenting Elizabeth and me with another pair of frosted glasses. I saw his inscrutable expression. I wanted to grab him and tell him this was not how I was.

◆ ◆ ◆

Elizabeth, like me, will be older now. We won't slip into that world. It is the blessing of youth that one is able to mix easily with all comers without the need for questions. It is only later that regret for the things we did decades before creeps in. Our choices then no longer fit with what we have become. Have those experimental Abu Dhabi teenagers grown into more conservative adults? Some will be part of the new powerbase, with responsibility to their people. I'm not sure how much their modern upbringing has helped them. This is a nation ruled by people living international and often double lives. Back then, little thought had been given to what it might mean.

11

The Song Remains the Same

From a distance I catch sight of Elizabeth. She's pacing back and forth outside the Hilton jazz bar clutching a vodka-tonic and talking into her phone. She is in tight jeans and a dinky floral blouse, a long bob bouncing on her shoulders. She's sucking as intensely on a cigarette as she used to. Her only concession to womanhood is a pair of towering heels. I run across and wave. She winks at me and finishes her conversation. 'Euch, LA.' She holds up her phone while drawing me to her chest. 'Same old, same old. I'm so over that place. It's the death of culture. I have *got* to get out.' And then, 'Oh, my God, Joanna. You're really here. The two of us back in old Abu Dhabi again.'

'Let's drink a toast.' She grabs my arm and whisks me inside to where Michael and two friends are sitting. He's on his phone but stands to kiss me while he talks. A Latin band is in from Rio and it's busy for a Friday night. Here, people dress to be seen: silky waistcoats, tight designer jeans and lots of jewellery. Style is a furiously competitive sport. Clothes have to be the newest, hair the biggest, heels the highest. Whoever has the most baubles or the most gold wins. Quantity and quality count equally. Women buff and primp themselves to the peak of perfection. I used to hope that one day, with so much sun and sand, the place might relax a little and take on the flavour of the Thai islands, or Nice after the season, with women in jogging pants and yoga shoes. But it's not a flip-flops kind of town. Yet for all this the night-life is still strangely gauche. Restaurants and expatriate drinking dens are an accepted aspect of life in Abu Dhabi, but nightclubs with quality DJs and international credibility are only just emerging.

Thinking back, Abu Dhabians have always been attracted to forbidden glamour. In 1980, flying back to Heathrow, the only unaccompanied English nine-year-old on the plane, I had watched women in black *burkas* haul huge handbags into the overhead luggage compartments. While they pushed along rows and wedged themselves into seats, men in *dishdashes* and rubber-soled sandals pulled out prayer beads and called on Allah for safety and salvation, then noisily lit Dunhills and Marlboro Reds.

An hour or so into the flight, when the captain announced that we had left Saudi and Syrian airspace, the women rose and, clutching vanity bags and other articles from the overhead lockers, set off for the toilets at the back of the plane. They never returned. Instead a series of denim-clad silhouettes, ablaze with Rodeo Drive and Knightsbridge's finest, in full disco makeup, appeared. They were the new jet set: rhinestone-studded stretch Farah jeans, spangled sweaters, shirts tied at the waist, gold pendants and gemstones nestling at throat and cleavage. As they wiggled their way back to their seats, some talked in cut-glass English accents.

The men set about transformation, too: jeans, chinos, Cardin shirts, topped off with pomade-slicked hair. They congregated at the emergency exits and waved down hostesses with requests for neat, iced Johnnie Walker and Rémy Martin.

Under a thick fog of tobacco smoke the party continued until the aircraft lowered its wheels for the descent into Heathrow. At Customs they bade each other farewell in a flurry of kisses and were gone, finding their drivers and teetering into waiting limousines that would deposit them outside houses in the grandest parts of town.

'Michael's landed on his feet,' I joke to Elizabeth.

'Hasn't he just! He wants me to come back and work for him – or, I shall rephrase that, *with* him.' She pulls out another cigarette and fishes between the wine glasses for a lighter. 'He's serious. He keeps pestering me to make a decision. What do I say?'

'Ask yourself why you wanted to get out the first time.'

'Exactly! I've grown up. Has Abu Dhabi? I just don't know if this is the place for a single woman of thirty-six, second time round.'

We talk as though we haven't been apart. It's the expatriate way, which requires one to dive in, but I like to think there's more to it than that. We share a desire to find a place in the world where we can settle. LA might not be the place for Elizabeth, but is Abu Dhabi?

'Thirty-six isn't old,' I say. 'Anyway, you've always done well for love here.'

'Yeah – none of them had the fairytale ending, did they? Do you know how long I waited for Hamed? Yup, no question, he was the one. Just assumed I'd marry him.'

Hamed was Elizabeth's greatest love. He was from a Palestinian family who had come to Abu Dhabi in the 1960s, laid the lights along the first Corniche, then made their fortune in pharmaceuticals. Educated in America, Hamed had settled into the family business and, after meeting

Elizabeth, had begun wooing her determinedly. She had
fallen for him. Rather than leave for Europe she had taken
a job with a Lebanese woman setting up a home-shopping
channel. It sold a little of anything fancy – clothes, shoes,
bags, jewellery, furniture, lampshades, cushions, hi-fi equipment, exercise gadgets and make-up – to Emirati women
who didn't, or couldn't, leave the house. From here, she
went to work with the Italian contractors on Sheikh Zayed's
grand mosque. Officially a translator, her role was more
to smooth the awkward, often stalled dialogue between the
Italian stonemasons working on the white marble façade,
the local partners and international construction firms. She
brought antagonists face to face and, where people would
not meet, counselled squabbling parties to a conclusion.

There were moments of strain in her relationship with
Hamed. Early on, when she had failed to win the approval
of his family, she knew she would have to woo them as he
had wooed her. They made it difficult. She found herself
excluded from family functions, and if she happened to
enter a party they were at, the sisters and cousins would
leave *en masse*. There were unfounded rumours, too,
besmirching her reasonably good name. But Elizabeth was
an optimist and, holding her head high, she decided to
counter the bad feeling with perseverance and dignity. At
least, as a Western girl, it was only her own pride that was
at stake, not the reputation of her family. When Hamed
insisted she come as a guest to a grand family wedding she
rose above the sniping and showed herself to the entire
clan. Joining the many hundreds of revellers in the reception line, wearing a crimson silk dress, with flowers to cover
the lack of diamonds, she prepared to meet Hamed's mother.

She climbed onto the platform and thrust out her hand. 'I'm Elizabeth, Hamed's *friend*.' She had given a great deal of thought to how she would introduce herself.

'Ah, *Elizabeth*. I feel as if I already know you. You are even more beautiful in the flesh than my son has said. I am very happy to know you.' Tears of relief sprang to Elizabeth's eyes as the tiny woman reached up for her shoulders and, in an instant, silenced the critics.

'When it ended I was devastated,' she says, pouring the last of the bottle into her glass. 'I went to LA and started looking back at photographs. I was searching for the moment when it had started to fall apart. I couldn't find one. He was always hugging me or holding my arm. I think he really loved me. We always had a good time together. But I noticed something terrifying. Necklines on my shirts got higher and hemlines got lower. I was covered with gold. I looked horrific – it's not my colour. But I hadn't even noticed. I loved him so much I'd stopped being me and was becoming exactly what he needed me to be.'

She crushes her Marlboro into the ashtray. 'It's a long time ago, huh? It's this place. It's for dreamers and people stupid enough to be seduced.'

'Don't you think it can work? There are plenty of successful mixed marriages.'

'Not everything is possible.' She pauses, then contradicts herself. 'Yeah, I know, there's a good percentage of the population here with a foreigner for a wife. Not so many husbands, of course. My mum's friend Paula is a great example.'

'See?'

'Damn this place, but I love it.'

We talk quickly. Time is short. Hello is soon replaced with goodbye out here. Elizabeth. Hamed. Friendships burn with the intensity that comes from knowing they won't last. The 80 per cent who come from abroad learn to live this way. A local woman tells me that her children keep losing their best friends as the families are posted onwards. Introspection is not part of the lifestyle. Reflection only leads to heartache. Abu Dhabi is not for ever. Most people stay a handful of years, five, six, sometimes more, sometimes not even that.

Until 2005 an expatriate could not become a citizen or own property. Now foreigners can buy into carefully designed, expat-friendly developments in al Raha, Reem and Yas, far from the local quarters on the west side of Abu Dhabi Island. But they can't have the land their investment stands on and people, like corporations, still need personal sponsorship before they are permitted to stay. The authorities want tourists to visit but foreigners shouldn't imagine that their feet will get too far under the table. Sponsorships can be cancelled abruptly, at whim, and often are. When I was growing up, we knew several people who were ejected without warning. Given only twenty-four hours to leave, there often wasn't time to gather possessions and money. Some had broken a law, others overstepped the line of trust, but whether it appeared justified or fanciful there were no second chances.

Against this unpredictable framework some expatriates seemed not to care about the rules. If they were well connected and discreet enough they could act with impunity, much like the locals they unwittingly aped. They would either be lucky or not. Such elasticity was part of the creed of tolerance espoused by the Abu Dhabian people. I had taken advantage of it in my own small way, running around with a Croatian boy, whose parents had escaped the Balkan War to save him from being sent to fight, driving his mother's jade BMW through the empty streets at night. It never entered our heads that we might be punished for speeding, or for parking on the sand behind the shopping malls to make out in the passenger seat. If we had been caught, we could have been arrested or deported. To the Sharia court, the display of love or lust between the eager young was a moral transgression. Romance and attraction were entirely private. They still are.

We were not immune, but the temporary nature of Abu Dhabi, its heat, the pace of the city and the constant changing of the guard, meant we threw ourselves into a racier way of living whether we belonged there or not. We behaved as if there was only today.

Our table is filling. Two Lebanese friends of Michael, a wind-dried Italian woman and Jon, his minder, an ex-Navy SEAL, who has drunk at least half of the six bottles of wine on the table. He is slurring something about his country's defence activities. Jon claims his job title is head of security at Michael's studio, but he seems to know a great deal more about the military ambitions of this city than the average inhabitant. He has spent afternoons with the crown prince discussing the UAE's defence and I have seen him striding about in his fatigues several times. The last coherent sentence he utters before sinking into complete unintelligibility is, 'Do you believe anything I've told you about myself?'

Elizabeth jabs me. 'That is so Abu Dhabi – no idea who anyone is, but can't trust 'em for the truth! Oh, my God.'

The wind-dried Italian has inched closer to Michael.

'She's a liability. She has a history of throwing herself at sheikhs. Now she's trying to make a go of it out here with a real job. I like her, don't get me wrong, but she's so not for Michael,' she mutters.

This sense of propriety guides the social landscape.

'You should feel for her.' I laugh. 'She's making a go of it.'

'I know. She's been resurrected,' Elizabeth concedes. 'It's all about reinventing yourself here. Just, please, not for my brother.

'Come on,' Elizabeth says suddenly, getting up from the table and grabbing me. 'Let's go and look next door.' She runs through the two sets of wooden doors and waves at the security guards sitting at the club entrance. They don't think of stopping her. The Hilton Hotel nightclub has grown up. Its cheap, tropical incarnation as Safari is long gone. Now it has a state-of-the-art sound system and a laser show. The wooden gazebos and tacky plastic palm fronds waving beneath a green and blue canopy of fairy-lights are nowhere to be seen: the new marble interior resembles a vast bathroom, a large open space with nowhere to hide. The DJ is at his altar, playing an Underworld remix. But there are no dancers on the floor. The place is empty, except for a line of posing men hovering close to the wall.

'Too early.'

'Yeah, maybe. It's only midnight.'

Two men, Egyptian or Syrian, perhaps, in artfully ripped jeans and greased ponytails slide almost imperceptibly towards us. One leans into Elizabeth and asks if he can buy her a drink. She backs along a vacant stretch of bar.

Slowly people saunter in, an assortment of drunken Australian naval officers and sober Lebanese men holding hands; they take to the dance-floor thrusting their matching stubble-lined jaws outwards in perfect synchronicity. The air thickens with smoke and aftershave, and the volume rises. It is an odd scene but people are beginning to have fun. The pouting, doe-eyed boys are untroubled by cynicism. It's why George Michael and Elton John are superstars here.

At the opening sounds of 'Thriller', arms are punched high into the air. Men prise themselves off the walls and strut to the beat. One goes to the middle of the floor and acts out the entire Michael Jackson routine, down to the last shuffle and pelvic lurch. The men are performing for each other and, suddenly, it seems, there isn't an inch of dance-floor to spare.

A decade or so back a group of Canadians retraced Thesiger's steps across the Empty Quarter. In the account of their journey even people from the most remote villages would stop and ask them if they had listened to Michael Jackson. Why didn't he write about camels, they would cry.

'My God, they love him, don't they?' I shout.

'Who? Wacko Jacko?'

Sara, a half-English, half-Lebanese girl, who has joined us, chuckles. 'Jacko's their hero.'

'He's more like them than any other person alive.'

'Yeah, he's a rich pervert,' shouts one of the Aussies.

'*Noooo*,' says Sara, over the noise. 'It's because he's a kid with too much money and nothing to spend it on. No one can tell him enough is enough.'

The palatial residences filled with houses for all the men and women of an extended family, brothers and their wives, cousins, aging mothers and uncles, contained by fortress walls and floodlighting, are hard to get into, and almost impossible to break out of. And behind the walls you can do whatever you like.

'These guys live in Never Never Land,' she continues. 'There are fountains and roads with mini-cars for driving around in. Golf courses, zoos, railways. Sheikh Mohammed has a go-karting track at his palace. Jacko's their kind of guy. It's no fantasy. He's more real than anyone else they see around them.'

'Just look at it.' Elizabeth gazes round the room. 'Weird.'

The male–female ratio may be even among Emiratis, but in the rest of the population men outnumber women by almost three to one. Arguing about precise numbers misses the point: hoteliers and property developers can design any trailblazing interior, with named architects, haul in the best DJs from Europe and the US, pump up the volume, the lights and the drinks menu, but the clubs will still be filled with men. As a child I was aware of the imbalance. From the expatriate Europeans in oil and construction to the Indian migrant workers, Abu Dhabi was, and is, a place for men doing greasy, ugly work. The city has been clad in the kind of modernity that makes most European cities look archaic, but the men have no one to preen for but each other.

It's likely to stay that way too, with hundreds of billions assigned to development over the next two decades. In the next five years alone Abu Dhabi's Chamber of Commerce is investing close to $354 billion in construction, tourism and manufacturing.

'It's the fault of the British,' I tell Elizabeth. 'They started shipping in Indians and Pakistanis during the fifties. Ex-Raj men were familiar and cheap.'

She isn't listening to me. 'Look over there,' she says, 'those guys at the table.'

Across the dance-floor a group of young Emiratis are sunk into their chairs. One raises his hand no more than a touch but the others turn to listen. After a few seconds their still faces break into laughter. 'Nothing changes. You remember how Khalid could take over a nightclub?'

'Abu Dhabi's answer to movie-star chic.'

On the rare occasions Khalid appeared in public, usually supplementing the dim lighting of a venue with dark glasses, he was trailed by fawners, sycophants and jesters, all struggling to gain favour. Waz would usher people in and out like a sweaty shepherd. And nobody ever refused the tap on the shoulder.

In this world things were done as the host wanted or not at all. I learned this during an evening pool party at a villa kept by a friend of a friend for occasional entertaining. Before the host made an appearance, he sent out a member of his entourage. The aide, in baggy hip-hop jeans and a back-turned baseball cap, had lumbered up to each of us in turn. 'Khalid wants his guests to enjoy all that he makes available this evening. And he wants to know he is among friends he can trust. Please go if you are not comfortable.' The words were veiled. The intent was not. Join in or leave. Being asked to agree to silence without knowing what, exactly, I was to remain silent about unsettled me. I might have meant nothing to him but, by staying, I was giving Khalid something over me. The air of fear and paranoia was stifling. They were probably only going to smoke a joint or two, something people did all over the world, but I couldn't do it. I lacked the bottle to throw myself into the ring.

Elizabeth leans over. 'You know what happened to the panther, don't you?'

I shake my head.

'It threw itself off the balcony.'

Before I can speak she nudges my shoulder again. 'It's like a modern *majlis*. Look at them.' She's right. Their culture is here. The same as it ever was.

The *majlis* is a centuries-old assembly, held by the sheikh or senior members of a clan or tribe for men to discuss the issues of the day. Anyone seeking an audience could appear at the door to the tent of their elders and plead their case. In an era before newspapers, books, radio or telegraph, when the tribes lived in almost total isolation from the outside world, it was the only forum for news. Anyone back from travelling outside the tribal territory would share what they had learned, and guests would be welcomed there. As well as the centre of governance, the *majlis* was an opportunity for men to learn, and talk to each other.

Like the Renaissance courts and French salons, the *majlis* has become an artful scene filled with invisible gestures, subtle cues and unspoken rituals. Over generations such assemblies have acquired a well-understood protocol, and as Abu Dhabi's society has reached into the world of business, the *majlis* has, to some extent, folded in outsiders, allowing newcomers to enter into a way of managing affairs that is not founded on contracts and officialdom but personal bonds. A few words can reveal enough to open or close the door of trust, opportunity and prosperity.

When my father arrived, he knew he had to throw himself into the fray or remain for ever a stranger. The *majlis* yielded its own rewards. It was never less than time-consuming, but without it he is certain that nothing would ever have got off the ground. He said it was the equivalent of the gentlemen's clubs in London, inside whose panelled rooms so much business was done. And it was right to pay your respects. The Abu Dhabians were watching. It always surprised him how few expatriates actually bothered to go. 'It's where you discovered what was going on, and who knew who. Around Eid people's troubles were fair game. It was the best time to push an issue that everyone had been trying to avoid.'

One of the first assemblies he attended was Sheikh Zayed's. Having removed his shoes, he entered the grand reception room at one of the palaces. It was edged with armchairs and cushions, and blanketed with richly woven, overlapping rugs of wool and silk. Servants walked between groups of men, wafting frankincense and *oud* out of the little silver cages that hung from their hands. He stood in line to pay his respects. When it came to sitting, he let Sami Suleiman direct him – choosing the right place to settle was all-important. Sami wanted them to be visible to others in the room. Spying a chair near the sheikh's, they sat down. After the formalities and the greetings, everyone hunched over tiny cups of *gahwa*, served from brass pots. The throat-strippingly strong cardamom coffee had become as important a ritual to my father as cigars and malt whisky.

The *majlis* is still a formal part of life in Abu Dhabi, but the open-door policy that once characterised the direct governance of the tribes has disappeared. Several people have told me that, since 11 September 2001, the upper echelons of Abu Dhabi society have closed their doors, too frightened to allow the uninvited through their gates. Abu Dhabi is no longer a small town of familiars, and those who might once have been open to their community now feel vulnerable to attack from outsiders who disapprove of a rich, Western-friendly UAE. It is not only fear, of course: the size of the population today prevents direct contact. While some Abu Dhabians have representation through the National Consultative Council, and invitations to specific influential *majlis*, such personal contact with rulers and laws could never extend to all of society.

Here, with men grouped informally round a table, I have a vision of the *majlis* as a loose cultural salon, a sense of how traditional practices might evolve to fit the future. Perhaps the open-door policy is being replaced by a *majlis* that can form and re-form itself anytime and anywhere. Suddenly those guys in jeans – in a club where their national dress is banned – seem to be bringing ancient customs bang up to date.

It's gratifying to see. Often, Abu Dhabi's culture feels fragile, and the citizens an evasive minority hiding from view, protecting themselves against the strangers that have filled their country. There are glimpses of an identity rising here and there like a refrain: straight-backed girls in slim-line *abayas*, silhouettes of men in robes glued to their phones, incense, flashes of homelife behind ornate compound gates. Many of the vast foreign population, recruited to execute specific professional assignments, never get much chance to meet and take part in the lives of their host countrymen at all. To be in modern Abu Dhabi is like being invited to someone's baronial pile for the weekend, and finding everything there, servants, guests, roaring fires, turned-back beds, except the owners.

12
We Also Set Them Free

The Masaood villa is a large stone ranch. Once it sat on the water's edge, with all the serenity of a sea view. Now the land that extended the coastline has left it marooned, half a mile inland on the wrong side of the six-lane mega-highway. People tell me not to mention it: it has broken Abdullah's heart.

I've dressed smartly: a black dress and patent-leather shoes. True to Abdullah's word, a car arrives to take me there. I haven't seen his family in a decade. He has grandchildren now and I'm looking forward to meeting them all, half hoping we will be served the signature lunch dish: a whole lamb, stripped of its skin, on a bed of rice, raisins and nuts.

The driver drops me off at the gates. I walk across the paved exterior to the house. The huge teak doors are open and I can hear voices. I move through a cavernous rose-coloured atrium into a huddle of family and friends. Moments later, a waiter appears at my side with a tray of drinks. 'Wine, water, juice, champagne.' He points at each. Such gracious hospitality makes it impossible to think beyond the moment. I take the wine and smile at a couple I dimly recognise before I catch sight of Abdullah.

'Ah, Joanna, hello.' He leads me through to a high-ceilinged carpeted room, with toys scattered on the floor. 'Come, you must meet the grandchildren.'

They are playing in a room adjacent to where the adults are gathered, small and bright-eyed, with nannies to care for them.

'Congratulations,' I say. 'The clan's growing, a whole new generation to look after you.'

'Of course.' He chuckles. 'The Masaoods are everywhere now.' And then: 'There are Masaoods in Dubai. Black Masaoods. They have our name but they are free.' The Masaoods he is referring to are the descendants of his family's slaves and servants.

Slavery was accepted across the Arab world long before Islam took hold. Islamic zealots and pirates were permitted by Sharia law to enslave anyone not from the *ummah* – the brotherhood of faith. For the millions brought from Africa, via Zanzibar and the coast of Oman, it was the route across the Gulf peninsula that delivered them to all the corners of the Arab world. They became part of domestic households, as concubines and maids, aides, harem attendants, guards and divers. Along the Trucial coast the need for slaves rose and fell with the success of the pearlers. A strong diver was an asset to any fleet. High prices were paid for slaves who could take on the deep waters.

The relationship between master and slave was characterised by strict codes of conduct: slaves called their masters 'uncle' and did not initiate conversation, but they were often well protected, becoming, in time, an extension of the family. Since Islam encouraged the faithful to free converted slaves many were given, or allowed to buy, their liberty. Even so, some chose to remain in their master's household. Freedom brought risk and uncertainty in an impossible clime and life in another's household guaranteed food and safety, at least. Without a motherland, adoption of the new culture was a way for them to belong. Pride in being part of a good local family spawned the saying '*Khadim al shaikh shaikh*', 'The slave of the sheikh is a sheikh.'

After legislation outlawed slavery in Britain, there were calls for overseas territories and protectorates to follow suit. But in Muscat trafficking was a highly lucrative cornerstone of the economy. While the Royal Navy patrolled the Trucial sea routes and the coastline, keeping the tribes at arm's length by allowing them to see to their own affairs, the slave trade shifted inland. Tribes brought the caravans through new land routes across the desert. During the second half of the nineteenth century, the Buraimi oasis blossomed as eastern Arabia's centre of slavery, with traders buying and selling them for money, pearls, gold, silver, food and guns. The British, who had no need of influence inland before the search for oil begin, chose to overlook what went on in the interior, rarely sending soldiers there. The runaways who found their way to British officers were issued with manumission chitties. In this way the trade continued more or less as it always had for another century or more.

The pressure to end it came after the Second World War. The hardship of the 1940s brought an increase in raiding as enslaved women and children from Trucial territories were transported to al Hasa in the Kingdom of Saudi Arabia, still an area of lively trade. But with a growing number of oilmen in the area, Her Majesty's Government knew it must address the reality of a flourishing market. In the late 1950s the British asked its Gulf protectorates to sign up to the 1956 Supplementary Slavery Convention. Following the lead of Bahrain and Qatar, the Trucial States assured the

Political Agent that slaves were 'at liberty to come and go at will' and in 1963 the Trucial Council signed a decree, with Shakhbut the last to acquiesce, outlawing the practice.

After 1971 any slaves who had not been formally emancipated found themselves naturalised citizens. With oil and new nationhood, slavery was consigned, without much record, to the Trucial States' history. Today, although many do not consider Afro-Emiratis true Arabs, they are part of the Emirates' history, testifying to the collision of cultures.

'To Arabs the slave was part of the family,' Abdullah tells me. 'They were slaves in name, but they lived with the family as a family member. They were in the middle of everything. And we made them free.'

'Do you see them?'

He shrugs his shoulders and opens his palms. 'They are there and I am here.'

Now, instead of slaves, there are Asian servants, who are still treated as members of the family. For instance, nannies travel everywhere with their charges, constantly on call, speaking broken Arabic and teaching them the ways of faraway homelands. And when they have reared the children to adulthood, they will leave.

In the city there is a feeling that Abu Dhabians have turned over too much of the responsibility for child-rearing to foreign domestic staff because, linguistically and culturally, children's lives do not chime with their parents'. As with the upper classes in Regency and Victorian Britain, it is increasingly the nanny who has the child's heart.

Abdullah's radiant American daughter-in-law sits next

to me, twisting the stem of her wine glass between tapered fingers. 'We want the children to do as they like. We want them to be loved by everyone.' She smiles. 'We want our children to be happy. Children who are loved always belong.'

Although she is young there is wisdom in her sentiment. Perhaps that is how a peaceful union of cultures will be achieved. I look at one of the nannies. The baby has fallen asleep on her shoulder and is being carried up to bed.

◆ ◆ ◆

When I was growing up, Peter, our houseboy from India, was part of our family. He was Keralan, long, lean and literate, and he managed the day-to-day running of our household six and a half days a week, shuffling about in his flip-flops. I picture him sometimes in the kitchen, chopping and wiping, his eyes so black they seemed to have no pupils. He lived, in monk-like austerity, in a tiny, oblong room at the side of the villa, with a single bed and bare walls. He had family in India, but no photographs or keepsakes on display, just a Bible and prayer book on his bedside table, and a small digital clock that my father had given him. On Sunday afternoons he joined a taxi share with three other Indians and they disappeared to St Joseph's, where the many Indian Catholics worshipped. The rhythm of his life troubled me with a feeling I couldn't articulate at the time but later discovered to be shame. Not only did he do all he was supposed to in the house, he helped Bill and me through countless childhood struggles, too.

When my parents were out on the endless circuit of cocktail parties and dinners, he was there to look after us. When I woke, alarmed by the churn of the air-conditioning coming to an abrupt halt or cockroaches scuttling across the floor, Peter came to my rescue. I would tiptoe down the stairs and there he would be, patiently minding the house on a small ebony stool between the kitchen and the hall.

I never cried in front of him and he didn't talk much to me. He acknowledged my presence by pulling out a little stool from the store cupboard and setting it next to his. There we would remain, side by side under the light, listening to the hum of the fridge and the tick of the clock. If I showed no sign of wanting to go back upstairs, he would retrieve his Bible and start to read.

Before Peter, I had known almost nothing of the grand warring and the poetry of the Old Testament, the meek pragmatism of love and faith behind the gospels' accounts of Jesus's trials were new to me, but I listened, tracking the indentations on the leather with my eyes and staring at his feet, which twitched in sympathy with the story. When he turned from the parables of the New Testament to descriptions of Solomon's palace, with its harems, eunuchs, asses, snakes and chariots dashing infidels to the ground, I would take myself back to bed and sleep.

Despite the intimate place he occupied at the centre of our lives Peter was barely recognised beyond his function. My father might have been contractually generous but he was pretty irritable with him most of the time. One painful lunchtime, Bill and I sat silently at the dining-table, waiting for Peter to appear from the kitchen. He had made a mistake and my father was not pleased. He had served the dessert on the gold-rimmed porcelain reserved for visiting dignitaries. 'Silly bugger. He just doesn't listen.'

We listened to the faint scrape of new bowls being taken

out of the cupboard, and then the quiet as Peter painstak-
ingly reconstructed each helping, his hands fishing out
brandy-snap, fruit and cream from one bowl and manoeu-
vring it into another, keeping the jellied glaze unbroken.
Bill and I crossed our fingers under the table, hoping he
would get it right and dissolve the tension.

Peter remained unfazed. He understood my father's keen
eye, which was far more attentive to detail than my mother's.
During meals Peter was on the alert to the ring of the little
brass bell my father sounded to signify the end of each
course. Washing dishes, brushing the sand that crept through
every crevice onto sills and into corners, hanging up
misplaced keys, polishing our shoes, buying prawns from
the fishing dhows at prices my mother would never have
been offered, Peter was my domestic prince.

When we left Abu Dhabi I wanted him to come with us.
My mother explained he was a servant and did not qualify
as one of the family. It was a hard lesson, but it seemed
that some were more equal than others. I know nothing of
what has happened to him or where he is now.

◆　◆　◆

In Abu Dhabi the value of human life has always been
inequitable. Tor, a Norwegian concrete engineer who had
lived and worked in Abu Dhabi for many years, told me
his story a few years ago in London. He had Nordic good
looks, a wide grin and a deep voice. Arriving as a young
man fresh out of college, he had intended to stay six months
but was there for a decade, involved in the construction of
several prestigious developments. He told me of the reckless speed at which the labour force was obliged to work

in order to meet punishing deadlines. I had seen this cavalier attitude many times myself. The sight of builders tightrope-walking the scaffolding at the top of twenty-storey blocks of flats, welding signs to roofs hundreds of feet up without safety ropes or harnesses, was all too common.

'So you tried to protect them?'

He shrugged. 'You did your best. But migrant workers were not considered to be worth much. You could never actually say so but it was the attitude of everyone. Yes, it was bad when one fell off or got injured but it didn't change anything. There were always more willing to step in. No one cared, really.'

Tor knew this from personal experience. He had been pulling away from a set of lights in the Tourist Club area when the accident had happened. He'd put his foot down sharply to get ahead of the other cars and cross lanes as they turned from red to green. An Indian man at the pedes-trian crossing decided to chance the amber light and ran out onto the road. He would have made it if he'd kept his nerve. But as the traffic shot forward he hesitated and stepped back towards the kerb, right into the path of Tor's jeep.

The man bounced onto the bonnet, smashed against the windscreen and dropped to the ground. Tor braked, the jeep stopped and the Simple Minds tape kept playing on the stereo. There was blood on the glass.

The road filled quickly with onlookers, crowding round the man, who lay perfectly still except for the shallow rise and fall of his chest. Within a minute the police arrived and took Tor away.

The prison, unlike the rest of the city, had not been the

beneficiary of oil money and Tor was surrounded by what seemed the entire criminal fraternity of Abu Dhabi. Inside, nothing separated executives, with their houseboys, drivers and thrice-yearly flights home, from the labourers who served them and slept ten to a room in the shanty-towns outside the city. Everyone was guilty until they could prove otherwise.

The arrest papers and charges were in Arabic. Tor's boss sent an Egyptian lawyer to the prison to represent him but no one had time to translate. When Tor tried to explain the turn of events the lawyer gestured for him to be silent and left. Later that day he returned and shook Tor's hand. 'Everything is OK. You can sign it, no problem, now.' He beamed. 'The man you ran over is only a jingly. You will get a *diya*, a fine. This will go to the victim.'

In court, the lawyer pulled something out of his file, spoke quietly to the judge and Tor was out in less than a minute. 'It was pretty obvious that my boss's boss, a national, had stepped in. I paid the fine and that was that. It was fifteen thousand dirhams, maybe a little more. It worked out at twenty thousand Norwegian *kroner*, less than two thousand British pounds. At the time I wanted it to be over. Now I think about the victim a lot. I never knew what happened to him.'

People still pretend not to notice the chronic mistreatment of the migrant labour force. They are omnipresent, yet invisible. In their municipal overalls they can be seen watering the gardens, sweeping the streets and cleaning hotel windows. Many work in hazardous conditions, facing years of indebtedness for the fees they pay to the recruitment agencies to bring them to the Gulf – despite the law that states such fees remain the employer's responsibility. Wages are routinely withheld and passports confiscated to ensure that they cannot abscond to look for less punishing, more lucrative roles. Domestic workers are still unprotected under UAE labour laws. In the old days of slavery a concubine might be freed to join the family with her children. Today Filipina housemaids bearing children by their employers are deported. The babies are frequently left behind, to be raised without them.

It is easiest to adopt a position of convenient blindness to the harsh realities. Many servants work upwards of twelve hours a day, seven days a week, with little prospect of getting home to see their families. Some expatriates argue that even the worst-paid members of the labour force have a better life in Abu Dhabi than they would in their home countries. The friend who had praised the ease with which curtains could be made explained how she saw things. 'We can't change anything anyway. For a girl from Sri Lanka to be supporting her family is a good opportunity.' It seemed the wrong time to mention the hundreds who, over the past five years, are reported to have run away from their Arab employers and turned themselves in as asylum-seekers in London. 'Even the Suez Canal was built by a slave force,' she adds. In a blink I realise that, like British shoppers who sidestep the discomfort of buying sweatshop-made clothes in order to snap up a bargain, only changes to the legal framework will move the hearts and minds of people in Abu Dhabi.

The Minister of State for Federal National Council Affairs acknowledges the gravity of the UAE's poor human-rights record, and is full of rhetoric about change. Yet the people's general lack of curiosity or outrage slows the efforts of human-rights organisations to push their agenda. Human Rights Watch have seized upon the development of Saadiyat Island as an opportunity to press the government towards meaningful reform. Dismayed by the gap between promises and observable progress they have sent letters to the Louvre and Frank Gehry, architect of the Abu Dhabi Guggenheim, imploring each to use their leverage and insist on working and accommodation conditions that conform to international law. Perhaps aware of the need to maintain the iconic standing of the Guggenheim, Gehry, I am told, has requested that workers' rights are protected on Saadiyat. Developers, desperate to avoid the kind of derailing publicity beginning to dog Dubai, are building workers' accommodation facilities that meet global standards.

Conflicts of interest, pursuit of profit and the widely held view that workers live a life of genuine choice all hamper change. But if the money spent on creating a squeaky-clean frontage for investors was diverted into solving the issues affecting migrant workers their place in the social order would be swiftly improved. This is a tiny, solvent country, run tightly from the top down. If it wanted to instigate social change, and encourage the ending of endemic discrimination, it could have its people mobilised in an instant.

The great irony is that for a society that talks about the collective few people actually belong. The weary workers squatting at the sides of the streets, watching the world they are not part of, are a constant reminder of the gulf between one stratum and another. Repelled by the smell of poverty and labour, it seems at times as if the genteel classes really believe that cleanliness is next to godliness.

In many ways, it feels like Victorian England. The poor

and less skilled are locked into a world in which they are dependent on the goodwill of those above them. The charitable obligation of Islam, *zakat*, does not often extend to the ghettoised immigrant communities. The size of the city is encouraging a regressive segregation. Once corrugated-iron shacks propped each other up in little clusters all over the town. Now, as workers are driven out of the plush city centre, semi-industrial areas like Mussafah have morphed into grimy shanty-towns for thousands. The cramped, dirty quarters are hot, pungent and a long way from the smart, iridescent blocks of the rest of the city. In jumbled passageways, men wash, cook, clean and socialise. Clothes are filthy, food is of poor quality, and people bed down in rows, crowded and yet alone, driven by worse prospects at home into being there. Many more no longer live in the city. The men who once ate at the cheap two-dirham joints and slept on the Corniche are bussed in and out of labour camps in the desert. Though many now have air-conditioning, there is nothing for these all-male populations to do: men borrow against their future earnings to buy TVs and satellite dishes, drawing themselves further into debt. When one is injured, his colleagues club together to repatriate him. When someone dies, they pay for the body to be sent home. In business terms these people are a cheaper commodity than the marble they work with, and almost infinitely replaceable.

◆ ◆ ◆

While I worked in Abu Dhabi, the only difference I could make was to act with kindness, which was how I'd come to hire Ewau. Elizabeth's mother, Kate, found her. Kate was one of those battling Americans, with the interests of all women close to her heart. She knew I was a soft touch. At one of her carpet picnics – tubs of hummus, tabouleh and wine served on the rugs in her living room – she persuaded me to give a Filipina in her forties a job. 'She'll be deported unless we save her.' I tried to tell her I had no need of anyone – I already had Ana, from Manila. 'You can do this for me, Joanna,' Kate said.

I brought Ewau in as an extra pair of hands to the Marina Club membership department. Miserable, obstreperous and utterly unsuited to the job, she relied entirely on me to communicate with other members of staff, refusing to answer to anyone else. She, Ana and I sat in the cramped, windowless office and I soon discovered there were no hidden reserves of charm beneath Ewau's awkward exterior. Although I never got to the bottom of what had happened with her previous employer, her undisguised venom for every man told me it had not been pleasant. Even in the calm surrounds of the Marina Club she would flare up at the slightest exchange, and I spent entire afternoons sitting with an arm round her shoulders while she sobbed into my lap and complained about some innocuous comment the squash coach or sales manager had made. 'He is an animal, an ape. Men are brutes.' I felt duped. But whenever I was on the brink of letting her go, she would offer me a tearful thankyou. It was impossible to regret my decision to take her on. She was twice my age and had nothing.

◆ ◆ ◆

During the time my father acted as adviser to Abdullah, he had an Indian PA, Georgina. She has lived in Abu Dhabi now for thirty years, transforming her family's destiny. I call her and ask if I can visit. I want to see how Georgina has made Abu Dhabi her own meritocracy.

I hail one of the new 'executive saloons' that have recently appeared across the city. 'Najda Street,' I tell the surly driver in his white cap. His henna-stained red beard shows he is a veteran of the *hajj*. He shakes his head and swerves into the traffic, then lurches back to the side of the road. 'Another taxi driver will take you,' he mutters, without turning to me. 'Yes, another one will be better for you.'

The next driver is from Peshawar, young, with a thick, well-trimmed moustache. In his neatly ironed white shirt, he looks as if he does a desk job. From his welcoming smile I expect he might brim with a little more optimism than the previous fellow. In passable English, he says he wants to leave Abu Dhabi. 'I like drive English man. Or lady. Locals very, very rude. Never have money to pay. Some get out end of journey and say, "OK, chase me if you want for your money." They take what they want. What can I do?'

Georgina has a conservative-looking office, filled with grey-beige cabinets and a small sofa. A couple of framed prints hang on the wall and there is a floor-to-ceiling tropical plant, but nothing that bears a personal touch.

'Georgina!'

'Joanna?' She registers mild shock at seeing me, then her slender Indian arms open with a welcome. She has a saintly aura of goodwill – the legacy of a lifetime in the Catholic Church – and her wide eyes are bright. I feel her absorbing everything I have become in the time since we last met. Henna glimmers on her grey hair and her skin is a little less translucent, but there is no doubt that like most Indian women, she has aged well.

I am older and more sensible-looking than she remembers. 'I have children,' I say, as if that is some explanation for my shift from excitable twenty-something to bona-fide adulthood.

'Ah, yes, your father said.'

She has been in Abu Dhabi since the mid-1970s. Knowing nothing about the city, except that it had a Catholic church, she left her large Bombay family and came on a one-way ticket to join her boyfriend and find a job before her tourist visa expired. Arriving on a Thursday, she spent Friday, the Islamic day of rest, kicking her heels. On Saturday she went to her interviews, and by the end of the day, she had been offered a full-time secretarial job in a construction firm.

In the first months she was filled with longing for India. After the bustle of Bombay, Abu Dhabi was a stifling backwater. But when friends who had gone to the Kingdom of Saudi Arabia wrote to tell her how lucky she was to be somewhere that recognised her religious faith she decided to apply herself to achieving her aims: saving enough for herself and her musician boyfriend, who now had a job in catering, to marry, and a little more to buy a home in India. As Abu Dhabians moved into newly built modern villas, they and other Indians took on the mud houses and slowly formed a new community. When friends acquired a car the four of them drove about town together on Friday afternoons. And they never missed the Sunday service at St Joseph's, where women appeared in glimmering saris and polished shoes, and afterwards disappeared to the beach with tea, biscuits and curry lunches, prepared and brought in carefully packed bags and tiffins.

By the time her CV arrived on my father's desk in the early 1990s she was long married, with three children, a host of glowing references, fine shorthand and fast, accurate typing. He viewed Georgina's arrival with relief. He had grown tired of the indolent parade of nail-filing time-wasters the recruitment agencies kept sending him, imagining he would want a British girl, despite his repeated insistence he wanted no part of the trend towards Western executive PAs. It was a match made in heaven. Georgina worked with him, on her Westerner's salary, until he retired.

She calls the Indian office-boy and asks for a cup of Lipton's tea, white, no sugar. It arrives, of course, thick with sugar and without milk, as the Arabs prefer it. She shrugs. 'Thirty years. Nothing changes.'

'It's a long time. Surely it must feel like home now.'

'In many ways, yes.' She inclines her head. 'It's maybe . . .' she pauses '. . . a little samey.' She is too steeped in Arab culture, and grateful to it, to criticise things directly, but I understand what she means. It is comfortable and easy, but no longer a challenge. She is a successful professional reaping the rewards of her perseverance. Her husband, too: 'He has worked twenty-five years in the catering department at the airport and now, finally, there is a new manager – a Brit – who has recognised the contribution he has made. The last manager, who was a Pakistani, destroyed every chance he had of being promoted. To be honest, Joanna, I despaired. He has tolerated so much snideness and bullying. Working the graveyard shift, you know, from eight at night till four in the morning for so many years, then having someone else take all the glory. Now he's cock-a-hoop. And he deserves everything he's got. It is two decades late, but it is there.'

Their sacrifices and the money they have earned have given their children choices. The boys who played football with the neighbourhood gang are now away at foreign universities. Only the youngest is still at home. 'She'll go to Australia, if she has her way.' She laughs. 'For me, the kind of education they are having was out of the question. I finished high school and that was it. We were out in the world. That's why I came here, really. I calculated what I was earning, and how long it would take to get anywhere if I stayed in India. I thank God every day for this place and all I have. I have faith and it provides answers. I want the boys to feel the same, but they don't have the conviction I do. It is because they can't see where we've come from.'

The phone rings and she takes a flurry of calls. The final arrangements are being made for an open golf tournament that the company is sponsoring. Few people had bothered to confirm, and now, at the very last minute, they're calling in and expecting to be able to add extra guests to their parties. 'You know how it is, here. No one commits to anything in advance, and then they want to bring five people on the day. I can't risk offending anyone.

'It was easy working for your father. He included me in everything and trusted me to make decisions on the hoof,' she says quietly. 'John and I were a team. There was give-and-take. Once when the baby had measles I had to take two weeks of afternoons off to be with her. When I told John, thinking he would say, "You're fired," he just said, "These things happen." To be honest, I was glad to have a boss who worked split shifts. It meant I could pick up the youngest from nursery at one and take her home, feed her, play with her, then put her down for a nap before I had to come back at four thirty. I always made sure she was asleep, and then the boys, who were nine and ten, came straight back to the apartment when they finished school.'

'You left her alone?'

'It was the only option. We could not afford a nanny. Even if we could have, there was no room for one in a two-bedroom flat. She was always still asleep when the boys returned.'

'But what if she'd bucked the routine?'

'She never did.'

The eldest son is now a scientist about to marry an American girl, settled in the US for good. 'I miss him. I wonder, did we send him off too young? But, then, I made that choice. And what else could I expect? I have to admire how he has taken on America.'

'Where does he belong? Is he an Arab-Indian? An Indian-American? An Arab-Indian-American?'

'I don't know! I get confused thinking about it.' She laughs but her eyes are mournful. 'All of them, I think.'

She sends the office-boy out again, this time for pastries. 'They are global children, I suppose. We knew when we made the choice to be here that this might happen. Of course, they were at school here with us, but none of them was going to settle for ever. Opportunities would have been limited for them here. And we are not going to be here forever either. I say to myself, "How can I be upset when I have set them on this path leading to new cultures? When

I consider where they are headed now?" The eldest, he is a real scientist. It's hard to argue with that.'

'What about you? How long will you stay?'

'The government here has not always made the most sensible decisions where Indians are concerned. There are a lot of us. They get worried about that. In 1994 they discovered we were more than forty per cent of the population and there was a frantic drive to get rid of us all. They pushed a lot out by raising the minimum wage at which someone qualified to sponsor their family. Many packed up and went home. Others stayed and started again as bachelors. It wasn't easy.'

I tell her about Marita, my former colleague at the Marina Club, who lived in a block of flats owned by the Islamic Bank of Dubai. The apartment next door had one bedroom but eight or nine Indian men lived there, against the rental-contract rules. It was easy for the police to catch them out. Since everyone took off their shoes before entering their homes, the police walked the stairwells counting the sandals lined up in the hallway. They deported them all for illegal sub-letting. 'That was in 1995, I think.'

'It happens still.' She nods. 'They run after people, but it is short-sighted. The economy in India is improving, wages are better and the benefits of coming to the Gulf are not as compelling as they were. It costs so much more to live here now that it isn't worth it for a lot of people, especially if they have to leave their families behind. But Abu Dhabi still needs people. Ninety per cent of the labour force is foreign, so they have to keep recruiting.'

'How much longer will you stay?'

'I don't know. But as soon as we are not working we

won't be able to stay. I can't complain. It has worked for us. Having the babies here was easy, raising them, too. We will go back after we retire, and see what adventures life holds at home.'

'You'll be returning as rather grand travellers.'

'That's what the family say.'

13
Don't Bury the Moon

The National Media Council is housed inside the Ministry of Culture, Youth and Community Development, a huge white concrete cube that sits at the dead end of Mohammed bin Khalifa Street. Formed in 2006, it assumed the responsibilities of the outgoing Federal Ministry of Information and Culture. I have been told it takes a far more enlightened outlook on media openness than its defunct predecessor. It would be hard for it not to: the Ministry of Information was renowned for heavy-handed and unapologetic monitoring of all print, radio and television. The new council, by all accounts, is more consumer-friendly: its remit is to share news on behalf of the government, issue bulletins, and defend Abu Dhabi's culture from those who would wish to compromise it. Nevertheless, it is far from being toothless. Alongside the courts it retains the power to take action against those falling foul of media laws.

I am here after another failed attempt to get to some records. This time I'd gone back to *Al Ittihad* to meet Juma'a, the sales manager, who told me that the newspaper's owners had been given money by the government to transfer all their back copies on to a microfiche system. Briefly I'd thought I was finally on to something. It turned out the microfilming department was a deserted room with a dusty machine wedged into a corner.

'Look, they are here.' He gestured to a pile of papers higher than me. Elsewhere, disintegrating fragments were strewn across the floor. 'Not everything is here. But some. I think.' He lifted the hem of his white robe away from the dust, and stepped over a pile of torn, dateless issues, explaining that dwindling funds had caused the project to grind to a halt. He laughed at my obvious disappointment. 'I didn't understand why you wanted to see these. They are dirty. You must go to the Media Council.' He paused. 'I am racing my boat this weekend. We have a team. This is what I like to do.'

The interior of the Ministry of Culture is hollow. It has the serene hum of people gliding in and out of elevators, acting with purpose but no urgency. A man in the lift fiddles with a string of prayer beads – an unusual sight: more often than not now it is a phone. I leave him at the second floor and walk along the glass-balconied corridor. This is a spacious building yet it is filled with old-fashioned corridors and burrows, rooms leading off rooms. The open-plan office is a long way off. I knock on the door. A woman's face looks up. Then, with one spin of her chair, she has pulled her *burka* over her face and resumed a diligent position at the keyboard. It is left to her warm, maternal-faced colleague to make conversation. 'Hello.' She smiles. 'Can I help?'

I tell her the whole sorry story: my visits to newspaper offices, non-existent archives, archives that did exist but weren't ready, of shrugs and numbers and names of those who 'should be able to help'.

'Aha,' she breaks into tinkling laughter, 'many have asked this. You must go to the newspapers.'

I feel defeated. 'But I've been to the newspapers. In fact, they sent me here.'

She looks at me with sympathy. 'I will give you my own contacts and telephone numbers. They will help.' She dips into a drawer for paper, then pulls out several packets of miniature crispbreads. 'You are hungry?'

I don't shake my head quickly enough.

'Ah, you *are* hungry. I am so sorry.'

She presses them into my hands and wraps my fingers round the packets. Then she writes some names and numbers on a sheet of paper. I take it. Her card, clipped to the top, has the logo of the New Media Council. The paper is old stock from the Ministry of Information and Culture.

'And what if they cannot help me?'

'Tell them Maha sent you. They will help.'

Later I make the calls. No one on Maha's list answers.

◆ ◆ ◆

I never thought I'd come to see the haphazard stacks of magazines, papers and cuttings I've been sent by my parents and friends as an archive. But in the context of what I'd managed to find it most definitely qualified as such. It's personal, of course, full of the random odds and ends that get squirrelled away in attics and under-stair cupboards – trade publications, annual reports, old newspapers, videos, consumer magazines, letters, cards, mostly from the 1970s and early 1980s. I pull out an edition of the *Gulf News* from 1976. It's relentlessly jolly, filled with trivia and the snobbish preoccupations of the expatriate community, the Queen's birthday celebrations at the embassy and inter-mittent pieces warning those with servants to be watchful.

I spot a story about a Gujarati maid who had given up everything to come to the Gulf. It's the closest thing to social comment I've seen.

It seemed that the corporation newsletters were more direct in addressing the issues than the papers. A 1977 edition of the Adma-opco newsletter cautioned oilmen newly arrived from Britain – a country teetering on the edge of bankruptcy, awash with punk, streakers at Lords, tube tops, hot pants and the Queen's Silver Jubilee – '*REMEMBER, YOU'RE LIVING IN ABU DHABI!*' The article called for respect towards the locals and demure behaviour from a new generation of expatriates; the men had specialist engineering skills but no clue how to handle themselves in a hot foreign country, and their wives, who had lived with the women's liberation movement, were full of ideas of personal fulfilment.

> *This is a Muslim country and, whether we like it or not, women in a Muslim society are treated very differently. Expatriate women living in Saudi Arabia are not allowed to go out unless they are covered decently and that usually means wearing a high-necked full-length dress with sleeves. In Abu Dhabi we are luckier, but this does not mean we should go mad.*
>
> *Wearing backless, halter-necked, revealing dresses, or clinging T-shirts, tight trousers or shorts to the market is not only stupid and ill-mannered – it is asking for trouble.*

It was a clear message to any woman who chose to flout the rules that she should consider herself a target.

There are here a large number of unaccompanied men of different nationalities. Crimes of assault or of a sexual nature are increasing. One can't really blame men who are driven to such crimes, especially when they are confronted by women who appear . . . to be flaunting themselves. Even your houseboy is probably here without his wife and family, so do be considerate about how you dress when he is around.

As I look through the piecemeal collection I am hoping that perhaps I will find something, anything, about the disappearance of the English girl. The lack of access to any real evidence is enough to make me question whether it ever happened. In the West, history is created from evidence. We require supporting material to be confident about our past: objects, books, photographs, documents. The heritage of the lithe, upright tribes is as different from this materialistic view on history as it is possible to be. They are a people who only ever carried what they needed to survive: a cooking pan, a coffee pot, a knife. Their history was held in their heads and passed on with certainty and clarity, if not a little bias. But we expect, and the modern world demands, something different. We live in a proof-driven culture.

At the bottom of the box there's a VHS tape. It is a BBC film, made in 1979, entitled *The Oilman's Wife*. I put it on. It's full of Farrah Fawcett hairdos and flares and mahogany tans. Leslie Chew, BP wife and friend of my mother, gives a frank and honest account of her life in 'one of the least believable cities in the world'. She shares her frustration that, sooner or later, when she is least expecting it, they

will be told to go. She is candid about the arguments she
has with her weary husband about arrangements for
weekend parties and dinners made while he was out in the
field. 'He just wants to stay in and watch TV but I've been
in all week . . .' Her eye meets the camera while she describes
the discomfort of being ogled by the Indian hordes out
shopping at the *souk*. 'It can be quite creepy here.'

But nowhere is she more emphatic than on the matter
of her children's freedom. 'Lives are limited. They don't
develop an adventurous spirit. They can't.'

Sitting upright behind her, on a peppermint-green three-
piece suite, two of her friends – in pale skirts and matching
tans – nod. And then silence.

The interviewer encourages her to elaborate. Surely it's
safe for children here, of all places. It's a small town, after
all. Leslie stares blankly into the camera, then turns to her
friends. The three eye each other in a mutual pact of silence.
They look nervous. Eventually one of the others speaks up:
'One or two things have happened here and it isn't, or we
feel it isn't, safe to let the children out any more.'

I rewind the film and play it again. This is it. This is all
I can find that even hints at the reality of the terrible event
I have held in my mind for more than thirty years. Just a
few veiled fragments of hearsay on a long-forgotten docu-
mentary, everything unspoken.

I recognise one of the women in the video: Christine
Nicol, also a friend of my parents. I call her. 'Ooh, no,'
she hoots, in a refined Scottish brogue. 'They'd never have
plastered anything horrible like that over the press or television. They hated bad news. You must remember, half the
time the Abu Dhabians would send a minion to deliver a

bit of bad news rather than have to do it themselves.'

She tells me that the episode went unreported: 'It was an expatriate issue, and they wouldn't have been interested in those.' We heard most things through the grapevine. There was an Arab-Israeli war going on, a civil war in Lebanon. Those were the problems and stories that afflicted the Abu Dhabians and their Muslim community. Those were the things that affected their standing – and OPEC, of course. They weren't interested in our business. We just weren't that important. They had quite enough to deal with. Even the embassy kept things close to its chest. We were there on the basis we wouldn't upset the status quo. They wanted people to like the place and report back good things.'

Criminality and tragedy were seen as a disgrace.

And yet stories always find a way to come out. People say in Arabic, 'Never try to bury the moon or a story because both will come out in the end.' Once the immediacy had faded, the story changed shape until it came to resemble one of those urban myths – closer to Ripley's Believe It or Not than anything hard and fast.

Marita worked for a spell in the 1980s at the Tawam Hospital up in Al Ain. She remembers a woman in a *burka* and stiff-beaked *niqab* being brought into the labour ward. A flurry of concerned relatives trailed in her wake. No one ever left her alone – there was always a posse of extended family beside her. When the *burka* came off, her skin was smooth and fair. She was a blonde Caucasian, speaking only fractured, childlike English. Others swear this incident happened at the Corniche hospital.

My father has his own authoritative version of events. 'Oh, yes, the family stayed on for many years afterwards, well into the eighties. I believe the girl was found two decades later, purely by accident, in Pakistan, living in a tiny village as someone's wife.'

Others offered sadder, darker versions of what had happened: her body was found in the desert; she was discovered by police in an apartment in the town centre, but the whole thing was hushed up and those responsible were never brought to justice. A few, including my mother, favoured a less sensational theory: not far from the girl's home there was a desalination plant; was it possible she had fallen into the gully and there was, perhaps, no mystery beyond it being a terrible accident? Her body might have been swept out by the tides.

In Abu Dhabi people are not so much amnesiacs as revisionists. When nothing is written down, the past becomes mutable. It can easily be reworked to fit the present. It is an entirely Abu Dhabi outlook on history.

Children's lives, especially, were touched by the tragedy. Open spaces were suddenly out of bounds; the stretches of sand we used to bike over were fraught with sinister possibility. Christine says, 'We didn't know where danger lurked. There were strange men everywhere. We had to change how we did things. You'd not so readily let your children out. You'd have to watch them play, and get them to call when they got to their friend's house just two doors down. And then you'd call the other mum when they returned. You thought that if it could happen to one, it could happen to another.'

'That was the start of us being compound kids,' is how one of my friends described it. 'I was *never* allowed outside the gates again.'

For Bill and me, it was confusing. We heard what the adults were saying. Were we supposed to think that Peter should be treated differently? How could we be suspicious of him? At some point, I suppose, we must have made up our own minds.

One autumn evening, back from our summer holidays, I slipped out of the house unnoticed. Bill had dropped a toy truck on the sand earlier in the day and I had promised to retrieve it for him. I ran barefoot round the corner of the yard, past the oil barrels wedged into the sand and onto the slip road, looking for the blue Tonka lorry against the pale sand. I spied it on the stretch of scrub a few hundred feet away, across the road. I wasn't worried about cars: whenever we cycled up and down or played chase, the road was usually deserted. Bill's best friend Tariq lived a little way down the slip road and they would sneak round the back of the houses, crawl over the building sites and sit teaching each other swear words in English and Arabic, pretending to smoke the butts left by the workers digging the foundations of the houses. At the bottom, before it turned out onto asphalt, there was a cluster of mud houses with corrugated-iron roofs and cock-eyed TV aerials where Arab workers lived. Aside from the children, only the stray neighbourhood dogs ever went there.

With the light fading fast, I reached the sand on the opposite side of the road and made for the truck. As if from nowhere a Baluchi man appeared, catching my eye as he stepped into my line of vision. Dusty cloth fell in great folds from his tall, lean frame and was twisted round his head. Tattered sleeves trailed from his hands. His face was the only part of him that wasn't covered.

I fixed my eyes on his. He had stopped, too. Even his

billowing trousers and *khameez*, usually sensitive to the slightest breeze, seemed frozen. In my head I heard the voices of the mothers on the beach.

I ran anyway. He ran in time with me, striding across the scrub, stopping feet away from where I stood. Only the truck was between us. Looking up at him, I reached out slowly and curled my fingers round it. Then I ran, pins in the soles of my feet as I hit the asphalt, gasping.

Bill lay on his bed scribbling on the underside of the bunk. Taped to his headboard was a picture of Sheikh Muhammad bin Isa of Bahrain in his lordly *bisht*, the dark, gold-edged cloak that hung, glinting, over his *kandura*. I gave him the truck and said nothing to anyone.

Bill was eighteen when he returned to Abu Dhabi. Barely having survived the English boarding-school system, he forsook his love of art and enrolled instead at Sandhurst to train as an army officer. He was expelled soon after they discovered him standing in a line-up puffing at a Ventolin inhaler: he had neglected to tell them he was a chronic asthmatic. My father's response was blind panic and frenzied phone calls. Was anyone prepared to take on his unruly son? Within days, news filtered back of an eccentric Swedish diving instructor living up in Khor Fakkan on the east coast. His company was looking for a Man Friday.

Despite the asthma, Bill threw himself into training for his diving certificates. He spent days fixing up the boat and pitching himself into the blackness searching for leopard sharks, in an attempt to keep busy and avoid depression about his long-term prospects. The simple life on the sea was a world away from the city. Occasionally he would be released for a weekend exeat in Dubai or Abu Dhabi. He'd visit the nightclubs filled with US Marines and hush-hush hostess girls, and sign up drunken sailors for his diving courses. He almost found himself playing the role of gigolo when he was offered as much as his monthly wage for tending to the needs of a bored housewife while her husband was away on the rigs. It was always a relief, he found, to return to the mountains of the east and the reassuring calm of life on the sea. 'It's old-fashioned up here. It's real and it's hard work. My body aches all the time. It's like we're adventurers,' he wrote in his diary.

Out east, beyond Abu Dhabi's rigid expatriate codes of the 'done thing', there was no culture of deference. Whichever Indians, Sri Lankans and Europeans were around would meet at the end of the day to drink beer and Scotch on the beach under the stars. Anthony Sunhil, and the other boys paid to sweep the sand, became Bill's friends. He would bring his portable Sony tape machine and they would lie about and listen to Def Leppard and Tamil pop music until the batteries died or the sun came up. 'You saved my sanity,' Bill once told Anthony, as they squatted on the newly brushed flats in the darkness. The Sri Lankan had merely chuckled and turned up the music.

They often ate together at the Star of Khor Fakkan. The manager ran this bustling diner on the main road as if it were a Mumbai boarding-house. He kept it simple and cheap. There was no menu, just two choices: vegetarian or 'meat', both simmering in giant aluminium vats on camping stoves. Whichever you chose, it came with rice, *chai* and the very hottest of hot pickles. Few Europeans and no local Arabs went there.

When Bill fell in love with a girl who took diving lessons

between stints as a stewardess on the private jet of Dubai's biggest business mogul, he took her to the Star. She was tall and attractive, and there had been a scramble to become her instructor. But, although he had won her approval, she was used to the high life. Her previous boyfriend, the driver of a black Porsche 911 turbo, had left her with a visible legacy of gold jewellery. Bill thought it was best to know from the start whether poverty would scupper things.

Their arrival set the place alight. Eric, Bill's Swedish diving buddy, had told him that taking Jane to the Star was a sure-fire way to ensure that she fled and never returned. But when the two of them slipped off their shoes and walked through the door it was not so much Jane as the manager who fell apart: 'Oh, my. A lady, a lady! Mr Bill, she is such a lady. We have never had such an honour. Come, come, now. Quick, quick, you follow me.' He spread his arms, as if to shield her from the eyes following her, and ushered them hurriedly into a discreet booth at the rear.

Bill, Eric and some of the other European staff who did stints in Khor Fakkan, when they weren't in Abu Dhabi or Dubai, had a great deal more in common with those Tamil men than they did with their fellow passport-holders in luxurious, air-conditioned penthouse apartments and gated communities. The Sri Lankans had been lured on a promise of money and security. Desperate to give their children the improved prospects that came with education, they endured years of separation from those they loved to achieve their aspirations.

Bill and Eric had come for the adventure, and because there was nowhere else to go, but they were united in poverty. Needy enough to benefit from resourcefulness, the pair once went after a swarm of termites gathering ahead of the rain. There were thousands, half the length of a child's fingernail and armour-plated, all over the villa yard. They caught them with bare hands and, after removing the wings from as many as they had patience for, fried them and ate them for lunch.

14
The Astronaut's Wife

The effort that goes into beautification in Abu Dhabi is unparalleled anywhere in the world. For many it is a full-time job. The wealthiest have salons in their homes. A perfect complexion, slender fingers and decorated nails are just the start. When the *abaya* comes off, everything else must be immaculate too. Alongside the smooth-skinned elegance of Emirati and Lebanese girls, it is difficult not to feel ungainly and lazy. I begin to feel the pressure to self-improve and take myself to the Filipina owner of the Violet Rose beauty salon. She talks quickly as she smears sugar paste onto my legs and briskly rips it off. 'Woman always have to look good here. I have many clients and I am seeing them every week. Doing this, doing that, even on Fridays sometimes, I will go to do one appointment with my ladies. They call me crying that they need me! I like to do well for my ladies.'

'You work very hard.'

'I love my husband. He is good man, and he like me to be happy. But I like to work while I can. Later, when we retire, I have problem. He will not go to Philippines to retire. I tell him I not go live in Damascus with his family either. He is Syrian, you know. So what can we do?'

'Why don't you retire here?' I say, turning the pages of a dog-eared copy of *Emirates Woman*.

She suppresses a titter. 'Ha! I like my business here. But retire? I don't know if this is good place. Need lot of money. And I miss Philippines.'

She pauses to pull up a sleeve. 'OK, so maybe option to stay in Abu Dhabi. I been lucky here. Come for job in big villa and one day later I meet husband. But the family will expect very much if we stay. I working all the time already. I think maybe it best to give business to my daughter, then she look after me. Many more opportunity for woman here than other places. It good if you are women here. Can work, no problem. And my husband, he very nice man. He not like Arab men. He not treat me like an Asian woman. I was young widow when I met him, with baby boy, but he like me to work and enjoy myself.'

I tip her extravagantly as I leave. Her story of loss, re-invention and new starts has moved me.

My phone keeps ringing. Texts have come through urgently, one after another, from someone calling herself Reem. 'Where the hell are you? We've been waiting three hours.' I don't recall having made any arrangement to meet Reem but I'm being ordered to 'get your ass' down to the Shangri-La Hotel. I call the number. She barks at me down the phone. 'Come on, you said you'd be here hours ago. How long does it take to get across this town?' Had I forgotten?

I hear a scuffle, then Elizabeth is on the line. 'Don't worry. I'm so sure you know her.' She gives a quick run-down of Reem's life. 'You know – Reem! From here, went to university in France, married now.' She's convinced we've met. The two of them are certainly speaking as if we've been close friends for many years.

'I'm coming,' I tell her. 'I'll be there as soon as I can.'

The Shangri-La makes a good attempt at living up to its name. Ostentatiously plush, even by Abu Dhabi's standards, this hotel prides itself on having created a world within a world. Aside from the long private beach, there is an excess of facilities – several swimming-pools, two gyms, shops, gardens and waterways – that threatens to overwhelm. It is glamorous but, like so much else in Abu Dhabi, a little confusing. I can see myself in every surface. Smiling people are there to help me at every turn and I spin through several lounges before making it up to the bar.

Elizabeth and Reem are in the far corner, across a sea of mosaic tiles. When we meet I'm relieved to find I've never set eyes on Reem before. Still, I am instantly in her thrall. She looks like an illustration from a box of Turkish Delight. Her skin is flawless. She wears loose layers that slide over her and throws the ends of her wrap over her shoulders with a theatrical flourish. Beneath her mane of hair her eyes are a glinting amber. She looks me up and down as though she is appraising a piece of cloth. 'Can't believe I never met you. I'd remember if I had.'

'Are you sure you guys never hung out?'

'You obviously didn't go out much. Not in with the in-crowd, eh?' She laughs, slipping from gossip to reapplying lipstick to ranting about politics and construction in her neighbourhood with an eccentric appeal that is all her own. From the instant I meet her it is obvious that few people ever say no to Reem. The phone messages and texts are an exercise of her right to do exactly as she pleases. But she is charming, funny, generous and filled with the sharp, spiky wit of an angry mind. Later, friends join us and a drunken argument ensues. There is a flamboyant walkout and an over-affectionate reunion. Five minutes later she flings a glass of wine over one of the group who has joined us because she discovers he has planned a fishing trip with her husband. 'You, yah. You've a lot to learn. Unless you know who you're dealing with, you'll never get on here. You son-of-a-bitch.' Then, turning to me with instant calm, she adds, 'You are coming back to my place, OK? It'll be brilliant. We'll have a little party.'

Reem's villa is welcoming. Pictures, photographs, cushions and expensive curtains fill it, with rugs, throws, wall hangings, Italian urns, plants and lamps. Silk cushions lie plumply on velvet sofas and carved *chaise-longues*. Spanish guitar music is playing on the stereo, and hundreds of incense sticks waft spirals of fragrance around the huge peach-columned rooms.

There are ashtrays, bowls of sweets and boxes upon boxes of tissues. I sink into the comfort and wealth. It is like lying in warm water.

Reem might have comic timing but her life is tinged with sadness and frustration. I remember Marita once had a client, Abha, whose idleness threatened to consume her too. After five years as a nurse and several more as the fitness instructor at the Marina Club, Marita had become a personal trainer pandering to the slimming whims of a number of Abu Dhabi's wealthiest young women. Back then, when most women were on their husband's ticket, she was one of the only self-sufficient women I knew. She had taken a chance in answering an advert in the Swedish press to work in Abu Dhabi, but she soon won people over. In her leggings and oversized T-shirts, with blonde, tousled hair and toned shoulders, she was a little bombshell, bringing the promise of Scandinavian sex appeal to her clients. Her women adored her, particularly clever, bored Abha.

Over the years Marita found their lives becoming more and more closely entwined. Abha was married to a young mogul but, from a powerful clan herself, was as wealthy in her own right as her husband. With him away on business or cruising the *majlis* circuit she had nothing to do from one day to the next, except issue orders to her many staff and compete with her inner circle over who was the thinnest, the best dressed, the youngest-looking. Until Marita came into her life the twenty-eight-year-old had never exercised at all. Abha wasn't fat, merely voluptuous – and excessively lazy. The taboo surrounding sweaty physical exercise gave her a convenient reason to live as indolently as she pleased. Even with Marita to spur her on, Abha wouldn't raise a finger unless Marita did the same. Her greatest motivation was her rivals. If one had dropped a dress size or returned from New York or London she would spend days jealously mining her contacts to find out what couture items they had bought. She was obsessive about outdoing their purchases and would plan trips to the same designer stores, jewellers and perfumeries they had visited on Bond Street, Rodeo Drive, rue St Honoré. Abha wasn't cultivating an interest in cardio-vascular fitness or a healthy BMI: she exercised to be thinner than her friends. She wanted social victory.

Marita was slowly absorbed into the household routine. She sat at chaotic family breakfasts and lunches, and was asked to return to the compound to join the women for late-night food and gossip on the rugs. Abha liked to include her in the long, repetitive couture evenings at home, when boutique owners came with suitcases of designer apparel and occasional pieces were tossed her way. After a couple of years Marita's wardrobe overflowed with D&G stack-heeled shoes and stilettos. A friend's wedding would yield a flurry of additional sessions in front of the mirror. Whatever devotion Marita felt for Abha, it was never enough. The calls came early in the morning and continued into the night. There was always one more thing Marita was needed for. Eventually, after a couple of years, she tried to withdraw. Rather than stay for dinner, she would tell Abha she was out on a date so that she could sit at home and relax. She reminded her friend she had other clients and couldn't spend all her days at the villa. But that didn't stop Abha, who thought nothing of calling at all hours pleading with her to come over, if not for dinner then at the end of the evening.

When Marita lost her temper – 'I'm your spy on the outside. That's all you want. You never leave the compound, Abha. No wonder you need me around' – Abha's response was to ask her to become her personal assistant. Marita gave up wondering when her friend would tire of her. It didn't seem to matter what she said or did. She might love Abha and have bought a house in Sweden on the proceeds of what she had been paid but the one thing she really wanted, to make Abha and her friends fit and happy, would never happen.

Abha's clique drifted about on a tide of constant *ennui*. They had everything, yet nothing seemed possible. Even those who left to study seemed merely to collect degrees from top universities and return home to be absorbed into idleness. As for taking a job, what possible reason could there be to get up every day and go to work? So many restrictions were imposed on them that finding rewarding employment was almost impossible, even if they had wanted it: they should not work in a place with men who were not family, or be absent from the home for meals or any other domestic duty that might require their presence. It was easier for Abha to live vicariously through the ups and downs of Marita's life: the lovers, the intrigues, the romances, the satin sheets and long summers in Scandinavia. Set beside the weight-loss and interior-design projects, the hours spent waiting for her husband to appear for the eternal round of family lunches, these were exotic and unimaginable freedoms.

Once, those women's lives would have been very different. It was they who kept camp when the clan was on the move, and ran daily life on the coast and in the interior. They pitched the goat-hair tent, cleaned the *barasti* and scoured the beaches for driftwood and strips of date frond to lay the fire. They cooked, drew water from the communal wells and made it potable by brewing coffee and tea. They took care of the livestock, farmed the land, ploughed the earth and gathered dates. On the coast it was the women who sold the fish the men had caught. A few traded haberdashery, incense burners and other trinkets, in the *souk* or among their community. Then there was motherhood, the menial drudgery punctuated with love. The care of their own children blended into the extension of a maternal hand for all others. A woman took in a sister's children when their mother died, wet-nursed for those whose milk failed, and shared washing or sewing. Invariably pregnant they would often bring their families together to eat, pooling all they had to make more of it.

When the men disappeared to hunt in the high desert or to sea with the pearling fleets, the women looked after the crops and managed the date groves. Together, they kept their tribes alive and defended themselves from raiders who rode in to take food, weapons and children to sell as slaves. In the absence of husbands, sons and fathers, the power rested in their hands. They could not afford to be anything less than formidable.

This time of vigour, of seeing the wide curve of the earth as they made passage from the coast down to the Liwa, was long gone. Aimless in the present, Abha filled her salon with sisters, in-laws, cousins and friends, and focused on the future. Madame Amina, a Russian *émigré* who had come to Abu Dhabi in the 1960s, counselled her on the time yet to come.

Amina came several evenings a week, and ate heartily from the spread on the rugs before she got down to business. One at a time the women would shake the bag of conch shells and wait to hear their fate from the way they scattered on the rug. Marita detested the pouches of broken shell pieces. She had asked Amina for direction a couple of times, but as not a word from the old woman's mouth had ever borne any relation to what happened in her life, she had written her off. But Abha wouldn't hear a word against her. And this was strange since as a rule Abha hated and feared the Russians. According to her, prostitutes flew into Sharjah from Russia on seventy-two-hour visas and didn't bother to leave their hotel rooms as they milked money and jewels from local men. Amina, though, was old and had been in Abu Dhabi so long it was debatable whether she could even be considered Russian any more. Besides, Abha was in thrall to the tales she told. Between the hushed anticipation and cries of disbelief, the old woman promised new futures and freedom.

I ask Reem if she knows of Amina. 'Of course. Everyone knows her. She is a strange thing.'

'Have you ever been to see her?'

'What do I need a fortune-teller for? I know exactly what I'm going to be doing in the future.' She shakes her head. 'But I know a lot who used to go. She gets everywhere.'

I, too, had visited at Amina's dilapidated house in the quarter of the town that money had forgotten. She was a drop of pure, pre-*perestroika* Soviet Union, perfectly preserved in her falling-down villa. Marita told me Amina had come to the Emirates after falling in love and marrying a UAE astronaut. A score of men had gone to the USSR in the 1960s to train with the Soviet space programme, and had wooed the girls with their dark eyes. 'Girls come here with husband, one suitcase, to find sand-blown tent is home and promise of a villa when the money comes,' Amina had said to me.

'I'm not sure he ever made it anywhere near space,' Marita had whispered, as we left. 'I'm not sure there were any real astronauts. I think maybe he was an engineer. You know how stories here go. But he got the girl. When he came home she came with him.'

What magic had they sensed, those strong-boned, statuesque women of the Urals? From the lonely interior of the Soviet Union they had packed their bags and let themselves be carried off to the desert.

Many hours later we're dancing around Reem's villa to the happy strains of disco classics. When someone mentions going to bed she begins to cry. 'We're out of wine, girls,' she wails. 'We have to get more or we'll sober up.'

While most expatriates are able to buy alcohol with a liquor licence, the quantity per month based on what they earn, nationals are not permitted a drop. It doesn't bother Reem. She suggests we go downtown for blackmarket supplies.

'But it's three thirty in the morning,' says Elizabeth.

'And we're not fit to go anywhere,' I add pathetically.

'Well, *I'm* fine.' She stands up. 'Come on.'

She may be more foolhardy and protected than we are but solidarity is the order of the day. We troop out to her Mercedes and strap ourselves in. She pulls out into the main road and we head slowly downtown. There isn't another car anywhere on the road, just our sleek black air-conditioned tank, piloting through the night. Reem settles into a steady pace, staying admirably within the white lines on the road. 'No, no, no.' She scoffs at Elizabeth's offer to drive. 'No freaking way. I'm the only one with immunity, yeah? Not having you being caught out.'

It's not so much a question of being pulled over by the police, I think, as of making it there and back alive. I'm thinking about my children. I don't want to find myself in an Arab hospital. Or worse. Reem lives here. She knows what it's like.

'We'll be safe, *insha'Allah*.' She fiddles with the head-lights. 'I'd never do anything stupid.' In her company it's easy to forget I inhabit a reality elsewhere. This place encourages expatriates to forget. With the right people there is still a purdah-like veil drawn over consequence. Abu Dhabians have been answerable only to God for so long that they seem not to care what outsiders think of them. Such self-assurance is a siren call to even the most sensible among us. It is easy to put aside questions and enjoy the thrill of being swept into a world in which someone else is at the controls.

We pull up in a shadowy back-street not far from where the old Corniche had been located and stop outside a goods-and-trades entrance Reem knows. She rolls down the blacked-out windows and waits for someone to come over. The men here run shifts between the back door and the dark corridors within. There is always a steady stream of buyers through the night, looking for black bin-bags of booze. One of the traders spies us and beams as he walks over. 'Good evening, madam. Welcome.'

'Hi, what have you got for us?'

'No champagne tonight, madam' – he wobbles his head – 'but Chardonnay, yes. Vodka, yes, madam.'

'I've got eighty dollars. How many bottles of wine do I get for that?'

They settle at four and Reem pays with a few straggly notes fished out of the glove compartment. 'I always forget money,' she tells Elizabeth and me – who have also forgotten to bring any. The man doesn't bother counting the notes she gives him. There is a curious tenderness about their outlawed exchange. The authorities are all too aware of people buying bottles in back alleys here and there. A couple of places have supplied illegal booze for decades. I guess someone with powerful *wasta* must be behind this tradition – at any rate the authorities choose to let it go. A minute later the man is back with an ice-filled bin-bag of bottles. Reem tosses it back for me to hold on my lap and reverses out with the same certainty she drove in.

'We're not far from where my parents' first house was on the beach,' I say.

'I loved all those little houses,' she says, 'so low-rise. We called them the Hanky-panky Cottages.'

We dissolve into laughter.

'I didn't know that,' I say.

'Because everyone has to have a vice, right?' Reem does a U-turn at a set of traffic lights and we sail back towards the villa.

When we return it's clear we've all peaked: nobody touches the wine and we make mint tea and lemonade instead. The trip was pointless, I think, watching Reem lie, steaming glass in hand, on cushions by the windows leading out to the courtyard. It is a beautiful haven of liberal expressionism, her walled residence, filled with comfortable, exquisite objects. Yet she says she's unhappy. She doesn't love her husband any more. And he stopped loving her long ago. But she cannot change a thing. She belongs to others now and always will do. With dawn eating away at the darkness we're ready to settle back into the Velvet Rut.

'The Sandpit, that's what the expats call this place,' she says, groping for her lighter. 'That's where we're at.'

15
'I Am Not My Country'

Reem's niece, Zain, is fourteen but has the composure of a woman twice her age. She wears sweatpants and a T-shirt, and petrol-blue kohl frames her huge dark eyes. She drapes herself over the sofa and reaches for the TV remote.

I can hear an American note in her voice. Her aunt has told me she loves to watch *Will and Grace*. She also travels more than most young teenagers. She likes to shop in Bond Street and eat out in the Bowery. She's international and well schooled enough to do polite party chit-chat with anyone. 'Where are you from?' she asks, in a nonchalant, teenage monotone.

'England, near London.'

'Cool. Europe. I want to go to school in France. I like art.'

'You've got sisters, haven't you?'

She snickers and fiddles with her rings. 'Yeah, four.'

'Wow, that's a lot.'

'Some of them are from my dad's other wives. They're half-sisters but I guess it still counts.'

'Do you get on?'

'They're OK.' She musters a smile but there's no enthusiasm in her eyes. After a minute's silence she confides that it's not the children so much as the other wives she doesn't like. 'They tell my dad I'm moody and I don't talk to them.

It's hard. They don't get what I'm saying so I don't bother much. It's hard. They speak Arabic all the time.'

'Does that make it difficult?'

'Yeah,' she says. 'I don't speak Arabic.' It's delivered casually, through braced teeth, without the slightest hint of its significance.

'Really? What about school? They teach Arabic there, right?'

'Not really.'

I'm dumbfounded. 'Perhaps you'll have the chance to do more later?' I want to hear that she loves her language.

She looks at me quizzically. 'I don't need it. Why learn something you don't need? I'm not my country's past. Facebook is easier in English.'

Zain is not alone. There are plenty of others her age for whom Arabic is a second tongue. It's a hotly discussed matter within government. All language evolves but the encroachment of English into the home culture has weakened the predominance of Arabic as the *lingua franca*. And, although letting things go is part of progress, language is a living record of the past. Change the language and you alter the thinking.

I get back to my apartment and lie down in the sunlight, feeling a strange sense of disorientation. It's not just language that's threatened: traditional songs, knowledge of old desert remedies, plants, cuisine, stories and dialects – the subtle distinctions between the ways of one tribe and another – are dying out. 'It's a library burning,' the commentator Abdullah Abdul-Qadir laments, in a book on Gulf folklore.

Many of the older generation are wistful about the past,

unable to entirely let go of the hope that some day a little of the stately pace of old Abu Dhabi will be restored.

Though I am inside, the sun has given me a headache. When I put on my sunglasses, the world seems a little less harsh. The words of a half-English, half-Iraqi friend come to mind, pinpointing the shift in Emirati identity: 'When we grew up here people just were. Now the place is too large and too full of foreigners to let everybody be. There's no room to be anywhere here. Emiratis have to stand up and be clear about who they are or else everyone's going to keep doing what they want. It'll only get more confusing.'

It seems the government has recognised this: 2008 was designated the year of National Identity in the Emirates after Sheikh Khalifa's announcement the previous National Day. In mid-April a two-day conference took place in Abu Dhabi, organised by the Ministry of Culture, Youth and Community. It debated the big questions: language, population, cultural iconography, Islam and history. The aim was to inspire an idea of a modern Emirati people.

Given the Abu Dhabi government's flinching sensitivity towards criticism this public debate was a significant break with tradition. It was an admission of inner crisis. In some quarters there was a great deal of doom-mongering. Many believe the population is too small to retain a true identity. Dubai's chief of police, General Dhahi Khalfan Tamim, made headlines in the local papers when he said, 'I'm afraid we are building towers but losing the Emirates.' He believes there will be a day when the social infrastructure becomes unsustainable: the sheer number of migrant foreigners will bury the regime.

Numbers have always been an issue. Despite financial rewards for nationals who produce large families some say the Emirati population is actually as low as 15 per cent and falling, but there is no way to reconcile Abu Dhabi's desire to grow into a city of 3.1 million by 2030 with its need to establish a stronger balance between nationals and outsiders.

I ask Saeed al Amri, the head of Cultural Affairs at the Ministry of Culture, if Abu Dhabi may come to resemble Singapore, where your sense of identity is based not on blood but on your contribution to the city's success.

He is silent for a long time, then sighs. 'Yes, we know Singapore, but we don't want to be too much like it. We are better than them. Emiratis do not want to become a small part of the nation they have made.' With this, he passes me on to his deputy, Sumaya al Ali, who talks about the identity workshops for a while before she too finds someone else for me to direct questions towards. 'Foreign workers are a valuable necessity. They are no threat to us. But, no, I don't think it will be possible to have a leader of the UAE from, say, India.' She laughs quietly.

'Sheikh Mansour and Sheikh Hamdan have both spoken of these things. They agree we have to accept the reality. We don't accept to live in isolation, on our island, preserving our values and identity. We are proud of our identity . . . We will make friends with the world. But we must be definite.'

So, what is being Emirati all about?

'It is the place where our national and indigenous traditions meet the modern world.'

As I listen to them circling the issue, I realise that they

are, like everyone I have asked, unwilling to nail their colours publicly to the mast. They talk of Islamic ways and family values, but in the most vague and general terms. No one feels comfortable expressing a personal view about what they stand for. No one will say because no one wants to get it wrong. Nearly forty years after independence they are only just beginning to address the question of who they are.

◆ ◆ ◆

My mother witnessed the first reachings for identity when, a few weeks after she arrived in 1974, preparations began for the third National Day. Strings of bunting and lights appeared between street-lamps along the newly paved Corniche. The new green, red, black and white UAE flag, its colours symbolising fertility, peace, oil and Arab solidarity, followed. A raised stand, for officials and other senior figures, was erected at the side of the road. Nothing had been announced, although there were rumours of a grand parade, a show of weapons and armoury, cavalry, tribal dancing, a fly-past of air-force planes and, in the evening, a majestic firework display. People kept guessing: the town was just a few streets deep but it was ready for celebration.

When the day came the new government staged a splendid show: military trucks and tanks draped with flags, soldiers and officers with pinned decorations and a cavalry of glorious Arab chargers flowed past. The parade's theme was new beginnings. The once distinct and independent Bedu tribes were speaking with a single voice and marching with one purpose: to build a strong and successful nation, as fast as the money would allow.

The sidelines swarmed with locals, expatriates and Indian workers. My father sat beyond the ropes in the official grandstand with sheikhs, ministers, diplomats, oil-company heads and government officials. My mother was in the women's pen. Families were always separated from their men. 'No Arab man ever associates with his wives in public,' she wrote home.

From behind makeshift railings she watched the parade. Men sang and danced in rhythm. Then, like a vast, drunken mob, they joined hands and surged forwards onto the road, cheering loudly with each push. In one exhilarated wave they crashed through the barrier into the women's enclosure. As men chanted and cheered, the women screamed. In a thick herd of black they ran for cover. My mother gripped my brother and me. Other children were swept protectively inside *abayas*. Men snatched and knocked each other this way and that. A minute later the police stormed the pen, beating the men out onto the Corniche in a hailstorm of blows.

The whole event was an exercise in *insha'Allah*, with success relying less on organisation than the goodwill of Allah. The entire town shuffled out a second time after dark, ready to mark a moment in their country's young life with the greatest firework display any of them had ever seen. At nine thirty their leader arrived, several hours after his scheduled appearance. As he emerged from a car to a mighty roar from his people, the first fireworks were lit.

Abu Dhabians, other Emiratis, Arabs, Indians, Baluchistanis and we British stared into the sky. 'Remember it,' my father whispered. 'It will never be so small again.'

◆ ◆ ◆

The management of history has become central to the creation of national identity. Intense efforts are being made to corral what is known of tribal history into easily digested snippets. Abu Dhabi's Authority for Culture and Heritage is collecting them and working them into the story of one nation. The previously disparate and isolated tribes and clans of Abu Dhabi now have a shared history, 'even if it is dominated by the Bani Yas and the story of the Al Bu Falah,' a professor at the Higher Colleges of Technology told me.

Sheikh Zayed is at the centre of it all. No longer merely a dead president he is an icon, the figurehead for brand Abu Dhabi and the UAE federation. Posters, musicals about his life, books about his achievements, all without a whisper of criticism, are everywhere. The people are grateful that the country remains glued together in the most unstable region of the world. Zayed can do no wrong. The new rulers know this. They are using him to legitimise visions of their own.

Though long dead, Zayed seems to have a relevant view on just about everything. He even appears to have endorsed the current fad for heritage and culture: 'History is a continuous chain of events. The present is only an extension of the past. He who does not know his past cannot make the best of his present and future, for it is from the past that we learn.'

Admirable though this much-quoted mantra of Zayed's is, most people choose not to live by it. One warm afternoon at the Cultural Foundation, rifling through books and papers on date-farming fertilisation, pearl trading and mountain warriors, I find a paper that cites Lord Clark. In his epic examination of Western European culture, *Civilisation*, Clark defined civilisation as a prevailing sense of permanence. 'Man must feel that he belongs somewhere in space and time.' He needs to 'move backwards and forwards within this framework' to explore and create his own history of ideas, to understand himself and have a sure sense of identity. Forwards and backwards. Abu Dhabi does forward, but what about the past?

Despite the efforts of Abu Dhabi institutions it is an uphill struggle to persuade people to appreciate their cultural heritage. Cities like Cairo, Oxford and Istanbul groan under the weight of ancestral achievement. History is in the worn stones and hand-stained window panes, the twisting lanes and cobbled streets. In Abu Dhabi only three buildings testify to life before the money. The oldest is the fort, Qasr al Hosn, or the White Fort, as it was known after it was mistakenly painted a brilliant white in the 1980s. Once the round watchtower erected to protect the island's freshwater well, it now sits safely inside the Cultural Foundation compound, a stately curio. The other two are a little-known coral and mud summerhouse built in the Bateen neighbourhood in the 1920s, belonging to Sheikh Shakhbut, and the Maqta Fort, which stands, like a giant sandcastle, in the middle of the tidal wash separating Abu Dhabi Island from the mainland. Erected in 1761 it marks the point where the hunters chasing the gazelle crossed onto the island and is also the place where the first Rolls-Royces and Bedford lorries rolled through the waters at low tide before the causeway was built in 1952.

Perhaps the growing archaeological heritage might convince people to look back. The dust at Tell Abraq and

Jebel Hafit is filled with the ancient marks of Mesopotamian, Persian and Assyrian empires. Al Ain is known to
have been inhabited up to seven thousand years ago. There
are archaeological sites: a Nestorian monastery on Sir Bani
Yas, the villages and grand tomb at Hili, dating from the
bronze age, the remains of Arabian life on the island of
Umm al Nar. In the mountains Portuguese fortresses tell
more recent stories of invasion. Old Islam can be seen in
the al Bidyah mosque in Fujairah, made from hand-packed
mud. It looks like a small cake with decorative domes.

But these icons and sites seem largely meaningless. In
Clarkian terms, the identity of the place and its people is
not yet fixed enough to offer the solidity of permanence
for the Emiratis to be considered a true civilisation. The
past is, to many, an embarrassing reminder of the struggles, the poverty and their insignificance. While the British
Arabists loved the pristine desert, the people who sprang
from it saw what they did not have. And when the oil
money began to flow they despised the lack. They felt the
eyes of the world on their bare feet. As Mohammed al Fahim
describes, in his history of Abu Dhabi, this was the arid
sheikhdom with less than any of its neighbours. Even
Bahrainis and Qataris had air-conditioning and shoes by
the late 1950s. The Abu Dhabians aspired to influence and
opulence. In a BBC programme I heard about the advent
of rock 'n' roll, Little Richard pondered a similar moment
of self-awakening: 'For the first time white people saw they
didn't have everything, and black people saw they didn't
have nothing. And they wanted to get something.' The dilapidated old villas, the ruined tumbledown towers and mud
houses, even the apartment blocks of the 1970s, with their

sub-standard foundations, might be the markers of an authentic culture to the first-world traveller looking for local colour, but to Abu Dhabians none of this is worth preserving for future generations. It is an uncomfortable reminder of poverty and regional simplicity.

The 2030 masterplan explores ways for the city to enshrine modern Islam. In some ways Abu Dhabi is standing at year zero. Its citizens have always been more conservative and risk averse than their mercantile rivals in Dubai. Holding back has allowed them to avoid precarious growth and over-extension. With Dubai on the ropes, Abu Dhabians are ready to recast their city exactly as they want.

◆ ◆ ◆

The identity of modern Abu Dhabi is being consciously considered, defined and redefined. The question, of course, is what role Islam will play.

There is a particular flavour to the Abu Dhabian faith, a devotion that sprang from the God the tribes found in the desert. He was a lord of endurance, and they beheld His divinity in every moment of life they snatched in the sand; His was the voice that answered from the silence. It was powerful and simple. In their surrender to such inhospitable climes, He was the only master.

At the Cultural Foundation its energetic director, Abdulla al Amri, smiles at me from across the room. He is wearing a dark grey *kandura* and red-and-white checked *ghutra*: unusual colours, these days. He looks like something of a rebel as he sits forward on one side of his corner sofa, his elbows on his knees. 'The thing is . . .' he pauses to open a huge gilt-edged glass box containing exquisitely gold-wrapped chocolates set in dainty paper petals '. . . we are Middle Islam in Abu Dhabi. This is what we stand for.'

He insists I take several before unwrapping one himself.

'Middle Islam?' I haven't heard the term before.

'That is what I call it. It is the Islam in which you know your God directly, as good Muslims do. You are good to those around you, but you are always able to deal with anybody, no matter what their faith. Those in Middle Islam are developed, as we are becoming here. We do not think only about who is and who is not Islamic. It is about ideas, not war and domination. This is the definition of being a good person. To become a good Muslim you must follow the rules set down in the Qur'ān. They come straight from God, so there is no arguing. But we can apply the meaning and the rules in a modern way. This is the Islam of Abu Dhabi and the UAE.'

Though the Abu Dhabians I have met haven't articulated it with the same simplicity this is the prevailing sentiment among them. They want a life in which piety allows for politeness and where discourse does not degenerate into argument and violence. It is a progressive form of Islam, founded on pragmatism and a belief in dialogue. The Qur'ānic message remade and remodelled for the times we live in.

When I met Abdullah Masaood he had said much the same: 'Religion is life. Do you know what I mean by this? If you live the life nicely, you are living a religious life. It is in all you do.'

I have heard this often. The connection with Islam, and with God, is in the air here. It informs every moment of every day, creating a wave through a person's life.

While Middle Islam may appeal to the majority of Abu Dhabians, conservative and extreme strains of Islam compete for primacy. 'There are influences coming from outside the UAE,' Abdullah Masaood had said. 'They bring ideas that are new for Abu Dhabi and unsettling for people. Too much time is spent talking about what religion means. Too many confusing voices coming in from abroad. For them, it is all about thinking, not being.'

Government policy is explicit on the matter of extremism. It seeks to 'promote harmony and peaceful coexistence among various ethnic and religious groups, and ensure their freedom to perform their religious rites in the UAE'. All must be free to worship in their own way. Faith of any kind is to be applauded.

Pockets of radicals are swiftly dealt with. A group of teachers at the Higher Colleges of Technology were recently suspended from their posts because they held what were perceived as overly Islamist views. Online, extreme religious content is firewalled. The authorities are only too aware of the power and influence al Qaeda and other *jihadi* groups have drawn from the media. And the Emirates Centre for Studies and Strategic Research monitors the movement of extremist elements outside and inside the Gulf.

Their more orthodox neighbours, the Kingdom of Saudi Arabia and Iran, do not share a belief in Middle Islam. Neither is tolerant nor open. A civil servant I met at a reception, whose family lineage is one of holy men, *mullahs*, explained that while the Wahhabi-based tribes of Saudi Arabia pledged to adhere to Muhammad's strictures and live life as it was in the first three generations after the Prophet, the tribes of Abu Dhabi worked in partnership to make ends meet, to bolster numbers and triumph.

Abu Dhabi is the little guy on the block, and it has acknowledged the shadow these two nations cast over smaller neighbours by adopting a position of greater public propriety. In the 1970s many Abu Dhabians exercised the choice to drink at public functions. Today the sight of a man in a *kandura* acting in an official capacity with a tumbler of whisky on ice is inconceivable.

It is this diplomatic ducking and diving that has allowed Abu Dhabians to carve a contemporary shape that allows other faiths their place in an Islamic state. The civil servant draws liberally from the tribal heritage for an explanation: 'Once alliances were made between families. Today those they wish to make arrangements with come from further afield and have to cross the boundary of religion.'

Before I leave I take one last walk round the library. In a row of several hundred neat, leatherbound PhD theses, one catches my eye: *Academic Freedom in Islam and the West: A study of the philosophical foundations of Academic Freedom in Islam and the Western Liberal Philosophy.* The student, Ahmed Othman Altwaijri, was at the University of Oregon and the dissertation was written in 1983. It is an exposition of cultural dissonance and collapsing identity. He warns of impending disaster. As Islamic society and the West become more entwined and reliant upon each other, so the canker formed under pressure of mutual dependence will grow into conflict. The Muslim world has reached a most critical stage in its history as it attempts to regain its identity and take part in the making of modern civilisation.

Today the challenges are greater than at any time before, with the need for co-operation extremely urgent and the potential for confrontation dangerously great. Muslims and Westerners are more antagonistic as they become day after day more dependent on each other. The seeds of conflict are sown in times of united co-operation.

Prescient, and written a quarter of a century ago. Perhaps the collision we all fear now has been a long time coming. It is a doom-laden prognosis. Had he known how fragmented Islam might become?

Marita once told me a story about Abha's son. At the end of the 1990s Abha hired a Western governess for him. Marita had advised her to send him to school, but she wouldn't hear of it. Five mornings a week, in an isolated compound, the boy concentrated on avoiding study. He kicked chairs and threw books about, and when his father was away no one had the authority to stop him. In the grounds he chased animals and threw stones at them. As soon as he was able to hold an air rifle he shot at them, peppering the compound walls with holes.

The governess's stint came to an abrupt end when he burst into his classroom and pressed a handgun to her head. He told her he did not have to listen to her because she was a foreigner, a Christian, a woman. 'You give the boy too much,' Marita told Abha, after the governess resigned. 'He hates himself already. And he hates the world because he doesn't know what to do with it.'

Ennui and self-loathing are still the preserve of many young men in Abu Dhabi and across the Gulf. Boys are rarely disciplined in the home. Freedom to play at being young lords may have created the fearless, decisive adults of the desert, but inside the vortex of Western consumerism, the lack of boundaries has propelled some into a cycle dominated by pointless excess.

The super-rich and powerful do as they please. Entourages disappear in and out of the country like mobile courts of kingly whim. They are above the law and accountable to no one. The annual *houbara* hunting tours are part of this slipstream. Since it is no longer possible to hunt in the UAE – the legendary and beloved bustard is an endangered, almost absent, species from the Gulf, and enormous sums are being poured into breeding programmes – the Abu Dhabians go to Pakistan instead, where vast tracts of land are given over to their use. The aristocracy hold sway over these virtual fiefdoms: Pakistanis are not permitted to hunt, but the Arab parties bag hundreds of quarry in the weeks they are there. There are limits imposed, but amid the funding of mosques and the feathering of officials' nests, they become flexible. Private planes arrive; men in dark glasses descend into smoky-windowed cars, no Customs, no questions. Generators are imported, wells dug and local women brought in while technicians scan and track the birds with radar. In Abu Dhabi 100 million dirhams are spent every year on breeding, training and protecting the falcon. The men want the hunting to be good. Many require hundreds of retainers to support the luxurious and high-technology interpretation of the old pastime. Once, a man was distinguished by his falcon, his camel and his strength of spirit. Now the size of his retinue singles him out.

People stay silent around the rich. There are, of course,

intermittent tales of whoring and drugs, but isn't that what the unbound and wealthy anywhere do? The excesses of the hedge-fund contingent and Russian oligarchs are something to behold if the British tabloids are anything to go by. It is the professed humility of a leadership in touch with its people – showing a grounded and thoughtful attitude – that does not sit with the reality of a more lurid, ostentatious and self-serving life.

Sheikh Mansour's investment in Barclays Bank and purchase of Manchester City Football Club demonstrate personal wealth and draw attention to the chasm between the royal family and their people.

But is this the true character of the Abu Dhabian society? Is it two-tiered, with a small élite making the rules and the rest following them blindly? Most people accept that the royal family have amassed a liquid wealth far beyond that of others. Incomes are undeclared but rumours set the family fund at close to $1 trillion. Yet the understanding has always been that they will not draw attention to their excessive fortunes. Now, partly as a result of the public investments, it is becoming more difficult to keep this private world from public scrutiny. The Internet and a global, fragmented media, with little concern for solidarity in a state far away, mean there is a group of commentators with no vested interest in keeping quiet about the riches behind the palace walls.

While Abu Dhabians still receive so much from the state, there is neither the need nor the will to complain. People have been concerned with their own good fortune. After the initial round of compensation paid to citizens whose *barasti* huts were torn down in the 1960s, there has been no let-up in the flow of goodwill: houses, land, untaxed income, cheaper utilities, living allowances, business gifts. As Reem said, 'Even state housing gives the people who are eligible a compound with five bedrooms, servants' quarters and a car port.' But amid a few rumblings about the introduction of tax, and the probability of comparatively harder times, will the people begin to question the heavily controlled status quo?

As the country grows and ordinary Abu Dhabians are given more autonomy in certain areas of their lives and access, through the media, to world opinion, won't they want a voice and the chance to make political and social decisions for themselves? Reem had told me quietly that now the golden age of Zayed was over there may come a point when things will have to change. Privately pluralistic but unable to offer alternative points of view in a political sphere, sooner or later the people of Abu Dhabi will no longer feel their true values are represented by the monarchy in its current form.

16
Women, Insha'Allah

The women in Abu Dhabi used to play almost no role in the UAE's public life, but it is harder to miss them now, sliding in and out of their four-wheel drives, controlling the Etisalat customer-service bureau, wandering in chattering groups around the al Wahda and Abu Dhabi malls. The young girls in cafés giggle a great deal. The women I have run into in a professional capacity are pragmatic and approachable. Unlike many of the men, who are afraid to shame me, they meet my eye. I am willing them to succeed in their pursuit of a developed Islamic state.

When I speak to Jocelyn Henderson on the phone, she tells me that a group of female students from the Sheikh Zayed University have been coming to her house as part of their undergraduate programme on the nation's history. It is a bold new step. One lecturer, at least, is attempting to give her students a real perspective of their own history by assigning them to people who knew it before they did. I decide to make another trip to the deserted stables that were once Sheikh Zayed's Arab breeding centre to talk to her about it.

It has been a few months since I saw Jocelyn. In the time I've been away the whole place has been redecorated, manicured and appears returned to its former glory. The roadside pavements are painted a chequerboard brown and white, the little mosque for the ground staff is brilliant white, the lawns are lush, green and perfectly tended. Swallows have settled on the trees and there are horses in every stall. Beautiful grey Arab chargers and lean, testy mares. A Baluchi stablehand sweeps the yard, and a few Indians are gathered to the side of a row of stalls, leading animals into the schooling ring.

Jocelyn is on her veranda. We sit facing a glorious, pink bougainvillaea and Lucky brings out a tray of tea with a plate of Waitrose biscuits.

'They're an energetic bunch.' She laughs. 'They still wear their *abayas* and *shaylahs*, of course, but beneath them it's jeans most of the time. Jeans and T-shirts. I get the feeling they've thrown on the *abaya* before running out to see me.'

'Someone told me she'd been out in her pyjamas,' I tell her.

We laugh. 'It's an ideal cover-up. Mind you, most don't skimp on the makeup. They usually look quite beautiful.'

For their observations of the life of an expatriate, Jocelyn takes them shopping at Spinneys, to the library or St Andrew's Church. 'I'm a bit of a curiosity but we rubbed along pretty well. I even took a group to the Queen's birthday party at the embassy. They went about taking photographs of themselves with the old sticks there to mark the occasion. They thought it was delightful. They were very sweet.'

She also describes to them the great changes she has seen in their country. 'They can't quite believe it when I tell them how their grandmothers lived. Some don't know the first thing about the conditions of their grandmothers' lives. Their mothers say they can't remember. It's because they don't want to, in my view. They've been shamed into having a very low opinion of their past. It's the education system here.' Her voice rises with frustration. 'Most of the teachers are Arabs from outside the Gulf. They come up from Egypt, Syria, Palestine and the Lebanon. They view the Emirates with disdain. They consider the people ignorant and backward, with no history worth speaking of.'

'But there's plenty that's known, these days. Surely the ruins they're digging up silence the naysayers. They must realise there's an ancient, peopled history.'

'Not much can compare to the Pyramids.' She shrugs. 'That's the view of the teachers.'

Bertie waddles out and settles by her feet, sniffing for biscuits.

The government has awakened to this deficit in pride and an overdue reshaping of the curriculum is under way. No one is quite sure what it will involve but education has come a long way since the first *mullah* school was established in 1960, when studies were confined to oral recitation of the Qur'ān and the transcribing of its vital passages. After that students were turned out because nothing remained to be taught.

'It ought to be far-reaching. The trouble is that teachers are paid such a pittance no national would ever consider doing the job. Two thousand dirhams a month is what some government schools pay.' Not all offer quite so little, but none the less educational reform is an urgent matter. In government schools salaries have been stagnant for years, and are a pitiful sign of teaching's low status. Pay-rises are on the horizon but they will need to be significant if teaching is to be propelled up a rung or two on the ladder of covetable vocations. Standardised salaries are hard to find: a person's country of origin makes all the difference in the employment package. But where a junior doctor receives 12,000 dirhams a month, an analyst not less than 20,000 and an expatriate teacher at a private school 10,000 or so, the government schools are a generally woeful comparison. Is this salary-starved vocation, where the government hopes to deploy a new generation of educated Emirati women? What better way to instil pride than to be taught by one of your own passionate enough to have devoted herself to sharing what she knows?

'Perhaps many will take up teaching but I think they want the choice, don't you? The situation has changed extremely quickly,' Jocelyn says. 'When their fathers and husbands don't intervene, many young girls show a keen intellect. It's a good family that makes the difference.' Her eyes burn with conviction. 'If the father is enlightened, then the daughters can get a very long way. There are more women graduating from university now than men. About three-quarters. Abu Dhabi has one of the highest percentages of female graduates in the world. Some are already married or nursing young children when they start their courses, but that doesn't stop them. They seem hungry to study. They have to be the future.'

In principle, education has been a dominant part of the government's strategy for making the best use of its people since the inception of the UAE. It is mandatory for every girl to be educated to primary-school level, with large numbers continuing into secondary and tertiary institutions. But this ruling may be overturned by a father's right to determine whether his daughter should or should not be educated. I want to talk to someone who knows about education in Abu Dhabi. There are no female Emirati professors, which I try to consider as only potentially ominous. The rise of women through the system is new and perhaps they have not yet filtered high enough to settle into university professorships.

Jocelyn gives me the number of Dr Kay Gallagher, head of Education Studies at Emirates College for Advanced Education, the UAE's first dedicated Teachers' College. She is behind the master's training programme to promote women into teaching positions in schools. A sweet-faced woman, she has been in Abu Dhabi for more than twenty years and has watched an entire generation take up the challenge of education. 'Many young women want their horizons broadened and they are ready to fight for opportunities. They know they can't walk into a directorship, an army commission or a good public-service position. It's easy for the men. They don't have to know anything much to get a good job. But the women must prove themselves, so they study to make sure they can. They're excited by knowledge. And there's a real gap opening up now. A lot of women are better educated than the men. They're really smart.'

According to Gallagher, female advancement in education and the workplace is characterised by a common tenacious streak. 'I have an MA student who comes from Tanzania. Her father stopped her going to school when she was ten because the secondary school was too far to be appropriate for her to travel. She married an Emirati in her teens, and after she'd had children she took up a place at the Sheikha Fatima "School of Second Chance". She learned to read and write and came top in her class, went on to do a degree, and now she's back again to get her master's and go into teaching.

'It's about pushing upwards. Sheikha Fatima, Sheikh Zayed's last wife, knew that. She was a great encourager, urging women onwards at every level. A few years ago she came to visit a class of girls training to be admin assistants. They were from some of the poorer Bani Yas families and the qualifications they were after would do their families a lot of good. She came and sat them in a huddle and gave them a real talking-to. "Work hard! Get good grades! I need you to take your place in society and match the men here." There was no question of them letting her down.'

It was with Zayed's public blessing that Fatima urged on the women of the UAE. She was behind the establishment of the Abu Dhabi Women's Association in 1972 and three years later the UAE Women's Federation. The education and learning, advice and consultation offered through this body have inspired thousands of Emirati women to improve their lives. Equality may be written into the constitution, with women afforded the same legal status as men, but competing legislation and cultural hegemony places stringent obligation upon women to put their families first. It is common for a girl to submit an essay late, saying, "I had to sit with my family." She can work on her studies only when domestic responsibilities have been discharged. Not even Fatima, with her UNIFEM Award for encouraging the women's movement in the UAE has challenged this: in a statement issued to the press in 2003 she praised the women of her country, and supported their right to consider whatever career they liked, but added that this should not impinge upon their most important role: motherhood. Since much of the traditional thinking about women has come from the Qur'ān, and criticism of its authority is illegal and unwelcome, it is difficult to discuss the role of women honestly. Fatima's words show what is expected of the women in a small, shrinking population, but she has helped them gather some momentum for emancipation by rooting change in practicality.

The government's enthusiasm for mobilising women is motivated by a longer-term pragmatism related to the population issue. Abu Dhabians need to make full use of all their people; to lose half is wastage they can't afford. As a result, in the past decade the landscape of the workplace has begun to change. Women take a majority of positions in the Civil Service, particularly in teaching and healthcare. In 1992 the first female soldiers graduated from Khawla Bint al Azwar Training College, and there are a number of powerful female public figures across the Emirates. Nine of the forty federal representatives, including Sheikha Lubna al Qasimi, the minister for Economy and Planning, are women.

'What women have accomplished in the Emirates in only a short space of time makes me both happy and content,' Zayed announced in a goodwill address before the millennium. 'We sowed our seeds yesterday, and today the fruit has already begun to appear.'

It seems that women have left the home without igniting a social revolution. On the surface, there is enough comment to believe that the country has begun to enjoy the best of both worlds; it is an evolution that has not broken the long-held pre-eminence of family. The story of the publicly demure woman who holds her own in the workplace and represents, with her exemplary behaviour, the reputation of her country abroad is a public-relations dream.

But the question remains: is this shift irreversible and meaningful? Are women, like their counterparts elsewhere in the world, moving irrevocably along the spectrum of liberation that might, eventually, lead to true equality? Or is it mere lip service to ensure the stability of the status quo and the dominance of the al Nayhans? The UAE is more progressive than most Arab nations. But women elsewhere in the Islamic world have known freedom only to have it snatched back, while many young women studying and working in the UAE still do so under certain conditions. In Abu Dhabi work experience forms a mandatory part of many undergraduate degrees, but most workplaces are mixed so fathers or male guardians are required to sign a permission form, acknowledging that a daughter or ward may work with men outside the family. While study is largely approved of, the employment market is a thornier issue. Kay Gallagher tells me of an IT technician who, after graduating, was forbidden to work by her father: he still had the legal authority to stop her pursuing a career. She sat at home for three years while her family brought in a stream of suitors. After refusing every one she cut off her hair in protest. Now, with her father's reluctant blessing, she works full time. She talks of her need to 'self-actualise' before she can consider marriage and a family. Other young Emirati woman echo this sentiment: 'If I got married I would feel restrained. I feel I should develop myself first.'

'I have all my weapons, my education, my degree, my master's, my car, my job. I don't need anything else.'

'I must know myself before I give myself away.'

While they are young, bold statements are possible. Some are obstinate enough to counter their fathers, putting off marriage for the chance to get out to work and study, but the call of children will lure this generation into the familial stage of their lives. Time will run out in the fight to end the double standard. Beyond the father figure looms the husband. Marriage brings with it a new set of permissions. A young Abu Dhabian woman I met who worked in property is soon to marry. She has been working with her father's blessing but after the wedding she will need her husband's permission to continue. A husband, like a father, has the final veto on all she can do: he can deny her the chance to work, prevent her travelling out of the country, divorce her with a few words and marry other wives she may not know or like, all of which she cannot do. 'I do not know what he will say,' she said. 'We will see. People don't like to talk about it. For the women, so many houses in the UAE are prisons.'

It was an off-the-cuff remark that made me feel faint for days.

17
Island of Happiness

Dick Hornby's business partner, Veryan, always had a wry, mellow air that made him attractive, if a little out of reach. An Olympian gold medallist in the 1988 Games in Seoul, he landed in the Emirates after finding that his achievement did nothing for his job prospects back in Britain. Now he writes environmental-impact reports and wears a rather more doleful face than he used to. He brightens visibly as we talk about the old days, diving for wrecks up the coast and hanging out with the seafarers, 'Ah, Bill! He was a character. Ask him from me if he's rolled any jeeps lately!' He laughs.

I ask him how often he gets up to the east coast now, or even the sea around Abu Dhabi. 'I've been speaking to the Tourist Development Investment Corporation about Saadiyat.'

He nods. 'You should go out there, see it now. It'll be a building site by the start of the year. In two years you won't recognise it at all.'

'I used to love it. We went a lot – you know, camping and barbecues.'

Veryan's eyebrows arch. 'It's nothing special, though, is it? There are plenty of genuinely beautiful islands out there. The only thing Saadiyat's got going for it is that it's close to the mainland. It's just a big bank of sand. They've been trying to find something to do with it for twenty years.'

Saadiyat is half the size of Abu Dhabi Island, but large enough to stand as a small desert state in its own right. Dotted with coves and coral inlets, it was shared by fishermen and colonies of small desert animals, *dhubs*, gerbils and the occasional trail of unhobbled camels, right up until I last saw it. I had dim recollections of having heard that sections had been turned over to experimental farming in the 1980s, rows of tomatoes growing in long poly-tunnels fed with desalinated water. When that failed they sank a huge air-force ground-to-air radar station into the sand at the bottom of the island. The military precinct is still inside the perimeter fence, the station long since abandoned. In 2000 the rest was more or less untouched. 'If something doesn't work here, they just reinvent it as something else.' He sniffs.

We meet at the marina the next afternoon. I bring a bag of Isostar, water and a handful of KitKats from the shop next to the apartment. Veryan and his wife have brought a few young environmentalists along for the ride, with coolboxes containing flat bread, hummus, chunks of pickled cucumber, beers, juice and water on crushed ice. For a moment it's just like the old days.

We streak out of our berth and into the open water but heading out to sea isn't quite the departure from the city it used to be. The coastline is built up, congested and largely unrecognisable. Half-built sand breaks run along the stretches of new coastal development where residential cities and landscaped parklands nestle beside huge tracts reserved for condominium projects, inlets for yachts and speedboat jetties. Steering towards the heavy steel skeleton and foundations of the ten-lane bridge that will eventually link Saadiyat to Abu Dhabi, it is as if we are merely cruising watery suburbs. Dredgers, supply boats and the odd coast-guard launch fill the waves. By 2012 the bridge will carry ten lanes of traffic, tramlines and aerial walkways. Pleasure boats are thin on the ground. It's all official now.

'What have they done?' I sigh. 'It's so ugly.'

Veryan's wife, Houry, is curt. 'It will be finished in a couple of years, and then we will have a perfect skyline.'

In the 1990s, Saadiyat was the great Friday getaway. A sizeable circle of expatriates had boats, and empty days were spent puttering around the island, drinking, fishing and scouting further afield for virgin stretches of sand. My father navigated our little boat in and out of the tidal shallows. A couple of decades earlier, in the 1970s, we had found oyster beds in shallow waters on the other side of the island. No one ever scooped a pearl, but we ate thousands of oysters. Many of the old pearlers still fished for pleasure. You would see them all chugging about in their launches. These small fishing dhows had outboard engines, their nets and traps piled at the back.

Veryan is headed towards the Cut, a channel sliced through the islands that is easy to navigate. 'Even the smallest of the little atolls is being developed now,' he says. 'Their owners are tearing down the tents and the *barasti* shelters. Look at it. Brick villas, jetties and landing strips.' We bounce past a couple of slipways that have jeeps and trailers parked under canvas awnings, waiting for their owners to drop in. An ugly line of giant pylons staples the sea between the islands, and there's a lot of litter. Rafts of rubbish bob about on the tide and wash onto the beaches in foamy slicks, fragments of polystyrene, cans and plastic. A coastguard launch steams past us in the other direction. With lights and loud-hailers, it guides stray boats back into permitted channels. This once watery idyll isn't just commercial, it's a mess.

The zephyr off the Gulf has blown the dry sand into drifts, creating rippled contours along the flat bank. We anchor at the far end of the island and wade to the shore with the cool-boxes. The rest of the party get stuck into the contents. I open a drink and walk up the beach into the interior. When we camped my first job was always to scour the island for kindling. Today I'm wearing a white tunic, stitched together in a day by one of the Indian tailors working from a hole in the wall near my apartment, to stave off the sun and keep me cool. I use my hat to collect shiny mother-of-pearl, strawberry tops and worm shells. Among the brush I see a couple of *dhubs* basking and bird tracks everywhere.

Wandering across the island I pass the signs of previous encampments: smashed bottles, Chiclets gum packets and squashed Pepsi cans.

On one occasion in my early twenties, I found a camel in distress. She was giving birth to a breech calf. Curled in a hidden dip with her legs tucked under her she made a sad shape. The calf's front and hind legs were out, hoofs first, but no little head. Lying on her side, the camel moaned, her large-lashed eyes gazing blankly into the distance. Her belly rose and fell only slightly, and as I crept closer I caught the smell of blood. She was exhausted.

I ran to my father. He listened, but told me that even if there was something we could do we would have to leave her. The camel belonged to a local. It was not our place to get involved. It would be positively reckless. We couldn't risk administering the wrong kind of help. 'We have to let nature take its course, darling.'

I knew he was right. Camels were considered almost sacred creatures, descended from the spirits of the desert. And as all swans in Britain belong to the Queen, so every camel belonged to someone.

With the falcon, camels have always been the most beloved of creatures in Abu Dhabi, and an old-time signifier of wealth. They were the beasts of burden that delivered the tribes safely across the wilderness, the first to be watered and fed along the way. They may no longer be needed as transport but they are bred for milk, meat and sport; racing is a huge industry, with large betting syndicates prepared to break human-rights regulations to ensure victory. Despite the controversy over the use of child jockeys, especially these kidnapped from Pakistan, and the recent introduction of the first robotic jockeys, which are lighter than the smallest child, respect for the camel is undiminished. The once modest beauty contests have grown into vibrant events. The 2008 Mazayina Dhafra competition, a part of the firmly established Dhafra Festival to celebrate desert heritage, attracted more than twenty-four thousand camels from across the region.

◆ ◆ ◆

That evening I email Bill: 'Guess what, I've just been to Saadiyat with Veryan. It's the same, just. But it'll be the last time I see it like that.'

He writes back: 'I think you should have a look at this.'

There are pages from his diaries, a newspaper clipping and an account of what had happened in the waters off Saadiyat. As I read, I realise how much it had mattered – and, from the way he writes, still does. I can see why he had never wanted to talk about it. Perhaps because Abu Dhabi is in the news and changing he feels he can now. It explains why he left in such a hurry, and why he hasn't ventured back since. He didn't want to live with the duality.

◆ ◆ ◆

At the height of the summer of 1994 when the temperature rarely fell below forty-five degrees, the city had emptied. Bill had come down the coast with his girlfriend, Jane, to go boating in Abu Dhabi. The humidity hovered around 99 per cent. Air-conditioning units groaned under the burden of the south-easterly winds blowing from the Rub' al Khali. People spoke only when they had to, and getting from house to car felt like a triumph. Even the beach wasn't much of a relief: people in the water found the shallows as warm as a bath.

Everyone knew the drill. Cool-boxes packed with ice, wine, beer, rotisserie chicken, fruit, chocolate, Isostar and plenty of water. While my father took off the covers and emptied the bilge, Bill admired a brand-new RIB moored alongside theirs at the marina. The commando-assault boat, made by the Australian company Osprey, had a huge dual-propeller Evinrude engine mounted on the back. 'Fancy one of those, old man?' Bill joked. Who wouldn't want to take something like that for a spin?

Hassan, the marina manager, wandered over to pass on the tide times as they refuelled. Then they were under way.

Cruising slowly up the outlet, round the tip of the island, my father steered the boat into the Cut.

They spent most of the afternoon idling in the shallows, drinking beer and moving with the shade. My father and the jocular British ambassador decamped to the beach and played boules on the damp sands while Bill and Jane floated lazily and gazed out at the passers-by: weekend fishermen standing to attention with rods, a huge yacht cruising sedately by, water-skiers waiting to take flight.

Around five, when the cool-boxes had been emptied and everyone was fuzzy-headed behind sunglasses and visors, they spotted the RIB from the marina blazing out of the glittering horizon, skimming across the platinum surface of the sea. Bill had half heard the high-pitched turbo whine earlier in the afternoon as it swerved and banked between the boats, charging the short breadth of the channel to and from the beach. It was full of drunken joy-riders in bikinis and shorts. The party over the horizon must have been large because the RIB kept picking up new passengers. It shot in and out of the shore, tearing up the surface of the water, the hull lifting clear as it bounced in tight, show-boat turns.

Bill was jolted into full consciousness by the grinding scream of the engine as pressure in the turbo-driven blades collapsed. He couldn't locate the sound at first. Then, looking into the sun, he saw the boat, faster than he could have imagined, spinning out of a turn and powering towards a small Arab fishing-boat coming slowly across the water in the other direction.

The RIB hit the fishing-boat and ripped lengthways through its hull, splitting it from prow to stern. The canopy poles flew like matchsticks and the fabric waved like a ragged flag as it hit the engine-house at the back. The RIB shot high into the air, its blades spinning furiously and the bronzed joy-riders, lining the edge of the boat, their legs hanging over the sides, screamed. The boat turned a perfect circle above the sea and fell with a slapping crack onto the water, right side up, bodies raining down beside it.

Bill watched as everything slowed to a halt: the blades with white water streaming off them; the wood and splinters from the shattered fishing-boat; the joy-riders suspended in mid-descent. It was like a reel of film turning forward frame by frame in his head. He caught sight of the pilot, unharmed. And everything was back to real time. The RIB ploughed on across the sea and people began to surface. Bill looked at the hull of the fishing-boat. He saw movement at the front. He called to my father and they were in the boat and driving over before either had stopped to think.

As they neared the fishing-boat Bill cut the engines and the boat drifted up to the split hull as it began to sink. People were in the water, moaning and crying out. Bill dived in and pulled himself up over the stern and onto the deck of the fishing-boat. The fisherman was curled up, holding his head in his hands. 'Are you OK, mate?' he called, and got no reply. The shock: he'd taken a few courses at the diving school and knew about first aid and shock survival. He could do mouth-to-mouth, staunch wounds and kick-start a heart if he had to. 'We'd better start pulling people out of the water.' He went closer. The man was an Arab. *Insha'Allah*, he would be able to get him off before the hull sank. 'Come on, mate.'

He was never sure afterwards exactly how he'd been fooled. All he could remember was the sight of his own hand reaching out to touch the man, and the realisation that everything he had seen was an illusion.

'The things the brain does,' he wrote in his diary. 'We almost believe what we see if we want it hard enough.' As he moved the man's hand away from his head he saw that the features had been peeled off and the skin on his face was flapping back into place, like a mask. There was nothing underneath. From the nose upwards the skull was missing. There was a moment of calm. He was looking at a human brain. It was a lighter grey than he had imagined, shinier too. He had always thought the curled ridges would have a dull, matt finish but it glistened like watery clay. In one last, dutiful attempt, he grabbed a towel and tried to apply pressure, to pull it all back together somehow, to provoke the thinking and feeling that would undo what he had seen. The man lay back on the wooden deck. He was still alive, bloody but breathing. Not for long. His was the serenity of a hooked fish that had finally stopped thrashing in the suffocating air.

Bill felt nausea rise from the core of his gut. Beer, sun, food and horror, like a bilious cocktail. He twisted to the edge of the boat and vomited into the water.

A black guy floated on the surface, moaning, with a long metal pole skewering his legs together. Bill closed his eyes. They were fifty minutes away from the marina and no one had a radio. The man dying on the deck was a national, he was certain. He reached out and touched his hand, then turned. There was nothing anyone could do to help now.

He threw himself off the boat. He seemed to be diving

and shouting at the same time. 'Get out of here! We've got to go!' he cried, thrashing through the water to my father. 'He's a local.'

To become involved in someone else's disaster was to step into the line of fire. UAE citizens defended themselves. If they needed someone to blame, would he not do as well as anyone else? He had a friend who had remonstrated with an Emirati woman in Dubai for blocking his car on the sand outside a department store. Within the hour he'd found himself in jail. She'd had the police arrest him for attempted assault. Bystander or Good Samaritan, who would care? However well connected Bill was, his association with the death of a national hung heavy. How would he ever explain he had been helping not hurting?

The RIB floated in the calm beyond the devastation. The driver looked back. Other boats were pulling up, Arabs shouting, men diving in robes, their skirts pooling up like crinolines in the water. Tensions were rising. Expatriates were shouting at the RIB driver too, as the injured were heaved into other boats. He was an Australian. 'Get the hell out of here! Get to the airport now. Go!' one European shouted. The man pulled back hard on the throttle and charged, as if into battle, back towards the city.

◆ ◆ ◆

When my father berthed back at the marina the RIB was there, empty. Bill looked at the boat for damage. There was none. Some unengaged part of his brain was in awe at how it had come through unscathed. He jumped in and felt along the hull for rips. It was diamond hard, a carbon-metal composite. The Australian boat-builders had done themselves proud. Under the seat he caught sight of a large stash of empty beer cans.

The others had begun lifting the cool-boxes out of the galley onto the service trolley. No one spoke as he led the walk up the pontoon. He was the first to see the police coming towards them along the marina boardwalk. Behind him, the ambassador whispered, 'Keep walking. Don't look back. Don't stop. Not a word.' The police were shouting questions. Bill held the trolley tightly, felt it bump on the wooden slats of the marina and rattle up the metal ramp that took him onto dry land. When he got to the car he waited, without moving, for a while. When he finally turned he saw Jane and the others in a car on their way to the police station.

◆ ◆ ◆

Jane did not expect to be released immediately. After she had been arrested for kissing a boy on the street at sixteen she had learned there was no point in watching the door. She sat in an interview room for hours. She knew she must remember to speak simply. The ambassador had told her what to say. She reminded herself to be calm, to trust that she was not alone. Eventually, the police would want to talk to all of them.

But she didn't get a chance to say anything. The officer looked her long in the eyes. 'You saw nothing,' he said. 'If anyone asks you, you saw nothing at all.'

◆ ◆ ◆

When I finish reading, I sit back and try to take it all in. I call Bill. It's a bright hot day in Abu Dhabi and the city looks as if it has been glazed. 'Why didn't you tell me?'

'I never talked about it with anyone, not even Dad. There never seemed a right moment to mention it. And after a while it feels too far in the past to bring up.' He pauses. 'Or even still to be thinking of it. And you get scared, don't you?'

'Why?'

'Because my version is different. It changes how things have to be viewed. They only want one version of events: theirs. Anything else takes away the control.' Bill speaks very slowly, leaving painful pauses, as if he's thinking it all through for the first time. 'Turned out the guy on the fishing-boat was a colonel in the army. I tried to follow it up – I wanted to know more about him, I guess – but I didn't get anywhere. No one would tell me anything and there's nothing in any records.

'They caught the RIB driver that night, trying to get on a plane home. He was an Aussie. I imagined they'd throw the book at him and he'd be in a UAE jail for the rest of his life. But a really strange thing happened. A few months later, not long after I moved to Australia, I was sitting in Canberra reading the newspaper and there was an article on the bloke being released from jail after killing an air-force colonel in a boating accident. He was being deported home from Abu Dhabi.'

'I don't understand.'

'Neither did I. So I asked a local friend, Mohammed, who'd been a diving buddy and was in the Special Forces to see what he could find out. Most of it was just bits and pieces. The guys in the boat were musicians from the Canadian jazz band at the Hilton. The dude in the water was the double-bass player. He'd been in the front of the RIB as it hit the colonel. The boat was really a military command boat, not a pleasure boat. I was right about that, at least. And the Aussie guy driving it was out there for the company that had made it. The only concrete thing I have now is the condolence page from the paper.'

I rifle through the piles of stuff I've printed out.

'It was published a few days after it happened.' He had cut it out when he'd seen it, as if knowing that one day he might need to remind himself.

I take the page and look at it under the light. There is a portrait of the colonel in the centre of the page, his cheerful bearded face smiling beneath the *ghutra*. There's a list of the businesses he was involved in, technical and industrial companies, equipment trading, property and advertising, and even-handed words of consolation from his staff, carefully arranged to avoid offence. There is no sense of how he died.

Condolence
We deeply mourn the sudden demise of
Col. Ibrahim A. al Mohammed.
We pray to God that his soul rest in peace.

'I had to get out after that,' Bill said. 'Everything worked in too mysterious a way. You have no idea what's going on behind the scenes. You start to get paranoid. I thought things would probably be OK because I knew the right people. But there were all these private conversations going on, deals done that no one ever admits to. I didn't want to live like that. I felt like I'd done something wrong. Suddenly it seemed I owed people because they'd done me a favour I should never have had to take. I had no control.'

Within a month he had left Abu Dhabi for good.

◆ ◆ ◆

I may not have much in the way of *wasta*, but Bill's story gives me another reason to return to the archives, to see finally perhaps if I can unearth a moment where Abu Dhabi's public face meets private truth. Ziyana might have put a stop to my search for anything in the 1970s but this incident took place in the middle of the 1990s and, by her own account, records from that period are stored in her centre. No point in waiting to be asked. If I'm charming enough, and as unyielding as she has been, perhaps I'll find what I'm looking for.

I take a copy of the condolences piece and head out to the new Centre for Documentation and Research. My early arrival takes her by surprise. 'Ah, you have really come,' she exclaims. Slender, with sad, brown eyes, she speaks softly, as most women do in public.

'Yes,' I say, allowing a slight smile. 'I came to see you.'

'But what you are here for?'

'There is something from the mid-nineties I'd like to look for. I thought it best to come straight up and see you. After the last time it was all very complicated—' I'm about to start running myself into circles, when she interrupts.

'Ah, but it is not possible. There is no access for outside persons.'

For an instant I feel a flash of unbridled irritation. People talk about a National Archive serving its people, but they are imagining reality where it does not exist. This remains a culture where access is more easily denied than given. What can they be so afraid of?

Still, although my search has taken on the air of a surreal pantomime, getting into an argument with Ziyana will not help my cause. She is a small part of a vast cultural-management system that Abu Dhabi has evolved to protect its public image. Besides, denial may not signify anything sinister. Perhaps, behind the five-star façade, it is simply the organisational shambles it was when I was growing up.

I look at her implacable face. She is very pleasant but she has surrendered no ground. I must appeal to her, person to person, in the Arab way. I need to show her I'm a friend, not out to undermine her. I look her calmly in the eye. 'I'd love to see anything you have from the summer of 1994. I do not mind if you would prefer me not to look. I can wait if you're able to do it.' I'm giving her control.

She narrows her eyes, searching my face to see if I have something to hide. I'm prepared to trust her and as my shoulders relax, suddenly she's smiling too. It's a wordless, instinctual moment: two pairs of eyes reading each other, the kind of connection that cannot be made by phone, email or text.

'Maybe it is possible for you to see,' she relents. 'You want to do it today?'

I nod. 'Today is best, I think, *insha'Allah*.'

Although there is no one to hear her, she draws closer and lowers her voice. 'OK. Wait here. I come back for you.'

Despite the hi-tech infrastructure that links the city, these are a tribal people who have never stopped operating on instinct. Trust is found in the 'good eye of a man'. Things are no different today from how they were in Edward Henderson's time.

Meeting face to face is the only way to get anything done. In Britain we have learned to mask our instincts with new technology, but here our rules do not apply.

◆ ◆ ◆

The archive room is heavily refrigerated. There are shelf units on casters. Everything is digitally operated, gliding in silence at the touch of a button. After finding bound books filled with Arabic papers Ziyana sends the clerk to bring the English equivalent.

We spread the documents across large boardroom-style tables in one of the galleried reading rooms.

'What you are looking for?'

When I tell her, she stalls with surprise for a moment before recovering herself. 'This is not a happy thing. Not good.' She talks instead about her job. She has worked in the centre since 1980. Back then it was housed in the old fort and very small. 'No one came, not ever.'

'And now?'

'We have more than a million pieces archived. They do it on the computer. Digital files. We have teams coming to try out new systems. We are a young country but now we are sorting everything out into one place. It is taking a long time. And soon this centre will become the official National Archive. They make the laws to change it over.'

Though the entire building is state-of-the-art with auto-mated cabinets, retinal scanners for logging staff securely in and out of rooms and a vast network of computers, the truth is that there is not quite a National Archive yet. There has been a statement of intent about a huge public facility but nobody has stopped to explain that it is not yet a reality.

Too much like bad news, an admission things aren't perfect? And yet, wishful thinking, wanting to please, refusing to communicate or whatever it is that has had me on this merry dance has only caused greater confusion.

'No one knows you are here,' I say. 'Not even the people who should know.'

'Yes, this is true. One day it will be better and people can come and search for whatever they like.'

'People like me?' I say to her.

'Maybe like you, but not yet.'

A colleague calls Ziyana into a meeting. She leaves me alone with the papers. The headlines and images look old-fashioned and irrelevant. Could these really have been the most important issues of the time? A future historian might gain a distorted sense of a trite, inconsequential people. 'Man Jailed for Bad Cheques', 'Bid to Steal Wire Foiled', 'Sri Lankan Music Group Set to Enthral Audience', 'President's Sail Boat Wins Race', '35 Poets to Participate in Mushaira'. And, of course, article after article marking the anniversary of Sheikh Zayed's accession. A real sense of the people, their struggles and triumphs, is missing. I move from the *Khaleej Times* to the *Gulf News*. The papers are as crisp as the day they were printed because no one has ever come to look at them. I stare over the balcony. There isn't a soul anywhere. This great temple to contemporary history is all but empty.

After several hours of fruitless trawling I pause to look at a large picture story of a Pakistani man who died while pushing his car out of the way of traffic. There, beneath it, is a small piece about the event I have been searching for:

Man Killed, Son Hurt in Sea Collision
A man died off the coast of Saadiyat on Friday when two boats each carrying two people collided at sea, sources at the General Directorate of Civil Defence confirmed yesterday.

The man who died, Ibrahim Abdel Rahim al Mohammed, was in a 27-foot fibreglass fishing-boat with his son, according to sources. He is said to have died instantly. None of the crew on board was injured.

It's the right story, yet nothing adds up. I find myself poring over the page. There is no mention of the man in the water, his legs pinned with a rod, nothing about the other people on the RIB, nothing subsequently about capturing and imprisoning the driver, no comment from the ambassador. It is clear to me now that there was a world above and a world beneath, two versions of the same thing that would never come together. Public and private were not designed to mix.

◆ ◆ ◆

Today nothing has changed. There are two separate streams, both necessary to how the country functions. The public sphere, filled with publicity-worthy initiatives and applause for what has been achieved, boosts the shiny veneer of Abu Dhabi and the power of the ruling élite. But it is the world beneath into which people tune for a more realistic perspective. This is where all that is complex and confused – and interesting – gathers. And it is here that significant details of a news story can be snatched, like feathers on the breeze, a barometer to the true culture. Abu Dhabians are varied and vociferous in their views and opinions, just not in a public forum. They rely on Channel Word of Mouth. And it is the only channel they will never forgo.

Over *shish taouk* in the Marina mall tower, Wasel Safwan, an artist, tells me how it works. 'Come on.' He wraps a bit of ripped bread round a chunk of chicken. 'There are many things that cannot be in the news, but people share what they know and things move around that way. My father learns a lot when he is in the sheikh's palaces. Then he tells me, I pass it on to some people I know, they tell their mothers. It gets around.'

'There is no such thing as being "in the public interest"?'

He laughs. 'Most of us get to know the truth sooner or later. I bet there are much naughtier things people say in public in England. More than here, right? About the Queen?'

'Our tabloids are merciless, but there's a lot of humour. And I think it's different for us. Making fun of people is a sign of affection. We might laugh at the Queen but we love her too.'

He gasps in disbelief. 'We could not do that here. In the papers? Never.'

The tradition of satire has largely passed the Emirates by. 'So how far could people go?'

'Well, there was a time, many years ago, when Sheikh Zayed drew up plans for a road to Al Ain. He sent them to Sheikh Rashid in Dubai, who took one look and sneered, "Who is this Zayed to build our roads?" and ripped up the plans. Everyone knows this story but it would never be written anywhere.'

I gaze at him. There *has* to be more than this.

'What about now, though? Dubai's woes, for instance. People must be talking about them.'

'Yes, of course. We all know Dubai is broke. And they are coming to their brothers down the coast. Abu Dhabi should help them, if they need it.'

Dubai has $10 billion in sovereign debt and is another $70 billion in the red from state-affiliated companies. Though it can't generate enough to pay off rising costs it denies having looked to Abu Dhabi for a bail-out. But reports on the Middle East business-intelligence network suggest it has been to the capital for aid. *The Times* in London has outlined an exchange of assets for cash, including a stake-holding in Dubai's flagship airline Emirates. And on the people's telegraph, the word is that Abu Dhabi will make a clean sweep: the whole airline, along with major property assets, including the Burj.

But whatever the private deal-making, the question is why Abu Dhabi has watched Dubai teeter and crash in full view of the world. And the devastation seems hardly to have begun: as buildings empty confidence plummets, work visas are cancelled by the thousand, debtors – including foreigners unable to pay mortgages without their jobs – are filling the prisons or finding themselves ejected from the country, losing deposits and other savings.

Abu Dhabi's image-controlling frame of mind should surely be reeling at such public turmoil. But it appears entirely unruffled by the halted construction projects, property-market breakdown and credit scarcity.

Dubai's misfortune is Abu Dhabi's great opportunity. The two cities may sit no more than a suburban corridor away from each other and present a united face to the outside world, but they are led by competing, antagonistic clans. Now the battle is not over strips of land and offshore boundaries but regional dominance and global reputation. It isn't war as we know it, but might Abu Dhabi have been playing a long game? In a time when some have begun to question the federation, and the role, autonomy and power of each state it would be the triumph of triumphs to draw even Dubai under its undisputed leadership. Always the influential partner in the federation, it may now be in a position to exact its price from a wayward Dubai: the falling-in of the Makhtoums to Abu Dhabi's aims, one strong federation with a newly pre-eminent city.

'They are brothers, yes, but always rivals,' Wasel says.

The idea settles easily. Isn't it impracticable to have two regional capitals little more than a hundred kilometres from each other? Abu Dhabi, floating on cash and oil, has always been the quiet authority despite Dubai's insistence on acting independently, and is beginning to look the more likely wielder of long-term power.

'Oh, yes.' He nods. 'You know what they are thinking here? Soon Dubai will be a suburb of Abu Dhabi.'

18
The New Islamic Golden Age

The Emirates Palace is built on an almost unimaginable scale. It sits on the western side of the island like a giant red monolith, a vainglorious testament to Abu Dhabi's inflated ambition. The Hilton and Intercontinental Hotels, once the big landmarks along the Corniche, now look like modest representations of a more provincial and understated age. Come night, the Palace domes are illuminated by an ever-changing spectrum of colours. Laser beams and spotlights light up the sky around them. Owned by the government, it cost $3 billion to build, making it the most expensive hotel ever constructed – a gilded palace fit for kings, heads of state and visiting pop stars. As the prime minister of Pakistan departed, following a well-publicised state visit, George Michael and his entourage prepared to arrive.

My taxi driver wipes the sweat from his brow with a grimy cuff as we turn in through the ornate iron gates and up past an acre of fountains towards the hotel. We leave the city behind and enter a world of fantastical opulence. With its tiered gardens, fountains and ornately paved walkways, this ritzy modern paradise is utterly unbound by petty considerations of taste. Lit from every conceivable angle by spotlights and uplighters set into the ground, it glows and pulses under a luminous halo of colour.

Hesitantly we join a cavalcade of absurdly expensive sports cars, Rolls-Royces, Maybachs and custom-order Maseratis waiting to be valet-parked by young, smooth-skinned attendants in immaculate white uniforms. I dredge a ten-dirham note from my purse and tell my driver to keep the change. It's the best I can do. He clicks his tongue. His own aspirations are on the rise. He thinks that because we are here I am wealthy, too, and that I should give him more.

As I walk in, the acres of polished marble shimmer with the reflection of gilded fittings and the vast ornate central dome above. All sound disappears upwards into the noth-ingness of this rounded golden space. Reality sways and shifts. There is nowhere quite like it. We are in another world, a place of grand flawless elegance and luxuriance on a scale I have never seen. Even the permanent smiles and elegant half-bows of the door staff have been finessed to perfection. Faced with these dimensions even the super-rich must feel humbled. The gilding is twenty-two-carat leaf gold, meticulously applied by hand, and it's every-where – even those places where no one would think to look. Somehow, the layers of soft luminous gold are tasteful: opulence achieved without the intent to overwhelm, a confident show of understatement. I walk through the atrium into one of the large tea lounges and slump into a champagne-coloured armchair to take it all in. Within seconds an immaculately turned-out Eastern European waitress appears at my side. I order a chocolate milkshake, the cheapest drink on the menu. It costs about the equiv-alent of a day's wages for a construction worker, and when it arrives in a tall glass it is dusted with flakes of edible gold. For the time it takes to drink it, I allow myself to believe I am a true part of the seven-star fairytale.

When the bill comes and I've paid the service charge with coins from my purse, I am, once more, an interloper, here merely to attend the opening of the Emirati Expressions exhibition. This glitzy showcase of modern Emirati artists is organised by the Tourist Development and Investment Corporation – the group behind the plans for the Saadiyat Cultural District. It is the largest showcase of home-grown talent ever staged in Abu Dhabi. 'Art from the heart of the Emirates,' the posters say. This is the third in a series of exhibitions aimed at preparing the resident population for the arrival of the Guggenheim and the Louvre in 2013. The first was an exhibition of Islamic art, the second an adventurous Picasso retrospective that brought together pieces never previously shown together. Both were extremely successful. Rita Aoun, the girlish, waif-like cultural adviser for the TDIC, says that fifty thousand people had come to see the Islamic arts exhibition, and more for the Picasso. 'It proves there is a real appetite for these things.'

The space is milling with the great and the good of Abu Dhabi society, royals, fashionable art collectors, dealers and gallery owners. Emiratis are in gleaming *kandura* and *abayas*, businessmen in suits. Female artists are accompanied by their fathers. Lebanese women wear spike heels and elaborate hairdos. Giggling European girls clutch each other in pairs and greet each other with kisses. The air is a heady mix of competing perfumes. Everyone gathers for the sheikhly opening and the moment when they will flood in and see the show.

Taking a plump date from an outstretched tray, I head

for the exhibits. Like a long velvety black hollow the space rolls on endlessly towards the mirrors that line the wall at the far end. I feel as if I'm inside an *abaya*.

'This is a space of secrets,' whispers a middle-aged Abu Dhabian woman, with lip-liner so thick her teeth shine milky white in the dim light. The work is full of surprises: unrepentantly modern, edgy and unsentimental, there is a mix of painting, sculpture, video installations, photography and graphic design. Steel rivets hold a lifesize outline of a man in a metal prison the shape of his own body. Graffiti scratched around it hint at delirium, claustrophobia, madness and hopelessness. Next to this, huge, rioting canvases are covered with reds and oranges so vivid they're almost neon. A calligraphic letter in black cuts like a scythe through scarlet. These stark contrasts of colour, emotion, intent, shape and size carry through the collection, challenging my preconceptions of what Middle Eastern art is all about. Only their bold modernity binds the work together.

Fragmentation and distortion seems to be the language artists use here. Down the centre a strip of fibreglass plinths display a collection of distressed, lacquered, graffiti-covered books, *The First and the Last*, *Time* and *Love*. Each ash-coloured tome represents the existential mystery at the heart of human existence, concealing wisdom we can only guess at. The artist's name is stencilled on each volume, reminding us that she is the only one to know the secrets contained within. At the far end, reflected in the smoky mirrors, like the moon across water, are several eerie grey astronomical photographs. Spread beneath the moon's pockmarked face is the shadow of Venus and a list of spatial co-ordinates. Reem al Ghaith has brought the science, as well as the wonder, of the lunar cycle into her art. The moon has always played an important part in life. Worshipped before Islam, it is an auspicious presence, heralding the major events in the Muslim calendar and guiding everyday decisions. Al Ghaith's silvery segments of lunar landscape explore this power and place the viewer in a small, earthly perspective. Then comes Wasel's enormous canvas, thick with lakes and rivers of paint. It looks like an abstracted earth observation photograph. It is called *Asr* or 'Afternoon'.

A large number of the works are portraits and semi-portraits. These would once have been the most contentious works of all. Islam has long forbidden representation of the human form. It is seen as an act of hubris and blasphemy: the act of creation belongs to God alone. But this tenet seems open to interpretation, at least here. There are humans all over the walls in any number of guises: voluptuous, thoughtful, aggressive, wretched, dejected and dead. Two oils by Maisoon al Saleh, showing a male and female skeleton in national dress and white bridalwear, are equally compelling and disconcerting. A set of six photographs depicting curved fragments of golden flesh – limbs, slices of torso, sloping shoulders – create a tantalising and sensual jigsaw of the human body. I have the impression that I'm looking at a whole person, as if through a kaleidoscope. On the opposite side of the exhibition, there are unnerving photographs of Indian labourers wearing Herman Munster masks toiling on building sites and operating heavy machinery.

Yusuf is a gallery owner from Dubai who helped organise this exhibition. 'Each artist must find his or her own place depending on their conscience. Perhaps this is new. But they are filled with fresh ideas and they should draw strength from each other and follow their own mind. Most artists in the UAE have spent their lives in isolation. A few of the older ones may know each other but this is the first time many have met. We have had no national museum or public space where they can come together. But now artists can begin to mentor each other.'

For some, like Rita Aoun and Yusuf, Emirati Expressions marks the beginning of a new artistic era for Emiratis. It is like the testing phase before a full product launch. The talk is of 'what if' and 'we could'. They want to turn creative expression into a new national obsession. Everybody will become either creators or consumers of art.

While confidence appears high, I suspect the mood may be more brittle than it appears. Rita had shown me a series of slides in preparation for the show: work by Emirati artists that either chimed in ideology or execution with famous pieces from the established canon of post-war modern art. Al Saleh versus Dix, Abdul Rahim Salim versus Pollock, Abdul Qader al Rais versus Rothko, Karima al Shomely versus Nan Goldin. When I asked about the purpose, she told me it was political: 'It proves the UAE can mingle with other cultures. They show we are part of a universal aesthetic expression.'

I can't help but think they're missing the point. Surely an artist doesn't create to raise national pride. Don't we seek to create things to find our place in the world? To tell people how we feel about life and events?

Artists in Abu Dhabi know they must embrace the contradictions of their world and not fear or hide the complexity. It is their duty to reflect things as they truly see them, to rise and meet the futures, presents and pasts that co-exist in this new hybrid state.

I may be mistaken, of course. When I talk to Faiza Mubarak, the young artist behind the distressed-books piece, and her sister, Khawla, they are quick to share their pride in 'doing a good thing' for their country. Faiza looks like a dainty gazelle calf, enormous eyes filling the top half of her face. 'I want to be an asset to my nation, to show people what my country can do. We want to show that we are like you.' Her sister nods. It is like listening to a Soviet-era manifesto, another example of how the needs of the collective drive the nation as if it were one family.

'But surely you're ambitious for yourself,' I say. 'Are there things you feel you want to say?'

She looks surprised and uncomprehending. Then she starts to giggle. 'My own work? Of course, yes, yes, of course.' Pulling her *abaya* tightly round her, she smiles jubilantly. 'You know, I have so many difficult ideas within my heart and I want to interpret them and share them. I want to share everything with others. When I am painting I am thinking of the hidden world that women everywhere inhabit. It is not just here. You have this, too, but different kind. It is called universal, no?'

As Faiza talks her sister listens, folding and refolding the ends of her *shaylah* compulsively. 'I love modern art. I read all the books, everything I can find on Internet.' Faiza nods. 'All night I like to sit in my room and analyse what others are doing and how they have reached the point of expression. I decipher the ideas that are in their work. That is the joy. It is a new discipline here, yes, but it feels as if it is the only way for me to interpret my life.'

'What do your family think?'

The sisters look knowingly at each other.

'We have brought our parents into the modern world. They used to like pictures of camels and deserts. We have shown them what modern art is, and how it fits with the life today. Now they love the symbols and all the parts it has.'

'Anyway,' Khawla adds, 'we have to keep up. Everyone has a duty to move with the life. There is no option.'

Faiza's public answer, which I do not doubt to be part of the truth, is the pride that comes from playing a part in the nation's journey, and of not letting it down. But as I look at her bank of small, painted wooden cubes, like learning blocks for adult life, I can see a private energy drawn from somewhere deep within, which she cannot see yet. Faiza is tiny against the sea of people. But she defies her size; at barely five foot tall, she is already a giant.

◆ ◆ ◆

The show is deemed a huge success. Celebrities, royals and businessmen have all come and are leaving satisfied. As the last of them go, Wasel offers to buy me a coffee. I warn him about the prices. 'It's OK. I'm celebrating,' he says. 'I think after today Abu Dhabi is a place where ancient and modern are together. This city is at a crossroads and we are crossing the boundaries of time and custom. There are two hundred and eight nationalities here. They have to be a part of who I am and a part of how the city is, no?'

The sides of his *ghutra* flap like elephant's ears. When he works he wears shorts and slashed T-shirts. But not out. The *kandura* is his social wear. 'Just listen to the way we speak. A bit of English, a bit of French, a bit of Urdu. We should cherish the mix, not worry about what it means. Our people have always adapted. That is our history.'

Though such a view would, surely, not meet with the approval of those behind the 2008 Identity Conference, Wasel and others are allowing themselves to explore new ways of being an Emirati. In his art Wasel weaves Western ideas of modernity with his own ideas of spirit and faith, life and mortality. It is more than a tacit admission that his world is complicated. Questioning it helps him to divine some kind of truth without becoming cynical, hypocritical or compromised in his present – at least, not too much. 'Every day I ask myself, "What is Wasel's place in this world?" And then I look around me and remind myself I can only create art from what I see. Anything else would be a lie.'

Wasel calls this newly forged response to his world 'UAE-ism'. 'The thought came from a painting. I had a canvas and I could not find a name for it. I really wanted to capture a sense of the diversity that is life here. Then I thought UAE-ism. Afterwards, I realise it is much more than the name for just one painting. It is all of my thoughts about this place, where so many opposites live together, but with happiness. Like ice and water or fire and ice.'

I wonder if UAE-ism will turn out to be an alternative mantra for the future of this city and the region, for artists and ordinary people alike.

For most artists the idea of devoting their lives to their art has not yet caught on. Wasel is one of only two Abu Dhabian artists working full time. 'Many are too nervous to let secure government jobs and status go in favour of an unpredictable life. For me, there was never a choice. I worked as a civil servant, then afterwards as an architect, which was a little better. But I was not living a good life. When I take risks in my art, it is frightening, but each time I jump further and something new happens. I was asked to go and do Art Paris, and now I have buyers abroad. People write to me with theories about what my paintings mean. I try to tell the other artists that this can happen to them but only if they take the risk. If a person gives everything they can, it will happen stronger.'

He talks with confidence, yet every so often his naivety shows: 'It is always unpredictable. When Ann Baldassari, the director of the Musée National Picasso in Paris, came to choose which painting of mine should be included, I showed her nine. I had spent weeks working on some of them, and on one in particular many, many weeks. Then she chose this one,' he gestures backwards, 'a painting I did in three hours.' Dwarfed by his canvas, it is as though he cannot quite believe in the skill of his unconscious. 'It's crazy.'

He has, he says, the blessing of God on his side, as well as his family. Tonight every one of his brothers and sisters has come out in support. Dotted about on chairs and sofas they clearly have little interest in the art, but they embrace him constantly and offer supportive words when he passes by. 'I was rebellious when I was young. I go to clubs and drinking, drinking, but my father, always he supports my choices. So I am with my family all the time when I am not in my studio. I still make my bed and rinse my own glass. In the end it is they and God who are the meaning of everything I do. When I wake I think, Wasel, God has told you, this is your place. Be positive. Everything we do is about God and love.'

I laugh. 'You make a great hippie.'

'Hippie?' He stares at me blankly.

I don't explain. 'Does art run in the family?'

He tugs at his *kerkusha*, the stringy piece of fabric that hangs like a tie from his neck and is peculiar to the Emirates. 'I never think about this before but I guess the answer is yes. My grandfather was a carpenter. He carved traditional chairs. And my father is an interior designer. No one had the tools or the permission to do art before, but perhaps these were the ways for them to be artistic. Their choices were simple. Many times I am confused about the purpose of my painting. But I must do it.'

'You are most definitely an artist, Wasel,' I say.

◆ ◆ ◆

In four short decades Abu Dhabi's people have walked in from the deserts and acquired every product and service they could ever need or want. The magic purse of Arab legend, the one that constantly replenishes itself, is a living reality for them. They have more cash per head of the population than anywhere else on earth. There is nothing that cannot be bought, no experience that has not been tasted, no vision, however unlikely, that has not been attempted by someone somewhere in Abu Dhabi. Their dominance over nature, their rearrangement of the coast-lines and the creation of halcyon islands for weekenders are the gestures of a people telling the world and themselves that they can do whatever has been done bigger and better, because oil money alone will never create respectability or cultural significance. In the main, people deal with Abu Dhabi because they have to. This hasn't gone unnoticed.

The physical development of the city has taken place at breakneck speed. Abu Dhabians have compressed six hundred years of economic growth into just forty. And at the end of it they have reached the outer limits of consumption and found there is nothing left. Instead, they have turned their attention to the new frontier of intellectual and cultural empire-building. They now appreciate the value of fostering an authentic and meaningful society. There is a deepening hunger for this, the ultimate badge of civilisation. They crave the respect and influence that comes with being seen as a culture of expression.

◆ ◆ ◆

I am packing my bags, preparing to fly home, when Abdulla al Amri's secretary calls. He has space in his diary. I am to be there at eleven. I have wanted to talk to him about what the development in culture means. Who is driving it and why? At the media manager's request, I had submitted a list of questions.

When I get there, I find I needn't have bothered. Abdulla is more cavalier and confident than anyone else I have met or spoken to in the whole time I have been back. 'I don't like to look at anybody's questions. I like just to talk. I have many thoughts about Abu Dhabi and the future, the purpose of the work we are doing here. Ask anything you like. I will answer you.'

Given that so much of my time has been spent trying to unravel the layers of fact and opinion, his openness is both refreshing and disarming. When so many people in Abu

Dhabi act only with reluctance, adopting a default position of natural suspicion, too nervous of saying or doing the wrong thing, this seems dangerously close to free-thinking.

'Why culture? Why not science or sport?'

'Abu Dhabi wants all culture. But we do not simply want to make the buildings. We are just starting to open up art and theatre and music for the people here. It is new, we know that, and we have to be patient. We are at the beginning. But we want to educate ourselves. It must become self-generating. Setting up university courses and qualifications will help people learn the skills to do this themselves one day. And we are not afraid to learn from others. In time our own abilities will grow. All the masters of art began in apprenticeship. The great painters of their day, Botticelli with Lippi, Michelangelo and those others, did the same. We are the apprentices now, but we are learning all the time.'

'Are you really telling me this is open to everyone? Me, say, or an Indian migrant worker, or a housemaid with a talent for painting? Isn't it likely that it will be only the Emiratis who are allowed to participate?'

He is unfazed. 'Of course art must be accessible. Making it, studying it, viewing it, buying it. This is the complete circle. We need everyone to be interested and excited. There are many kinds of art here, and artists practising. There are exhibitions with Indian artists already.'

I can't see a Baluchi artist sitting alongside an Abu Dhabian, like Reem al Ghaith, or being welcomed into the splendour of the Emirates Palace to exhibit – it simply wouldn't happen. But then one can't judge the end by the beginning. Maybe this is the start of a journey that will draw his people towards a new ideal for living. 'And who is driving this? Is it the royal family? If it is, what are they trying to achieve? If you had to spend money on anything, surely it would be to ignite thinking in science and technology. Isn't that the key to future success?'

He hitches up his *kandura* and leans forward with a wry smile and a flash of his eyes. 'You keep asking why we want culture, why so much money spending and why now. So I will tell you everything. It is Sheikh Mohammed. He has been reading history. He has seen how civilisations rise and fall. He knows that art creates influence and that is why he wants the arts to flourish here in Abu Dhabi. Any civilisation can exalt or degrade its people and its descendents. There are some who leave legacies of beauty, truth and honour. Others leave nothing but destruction and ignorance.

'He has set us on this path. And to know where we are going we must look back to the great achievements of the past. In the great Islamic expansion after the seventh century the Muslims discovered many other cultures. They went to Morocco and conquered Spain, and at the edge of their empire they found new ideas and took them. There was a little of everything. This became the Islamic Golden Age. By the end of the eighth century Córdoba was filled with libraries, mosques and places of scholarship and learning. Many great minds converged from across the cultured world, including the philosopher Averoes, and the musical and cultural revolutionary, Ziryab, who brought the lute which became the Spanish guitar, New Year celebrations, glass tableware and seasonal fashion to Iberia and Europe. Córdoba, like Baghdad, was a jewel in the Islamic empire.

This is what he sees for Abu Dhabi. Just as the Medicis spawned the Renaissance, there are minds, families and cities whose reputation has lived on for centuries.'

'You are saying that Sheikh Mohammed wants Abu Dhabi to light the dawn of a second Islamic Golden Age?'

Al Amri smiles. 'Why not? The world is ready for it, no? Then there can be a new age of excitement and learning everywhere. There was once a time of tolerance. We want that. We believe it is what the world needs – dialogue between people who wish to progress the boundary of human expression.'

And there it is. The frenzied aspiration on the streets has a singular source. Like his father, Mohammed has a dream. Where Zayed strove for physical permanence, Mohammed wants to go down in history as the man who took his people into a new age of Enlightenment.

'What about Sheikh Khalifa? Is he a believer?'

'Of course. It is like your prime minister and your Queen Elizabeth. One is the figurehead, the other is doing it.'

'Like father, like sons.'

'It is good to dream. We know this here.'

◆ ◆ ◆

The first Islamic Golden Age suffused the young Muslim empire with knowledge and culture at a time when the fog of religious dogma hung low over most of Europe. In a century and a half, Islamic conquistadors had pegged their new religion and way of life across a vast terrain, from India in the east and Abyssinia in the south to Spain in the north-west. The best minds of these disparate lands came together and ignited a bold, optimistic civilisation based on open exchange and possibility. Innovation in the arts, technology, science, astronomy, philosophy, trade and geography, drawn from all corners of the empire, was welcomed and folded into the Muslim way of life. The Prophet Muhammad's declaration that the ink of scholars was more powerful than the blood of martyrs seemed to embody the spirit of open-minded advancement. The House of Wisdom, a vast institution dedicated to learning, brought together not only Islamic scholars but Christians and Jews, too. The liberal Muslim kings of the Abbasid and Umayyad dynasties fostered an environment in which scholars were free to exchange and explore, to build on the thinking of the ancients by launching a translation effort never so comprehensively repeated, to break the boundaries of scientific thought, sharing and safeguarding their knowledge, all of which was, in the end, passed to a post-Renaissance Europe propelling Western thinking forward in an electrifying leap. Pure distillation, stained glass, Avicenna's Canon of Medicine, ballistic weaponry, essential oils, toothpaste, psychiatry, hospitals, quarantine, glass fountain pens, observatories, libraries, schools, bridges, dams, tar roads, jury trial, sugar refinement, windmills, ceramic lusterware: there has, perhaps, never been a time of greater ingenuity and experimentation.

But the people who had thrived on debate, independent thought and *ijtihad*, ended their centuries of advancement as suddenly and inexplicably as they had begun. The thirteenth century brought a new era of restrictions. The cherished climate of openness was suddenly stifled and conformity and closure hushed lively debate in just a few short years. No one is clear what brought such a complete paralysis to this vast empire. Some historians suggest that it grew too large and disparate to sustain innovation and growth, others that as Islam was besieged, by the Crusades from the west and the Mongols from the east, the increasingly fragmented doctrine of Islam – in danger of being lost in a wave of invaders – was distilled into a rigid orthodoxy that held followers fast.

Al Amri makes the idea that we might be about to enter into a new age of liberal Islam sound easy, glamorous even, but the truth remains that artists in Abu Dhabi are not free. Neither they, the writers nor the ordinary people have the autonomy to say what they want. The restrictions are not rigidly imposed but that does not mean they do not exist, or that there are not great consequences for flouting them. It is the culture of self-policing, so ingrained in their collective psyche, that keeps people in line. This quiet strangulation of expression is what most endangers the chance of Abu Dhabi developing a powerful, believable voice. Art requires irreverence and the willing exploration of the untried thought, the reaching towards some kind of transfigurative experience. It will take years to change that mindset – if it ever happens.

It had seemed throwaway at the time, but at the exhibition Khawla had looked me up and down enviously: 'You are so lucky,' she said. 'You can choose to wear whatever colour you like in the morning. I have to dress in black. If I go to London I can wear blue.'

There is a risk that the expansion of apparent freedoms and the encouragement of a new liberalism may be shut down as fast as it has opened up, because it is the vision of one man, Sheikh Mohammed, and he is driving the pace of change. The sanction is his alone. He cancelled the 2008

New Year's Eve celebrations in sympathy with the people of Gaza. There was great public support, of course, but it was still a symbol of the limitless power of the monarchy to affect the mood of the country.

I ask al Amri whether things would continue if, God forbid, Mohammed was no longer there to push them through.

'Yes, of course. It is his personal dream to see this happen.'

◆ ◆ ◆

Abu Dhabi is nothing if not a place of shape-shifters. People there are used to playing whatever role is necessary to get where they need to be. In finance and business, they did what they had to in order to achieve influence. Now they are after cultural dominance. To grasp it they have assumed the mantle of liberalism, like a new suit. But on the ground there is still a conspicuous rift between the word and the deed. My time here has shown me that, like everyone else, I'm still constantly rearranging myself to fit: soft with the Filipinas, entertaining and lively with Reem, demure and courteous with the local women at the Ministry of Culture, Youth and Community Development, and deferential enough to adjust my scarves for modesty in the company of Abu Dhabian men.

From Thesiger through to my parents, the good of the community remains at the heart of how Abu Dhabians think. Now more than ever, when they are so outnumbered, the desire for stability overrides just about everything else. Out in the desert or on the waters of the Gulf, security and a better future means acting always for the good of the many. All for one.

Western democracies are consumed with enshrining the

rights of every person to bear arms, to have children, to be free, to receive compensation, to express themselves sexually. This is where the cultures divide. Ours places an ever-greater emphasis on the cult of the individual. In the tripartite of liberty, equality and fraternity, it is the last to which Abu Dhabi is most attuned. People cannot suddenly make the shift from a communal to an individual stance by buying iconography off a shelf or learning it as theory.

Still, exhibitions like Emirati Expressions demonstrate that the winds have stirred the pace of change at the top. After years of control the state has turned to its people and is asking for ideas. UAE artists have been given a mandate to explore. The state wants to hear what its people have to say. But the simple truth remains that anyone who runs counter to the objectives of the monarchy will get nowhere. That is how Abu Dhabians deal with views they don't like. They don't attack people. They shut them out.

Even if people can change their ways quickly enough, do they, deep down, really want to? Many do not want their lives altered any more than they have been already. Culture must offer more than a seven-star façade. The question to ask is not the one most frequently posed – of whether nudes will be exhibited in the Guggenheim – but, rather, what can take root and flourish in Abu Dhabi itself. There is a lot of talk about making one's country proud, and government enthusiasm may ignite a spirited rush at the outset, but momentum must eventually devolve to artists and their audiences. Artists must trust in the power of their voice. It must be the audience and critics who shape the country's talent, not the authorities. Like all diviners, artists guide societies by representing what has yet to come. They are the mainstream of the future. And since not even the most enthusiastic leadership can know where such release will lead, those who would be artists should not be waiting for their sheikhs to offer them exhibitions, but rather fighting to say all they must say, trusting they are free to continue.

The high-profile series of talks by respected international artists are as instructive to those invited to talk – such as Anish Kapoor, Jeff Koons and Anselm Kieffer – as they are to the emerging group of Emirati painters and photographers eager to listen, but there is plenty more that could be done: an art school, studios, a district that becomes the city's creative quarter, even professional art supply shops. The government cannot create an authentic art scene, merely allow one. And Abu Dhabians will soon be judged. Whatever they decide to produce it must be the art of the people, rather than the art wanted by the leaders.

Beyond its vast oil wealth, Abu Dhabi is a tiny, vulnerable country. If its financial or political stability was threatened, would the government care what it means to have unfettered artistic expression as a founding principle of their culture?

Perhaps getting into the culture game is another wise ruse. What was it Wasel had said the night before? 'Abu Dhabi is a cute town. It has money and a good look, but it isn't weighty enough to be powerful. Not yet.'

'He is right, of course.' Abdulla grins. 'We *are* a tiny country. We have a tiny army. We can never be the biggest. That is why we will take power in another way.'

And there it is: the real reason behind all of these huge

public initiatives. Power. And a quest for a serious legacy. Art, like the creation of wealth and the newly announced desire to be among the top five governments in the world in another half-decade, is merely a stepping-stone to the influence and credibility the rulers of Abu Dhabi have set their hearts on.

But the quest for such power demands national effort to replace lingering unfavourable perceptions of their society with a more palatable reality. People live many lives in Abu Dhabi, none particularly truthful. The government will need to look at the fundamentals – in particular, the rights of the individual in law, the role outsiders play in future development, and how to release a culture from the self-confessed grip of stringent self-policing.

The challenge of engendering a genuinely receptive society is enormous. Books are still banned as media laws outlaw criticism of the rulers, profanity and obscenity remain criminal offences, and the fear of homosexuality casts a dark shadow over freedom of thought and deed. Other deficiencies may be more easily ironed out: the recasting of the education system to raise the quality and bring a generation home, the question of transport in a city that has cars backed up on every road and precious few spaces in which to park, even the potentially seismic issues around the long-term health of the federation – the matter of how Abu Dhabi, as it presses ahead with its own vision, will find a place for the voices of the six other states – all seem surmountable problems, compared to the adaptation of a culture.

Many expatriates are doubtful about whether the government can, or will, follow through on the changes that would transform Abu Dhabi into the kind of place to which people would come regardless of the money. By giving their people financial support and social privilege, the ruling family has managed to navigate forty years of change without profound political reform. They have held the reins of power tightly, controlling their wealth and their people, protecting a way of life that serves them well. It has the veneer of modernity but, like all face cultures, it is more concerned with how things appear than how they are. Most outsiders cannot see the leadership relinquishing the authority they have at home.

And yet, Abu Dhabi has chosen to corral culture and governance as the two spheres in which to generate lasting global influence. And the rulers have made a very public statement of intent about their ambitions. After taking such a gamble they can't very well back down.

It seems that the leadership may be prepared to sacrifice total control over its people to attain a higher level of power: a place at the global table. There is certainly a great deal of excited talk around the Saadiyat venture and other media and cultural partnerships that will help give the city a bit of 'Dhabiwood' pizzazz. Abu Dhabians form a small, easily mobilised population, with enough money to invest in restructuring, reskilling and improvement. The noises about freedom of expression suggest that there is some will for change. But with fame comes scrutiny and accountability. If ministers don't want these vast art sheds and eco-cities to remain empty once they're built they must do more than talk or simply make it appear that there has been a shift into an epoch of open expression. This is no time to fudge, fake or offer half-baked freedoms.

Abu Dhabi is entering a grace period. The president and crown prince are on notice. Youth and inexperience can no longer stand as the explanation for intent without action. As their country buys into the cultural equity of world, others will be watching to see what they do with it. They have five, perhaps ten years to confront and erase the issues that threaten to undermine their chance of acquiring genuine credibility and moral admiration. It is not so much what they do with money, but what they do in spite of it. The success of their cultural plans, and the vast investment of the 2030 initiative, hinges on whether shared aspiration can draw together the distinct public and private realms and create a dynamic heterogenous society that is not plagued by the need to preserve face at the expense of liberty. The West needs Abu Dhabi to triumph: the threat both the UAE government and people feel from Iran and Saudi Arabia, and from a more aggressive fundamentalism, is our threat, too, and perhaps this is why we leave them alone, aware of the imperfect trade-off of small freedoms for larger ones. But though many may be intrigued by Abu Dhabi's plans, and delighted at the prospect, in principle, of entering a dialogue with a city that wants greater understanding between East and West, intellectual and artistic communities are unlikely to tolerate social hypocrisy. Not with a leadership that put itself forward for the honour of exemplary government and rich cultural capital. That Abu Dhabi's attitude to the expression of ideas and the treatment of the vulnerable could shatter the kudos of cultural giants like the Louvre and the Guggenheim is a reminder of how far it is from being the kind of culture that engenders the creation of such icons.

I open Thesiger's book and look at some of the pictures he took of the Liwa when he travelled through it, the first foreigner to do so, in 1947 on his way out of the Empty Quarter. There was nothing, just a few patches of palm trees against an endless curve of dust.

These people, who hovered delicately on the brink of extinction for so many generations, have come a long way. In half a lifetime they've gone from being hidden from the eyes of the world to wealthy, successful city dwellers. The transformation terrified Thesiger: Arabia had been an almost mythical place. The Liwa was another lost Atlantis, a place no foreigner had been able to locate until the 1920s. Now, if the rulers and their emissaries, men like Abdulla al Amri, are to be believed, the country is taking the first step towards becoming a global powerhouse. Building on what they share with other nations, their second great transformation is under way. The buildings, partnerships and media ties may be in place, but it is the mindset of the people that will demand the greatest change. Though Abu Dhabi's people are building on what they share with others, rather than what divides them, to find a place among the cacophony of global voices is a much bigger and more difficult task than they can know.

If I return again in ten years' time, Thesiger-like, I may find the society and the city unrecognisable. If Abu Dhabi's plans succeed, it will be because the Bedu spirit of purpose and survival has brought them to a resting-place somewhere quite different again. Such determination as they have needed in the past will help them become the bridging point between the Middle East and other cultures. They want peace. They want to flourish and take the wandering Bedu spirit to the world. They have always led with diplomacy.

Beneath the glitz, the razzmatazz and the investment, the fact remains that their existence is no less precarious now than it has always been. The stakes are higher. They live in one of the most infertile and inhospitable places on earth, in a gleaming Babylon built with money from resources that will eventually run out. The government and business élite are busying themselves creating reasons to exist beyond oil, preparing people for a future that will be more different than the past is from the present.

The day I journeyed out to the Liwa with Safwan we had pulled off the road to watch the sunset. The colours changed fast. Shadows rippled across the dunes and the sun softened to yellowish gold, then amber, as it dropped towards the horizon. Against this reddening sky, two black camels appeared high on a dune. They watched us, like emissaries from the past, still and silent, almost quaint.

When the desert had turned a dusky umber, we heard the hum of a vehicle approaching, unseen. A Land Cruiser ploughed round the side of the slope and parked on the incline below where the camels stood. A camel-master emerged, long stick in hand, to check his animals.

His long white robe caught the wind as he reached the crest, billowing against his legs. The beasts turned towards him slowly and lowered their heads in submission. He patted each in turn, and for a moment the three were joined, the old and the new, in silhouette, looking over their dominion of emptiness.

Acknowledgements

I owe a great deal to the numerous friends, old friends, acquaintances, business colleagues and establishment figures who let me into their lives, sharing their knowledge, stories, thoughts and experiences, and to those in Abu Dhabi who played landlord, guide and mentor during my visits, making me welcome at every turn. (In the interests of privacy I have changed some of their names within the book.) In particular I would like to thank Abdullah Masaood, who remains an inspiration on how to navigate transformation without losing balance. And L, for living as if she were free, and for becoming half the reason I pursued this book in the way I did.

Through the accounts of Jocelyn, Georgina, Marita and Reem I hope that, in some small way, I have provided an often neglected female perspective. It has been an honour to do so.

Thanks also to Wasel Safwan, Faiza Mubarak and all in the artistic community I met, whose incisive analysis, wonder and openness are a great cause for optimisim.

I'm grateful to the teams behind the Saadiyat development, who dealt with my many questions, to those working in the Cultural Foundation and Ministry of Culture, to Dr

Christopher Davidson at Durham University for being a sounding board along the way, and to the team at Human Rights Watch and Nicholas McGeehan at Mafi Wasta.

If there were something more than thanks I would offer it to Kate Jones, who believed in the idea first, and in me as the one to do it. To Carole Welch for her superb editorship, pushing me, encouraging me, insisting on more. To Ruth Tross and Hazel Orme too. And to Karolina Sutton for being there.

I can't begin to thank my parents, John and Sarah, for having the faith to turn their memories, thoughts and feelings over to me so wholeheartedly and without question. And to Bill, too, for the same honesty, and for his courage in looking back and asking the awkward questions about the way we lived.

And to Cliff, whose enthusiasm for a place he didn't know and sympathy for my obsession with it lifted me off the floor countless times. His passion – not to mention guidance in all aspects of the process – has made all the difference. And finally, to A and X who, I hope, will be part of that third culture which has to be the future, for geeing me up with words of inadvertent wisdom.